DESIGNING WITH LIGHT

AN INTRODUCTION TO STAGE LIGHTING

SECOND EDITION

J. Michael Gillette
University of Arizona

Mayfield Publishing Company
Mountain View, California

Library of Congress Cataloging-in-Publication Data

Gillette, J. Michael.
    Designing with light : an introduction to stage lighting / J. Michael Gillette. --2nd ed.
      p.   cm.
    Bibliography: p.
    Includes index.
    ISBN 0-87484-853-9
    1. Stage lighting.   I. Title.
PN2091.E4G5 1988
792'.025--dc19   88-21660
                                                                        CIP

Manufactured in the United States of America
10 9 8 7 6 5 4 3 2

Mayfield Publishing Company™
1240 Villa Street
Mountain View, California 94041

Sponsoring editor, Janet M. Beatty; production editor, Linda Toy; manuscript editor, Joan Pendleton; text designer, Juan Vargas; cover designer, Janet Bollow; cover photograph, © Ron Scherl, 1988; The text was set in 10/12 Palatino by TCSystems, Inc. and printed on 50 Finch Opaque by W.A. Kreuger Co., Inc.

P R E F A C E

The purpose of this book is to introduce students to stage lighting design, which is an amalgam of technology and art. Without an understanding of the technology used in the craft, it is difficult to design with light. And without an understanding of the theory and processes of design, it is almost impossible to design with light. To be successful, a designer needs to know both.

As with any art form, the basic elements for a successful creation are an understanding of the chosen artistic medium and the inspiration to create. I hope that this text will provide that basic understanding of the design potential of light and give an insight into the sources that inspire a lighting designer to create.

Organization

Because the study of theatrical lighting design covers two basic areas—technology and design—this text has been divided into two sections. Chapters 1 through 8 present practical information that is essential to developing an understanding of the technological aspects of designing with light. Chapters 9 through 16 provide information on how to design with light as well as how to draft the light plot and execute the other paperwork used by a lighting designer.

New to This Edition

In the ten years since *Designing with Light* first appeared, changes have occurred in the field of lighting design. The technology has become more electronically based; lighting designers now have the means to achieve their every desire in terms of controlling the timing, intensity, color, and movement of the lights. The second edition reflects these significant technological advances.

Although *Designing with Light* covers the same basic information as a number of other texts on lighting design, a number of features set this text apart.

- **Content** New information has been integrated into every chapter. Chapter 10, "Color," has been expanded extensively, and color plates have been added to demonstrate the applications of the theories discussed. Chapter 3, "Electrical Theory and Practice," has been greatly expanded to provide the thorough understanding of electricity now imperative because of the extensive use of electronics in almost every phase of theatrical production. Chapters 7 through 9, "Projections," "Practicals and Effects," and "The Design Process," contain practical information, new to this text, that will help students create better lighting designs. Chapter 14, "Drafting for Lighting Design," is also new. It introduces students to the USITT graphic standards for lighting design and provides practical information on how to draft a light plot. Because lighting designers frequently find employment in musical theatre and dance, examples of each have been added to Chapter 15, "Design Examples."

- **Philosophy** The underlying spirit of this text is firmly rooted in my belief that learning about, and working in, theatrical production can be, and should be, fun. With that in mind, I've tried to make this text not only informative, but enjoyable and easy to read.

- **Color Section** The eight-page color section provides a discussion of the practical applications of color theory as well as the analysis of the color choices for the lighting design of an actual production.

- **Safety Tips** Safety tips are discussed throughout the text. They have been placed in special boxes adjacent to the relevant text to help readers integrate learning about a tool, process, or procedure with its safe use.

- **Running Glossary** To help students learn and remember the vocabulary associated with stage lighting, new terms are defined in the margin on the pages where they first appear.

- **Boxed Material** Additional material that provides further depth and practical information has been placed in boxes outside the mainstream text. This added material is included to enhance student understanding by providing insights into and solutions to real stage lighting problems.

- **Illustration Program** An extensive photo and illustration program provides a very strong adjunct to the text.

Acknowledgments

I'd like to thank all those people—students, colleagues, and mentors—who helped me develop my love and understanding of the theatre, and specifically, of stage lighting.

I also want to thank Jan Beatty, sponsoring editor for this book, for her friendship, enthusiasm, and unfailingly professional counsel and advice.

I would like to acknowledge my appreciation to the following reviewers of the text for their many excellent suggestions: Terry R. Hayes, Davis and Elkins College; Edward C. Houser, George Mason University; Terry L. Price, United States International University; Michael F. Ramsaur, Stanford University; Bernard J. Skalka, California State University at Long Beach.

C O N T E N T S

CHAPTER 4

LENSES, LAMPS, AND LIGHTING INSTRUMENTS   34

CHAPTER 5

CABLES AND CONNECTORS   62

TO MY DAD

AN INTRODUCTION TO LIGHTING DESIGN

ny dramatic production, unless it is performed outdoors during the day, needs some kind of artificial light. If illumination were the only function of stage lighting, however, you could hang a bank of fluorescent lights over the stage and forget all about the **dimmers, control boards, cables,** and **instruments.** Obviously, there is more to stage lighting than simple illumination. Effective stage lighting not only lets the spectators see the action on the stage but also ties together all the visual elements of the production and helps create an appropriate mood and atmosphere that heighten the audience's understanding and enjoyment of the play.

DESIGN CHARACTERISTICS OF LIGHT

As you begin to study stage lighting, it is important that you understand what lighting design is, as well as what it is not. Theatrical lighting design is a process and a craft for creating an artistic result. While the lighting design first of all allows the audience to see the stage, it is more than an exercise in illumination. The **lighting designer** uses light to achieve three primary goals: (1) to selectively illuminate the stage; (2) to sculpt, mold, and model actors, settings, and costumes; and (3) to create an environmental atmosphere that is supportive of the play's **production concept.** To achieve these goals the lighting designer uses the tools

Dimmer: An electrical device that controls the intensity of a light source connected to it.

Control board: A console containing controls for a number of dimmers. Also called a control console.

Cable: An electrical extension cord used to connect instruments to dimmers or instruments to permanent stage circuits.

Instruments: Lighting fixtures designed for use in the theatre.

Lighting designer: Person responsible for the appearance of the lighting during the production.

Production concept: The creative interpretation of the script that will unify the artistic vision of the production design team.

Color media: The plastic, gelatin, or glass material used to color the light emitted by lighting instruments.

of lighting design—the instruments, dimmers, **color media,** and so forth—to create a design that works to support the production concept.

Any creative art, whether in theatre, painting, or sculpture, comprises—in equal parts—inspiration and craft. Inspiration in this case refers to the creative element, the process used to create a conceptual image that the artist "sees" in his or her mind. Craft refers to a mastery of the tools and techniques used to re-create the conceptual image in physical form. Michelangelo is reputed to have said that he released figures that were trapped in the blocks of stone that he sculpted. He first studied the stone, saw the figure entombed within it, and then used chisels and mallet to sculpt away the stone to reveal the form trapped within. Michelangelo's statues are the result of the two qualities that any artist has to possess: artistic inspiration or vision and skill in using the tools of the medium to re-create the inspiration.

Actors also use both process and craft. An actor uses many sources to develop the interpretation of a character. Although the character is based on elements in the script, a good actor also uses other sources to conceptualize the role in an effort to make the character portrayal seem more "real" and to create a life beyond that contained in the script. For example, an actor may recall and use characteristics of people he or she has observed; perhaps characters from literature will serve as models for certain aspects of the role; parts of the characterization will certainly be based on emotional memories from the actor's past. Although the process of analysis can lay the foundation for creating a conceptually brilliant character portrayal, if the actor doesn't have a mastery of his own body and voice so that he can move and talk as he has conceived the character would, then it will be impossible for him to fully realize his

---

DEVELOPMENT OF THE PRODUCTION CONCEPT

The production concept is the coordinated artistic vision that the members of the production design team—the producer; director; and the scenic, costume, lighting, and sound designers—develop. This kind of development is only possible if all members of the team freely share their ideas and visions for the production. A regularly scheduled production meeting (discussed more fully in Chapter 2, "Lighting Production Team: Organization and Responsibilities") is probably the most effective method of ensuring that every member's ideas, thoughts, and opinions are heard and understood by every other member of the team.

brilliantly conceived portrayal. To create a great character an actor employs both process and craft. The intellectual process of character analysis can neither supplant nor negate the need for a basic under-standing of how to move and how to talk and vice versa.

In the same way that an actor uses both process and craft to create a character, the lighting designer uses process to develop an under-standing of how the lighting should look for a production and uses craft to re-create those images in, hopefully, an artful manner. (A technique used to help the lighting designer "see the light" is discussed at length in Chapter 9, "The Design Process.")

CONTROLLABLE QUALITIES OF LIGHT

Tharon Musser, a prominent professional lighting designer, has said, "If you ask most people who walk in and tell you they want to be lighting designers, what kind of weather are we having—what's it like outside?—half of them won't know how to describe it, if they remember it at all. They simply don't know how to see."[1] Learning how to see—understanding how light shapes and modifies people and objects—is absolutely essential to learning lighting design.

A lighting designer can "see" how the lighting should look for a production only if he or she has an understanding of the controllable qualities of the medium. These controllable qualities of light are divided into four categories: distribution, intensity, movement, and color.

Distribution

Distribution is a catchall term that refers to several elements: (1) the direction from which the light approaches an area, actor, or object; (2) the shape and size of the area that the light is covering; (3) the quality of the light—its cohesiveness (clarity or diffusion); and (4) the character of the light—its texture (smooth, uneven, patterned, hard- or soft-edged, and so forth). The **focus** of the lighting instruments determines both the pattern and position of highlights and shadows cast on the actors and their environment.

Intensity

Intensity is the actual amount, or level of brightness, of the light that strikes the stage or actor. The lighting designer can control the intensity of all lighting instruments by adjusting appropriate dimmers. The range

Focus: In this case, the location onstage where the light from an instrument is directed.

[1] "Tharon Musser," *Lighting Dimensions* 1(1977):16.

Light cue: Generally, some type of action involving lighting; usually the raising or lowering of the intensity of one or more lighting instruments.
Followspot: A lighting instrument with a high-intensity, narrow beam of light; mounted on a stand that allows it to tilt and swivel so that the beam can "follow" the actor.
Production design team: The producer; director; and scenic, costume, lighting, and sound designers who develop the visual and aural concept for the production.
Unit set: A single set in which all of the play's locations are always visible and the audience's attention is usually shifted by alternately lighting various parts of the set.

of intensity can vary from total darkness to painfully brilliant white light. The range of intensity normally used lies somewhere between these two extremes and is modified to suit the needs of a particular scene or moment in the play.

Movement

Movement can be divided into three general categories: (1) the timed duration of a **light cue**—that is, the length of time it takes for the lights of one cue to come up or go out; (2) the movement of onstage lights, such as a lantern or candle that an actor carries across the stage; and (3) the movement of an offstage light source, such as a **followspot**.

Color

Color is an extremely powerful tool that will be discussed at length in Chapter 10, "Color." Color media allow the designer to use the full range of the rainbow. The judicious use of colored light onstage can enhance a scene immeasurably. Happy, pastel colors can help to create a pleasant, friendly environment for the production of an old-fashioned musical comedy like *The Boyfriend*. Stark white light etched against a black background can help reinforce the sense of conflict in Anouilh's *Antigone*.

FUNCTIONS OF STAGE LIGHTING

Stage lighting design can be defined as the creative use of illumination to enhance the spectator's understanding and appreciation of the production by visually supporting the production concept. To achieve this goal, stage lighting must perform several basic functions.

Visibility

The lighting for any production must make the actors, costumes, and sets clearly visible to the audience. At the same time, it is equally important that the audience see those actors and objects only as the designer, director, and other members of the **production design team** want them to be seen. The dark, brooding, heavily colored shadows that we usually associate with murky tragedies would call for a completely different type of visibility than would the bright, happy look of a farce or musical comedy. One of the real challenges of lighting design is to create a selective visibility that subtly directs the audience's attention to a specific area or location. The intensity of the light as well as its direction and color all affect the visibility of a scene.

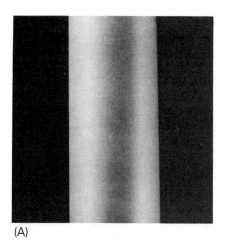
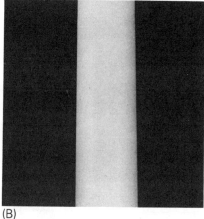

(A) (B)

Figure 1.1

The modeling effect of light: (A) a column lit from the side; (B) column lit smoothly edge to edge.

Selective Focus

Selective focus means directing the audience's attention to a specific area of the stage. The lighting designer can selectively focus attention in a number of ways but frequently does so by increasing the intensity of the lights on the desired area of interest. When this happens, all areas that are less brightly lit become of secondary importance. A common example of the use of selective focus occurs when the lighting designer reduces the intensity of lights on one area of a **unit set** while simultaneously increasing it on another. Instinct literally forces the audience to look at the brighter area. A more subtle use of selective focus can be seen in the lighting designs for most interior settings. In these designs the lights are usually brighter in the major acting areas than they are in the upstage corners of the set where there is little, if any, action during the course of the play. The most extreme use of selective focus can be seen in almost any musical, where the audience's attention is directed to the lead singer by one or more followspots that focus on the singer while the rest of the stage lights dim or change color to emphasize the mood of the song.

Modeling

Light can be thought of as a plastic, sculptural medium that is used to reveal form through the creation of a pattern of highlight and shadow. A column is perceived as round because of the smooth gradation of light from the highlights on the sides of the column to the lowlight, or shadow, area in the center (shown in Figure 1.1A). However, if we light the shadow area, effectively creating a smooth, unvarying wash of light over the whole column (Figure 1.1B), then the column appears to be a flat, board-like rectangle with little or no apparent depth.

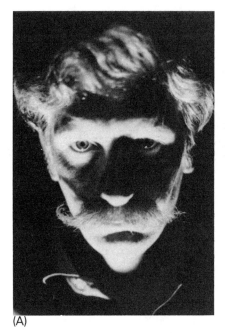 

Figure 1.2

The modeling effect of light: (A) face lit from beneath; (B) face lit from in front and above.

(A)   (B)

Almost all of us, at one time or another, have placed a flashlight under our chins and impersonated a monster by shining the light up into our faces. Lighting the face from beneath, as shown in Figure 1.2A, reverses the normal and expected patterns of highlight and shadow that are illustrated in Figure 1.2B. In Figure 1.2A, areas of the face that are normally shaded—the bottom of the nose, the eyebrows, below the chin—are highlighted, while areas that are usually highlighted—the cheekbones, bridge of the nose, and brow—are shaded. This simple example demonstrates the dramatic changes that can be made by reversing the normal pattern of highlight and shadow. In the same manner, the forms of actors or dancers can be changed or modified by controlling and manipulating the patterns of highlight and shadow on their faces and bodies. The use of **sidelight** highlights and accentuates the edges and vertical line of the body and makes those actors or dancers seem taller and thinner than they are in reality.

Direction is the primary element used in modeling, although intensity, movement, and color all affect modeling to a lesser degree. A change in any or all of these variables will inevitably result in an apparent change of form and feeling in the object being lit.

Mood

Creating a mood with light is one of the easiest and, at the same time, most difficult aspects of stage lighting. It is relatively easy to create a spectacular sunset effect or a sinister feeling of lurking terror; the difficulty comes in integrating these impressive effects with the other elements of the production. Effective stage lighting is subtle and rarely noticed. Although it is fun to create a sunset or similar breathtaking visual display, the opportunity to do so legitimately doesn't present itself in very many plays. Within the parameters of the production concept, stage lighting is usually designed to enhance the mood of the play as unobtrusively as possible. Intensity levels may be varied slightly to shift focus, change color, or create a mood, but the movement of the light must be so restrained that it will be felt by the audience rather than seen. Lighting handled subtly and with precision can be used to create or shift the environmental mood without distracting the audience or calling attention to itself.

An understanding of the functions and controllable qualities of light will enable the designer to blend and manipulate light with the subtlety and precision necessary to create a lighting design that uniquely enhances the audience's understanding and appreciation of the production.

PSYCHOLOGICAL EFFECTS OF LIGHT

In lighting design, just as in literature, the concepts of good and evil are often associated with light and darkness. When a scene is lit with dark and murky shadows, most people instinctively react with a sense of foreboding. The suspicion that something could be lurking unseen in the shadows is almost universal. When a scene is brightly lit, we instinctively relax, because we realize that nothing can sneak up on us unseen.

To more fully understand how we see and how we understand what we see, you might want to take courses in perception from your school's psychology department. These courses are appropriate, effective, and necessary to the training of a lighting designer. After you understand the nature of our learned and instinctive responses to light and our environment, you will be able to apply that knowledge to create lighting designs that will effectively manipulate the audience's response to the environment of the production.

Additional information on the psychology of color can be found in Chapter 10, "Color."

Sidelight: Any light striking the side of an object relative to the view of the observer.

LIGHTING PRODUCTION TEAM: ORGANIZATION AND RESPONSIBILITIES

n some professional theatres, such as the Broadway theatres in New York, unions stipulate the individual jobs for which a **lighting production team** is responsible as well as the number of people necessary to perform a particular job. In regional professional theatres and professionally oriented educational training programs, the demarcation of these responsibilities becomes a little fuzzier. However, this chapter's discussion of the lighting production team's organization and responsibilities generally applies to both professional and educational theatres.

LIGHTING DESIGNER

The lighting designer is responsible for the design, installation, and operation of the lighting and special electrical effects associated with lighting used in the production. Because light is a nontactile sculptural medium, it is all but impossible to build a model to show what the lighting will look like. However, it is possible to draw or paint sketches that show the results of the lighting onstage, and an increasing number of designers are choosing to do so.

To show where the lighting equipment is to be placed, the lighting designer produces a light plot, which is a scale ground-plan drawing that details the placement of the lighting instruments relative to the physical structure of the theatre and the location of the set (see Figure 2.1). The designer also produces the lighting sectional, which is a composite side view, also drawn to scale, that shows the location of the instruments, the set, and the theatre (see Figure 2.2). Additionally the lighting designer compiles the instrument schedule or hookup sheet, which is a form used to record all of the technical data about each instrument used in the production (see Figure 2.3).

Lighting production team: The personnel who work on lighting for a production.

ASSISTANT LIGHTING DESIGNER

The assistant lighting designer functions as a general assistant to the lighting designer. He or she may draw any or all of the associated paperwork—light plot, lighting sectional, instrument schedule, and so forth—as requested by the lighting designer. Depending on the nature and disposition of the lighting designer, as well as the complexity of the show, the assistant lighting designer may focus or participate in focusing the instruments, write cues, update paperwork, or perform any of the other myriad tasks necessary to make the lighting design come alive onstage.

PRODUCTION MEETING

For any theatrical production to be successful it must be well organized, and communication within the group must be excellent. The production meeting is probably the single most important device for ensuring smooth communication between the members of the production design team—the producer; the director; and the scenic, costume, lighting, and sound designers. The initial production meetings will probably be attended only by the production design team. The purpose of these early meetings—ideally held on a daily or relatively frequent basis—is to develop the production concept. After the designers begin to produce their drawings, sketches, and plans, the production meetings decrease in frequency to about once a week, and their main purpose is then to keep other members of the team informed about progress in all production areas. At this time the stage manager normally joins the discussions. The last production meeting is usually held just before the opening of the production.

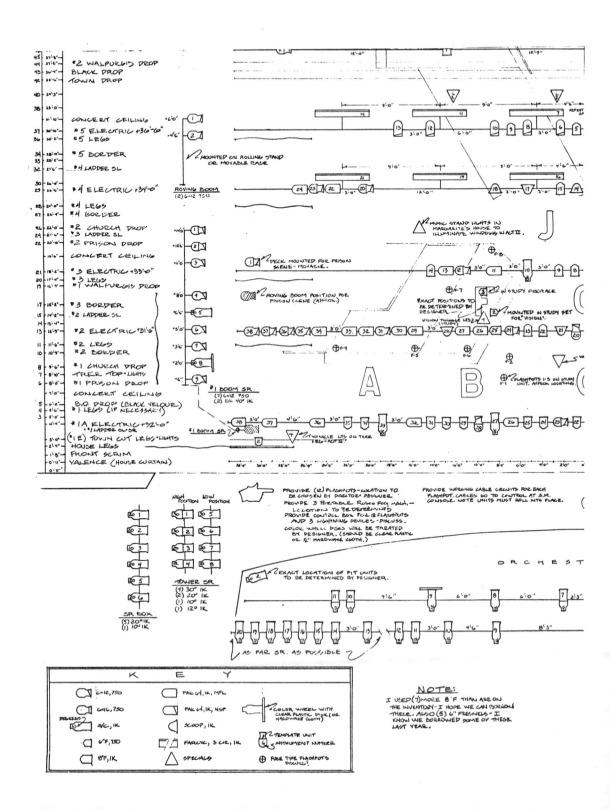

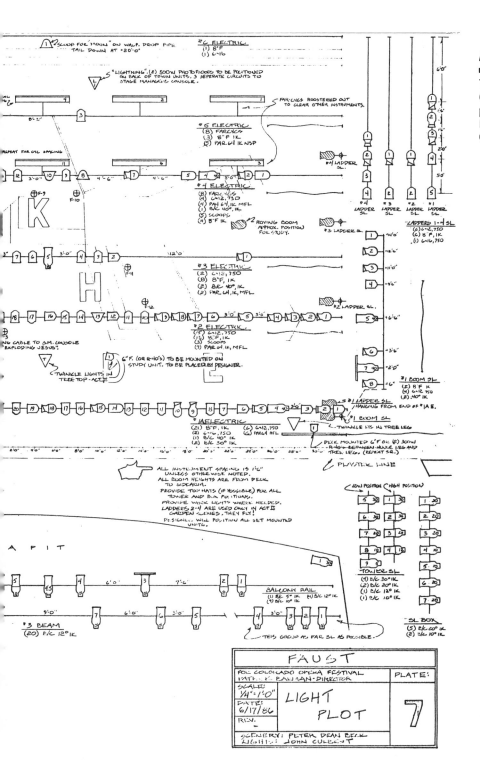

Figure 2.1

The light plot for the 1986 Colorado Opera Festival production of *Faust*. Lighting design by John Culbert.

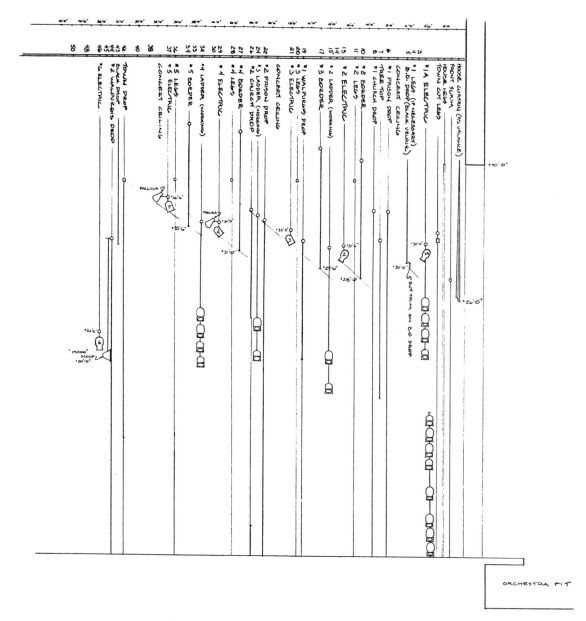

Figure 2.2

The lighting section for the 1986 Colorado Opera Festival production of *Faust*. Lighting design by John Culbert.

HOOK·UP

SHOW: FAUST
DESIGNER: J. CULBERT
FOR: COLORADO OPERA FESTIVAL

PAGE 1 OF 15
DATE: 6/86
THEATRE: PIKE'S PEAK CENTER

Figure 2.3

A sample page from the instrument schedule (hook-up sheet) for the 1986 Colorado Opera Festival production of *Faust*. Lighting design by John Culbert.

CHAN	D.	POSITION-NO	TYPE	FOCUS	COLOR	NOTES
1		π 3 BM (Eirm) 20	12° 1K	FILL WM A	R-30	✓
2		π 3 BM 19	"	B	30	✓
3		π 3 BM 18	"	C	30	✓
4		π 3 BM 15	"	D	30	✓
5		π 3 BM 11	"	E	30	✓
6		BX R (40%) 1, 2	20° 1K	F, G	30	✓✓
7		BX R 3	10° 1K	H	30	✓
8		π 1 E 27, 33	30° 1K	J, K	30	✓✓
9		3 BM 6	12° 1K	A	R-03	↖
10		3 BM 4	12° 1K	B	P-03	↖

MASTER ELECTRICIAN

The master electrician, under the supervision of the lighting designer or assistant designer, implements the lighting design. He or she is directly responsible for the acquisition, installation, and maintenance of all lighting equipment and the supervision of the crews who hang, focus, and run the lighting equipment during the production.

Hanging: The process of placing lighting instruments in their specified locations.

Circuiting: The process of connecting a lighting instrument to its specified stage circuit.

Running: Controlling or operating some aspect of a production.

Pipe: A counterweighted batten or fixed metal pipe that holds lighting instruments or equipment.

Boom: A vertical pipe with a heavy base that holds lighting instruments or equipment.

Lamp: The stage term for "light bulbs" used in stage lighting instruments.

Patch: To connect a stage circuit to a dimmer circuit.

Gel: To put the color media into color frame holders and insert the frames in the lighting instruments.

Light board: A generic term used to describe all types of lighting control consoles.

Cue: A directive for action; for example, a change in the lighting.

Fade: To increase (fade-in) or decrease (fade-out) the intensity of the lights.

As head of the lighting crew, the master electrician is responsible for **hanging** and **circuiting** the equipment used in the lighting design. Each instrument is hung in the exact position shown on the light plot and is checked by the master electrician and crew to determine that it is functioning and circuited according to the instructions of the lighting designer.

ELECTRICIANS

The work of the electricians can be divided into three areas: hanging, focusing, and **running.**

The hanging crew places the lighting instruments and associated equipment in the positions designated by the light plot. This job is very important because the accurate placement of the instruments on the **pipes, booms,** and other locations affects the distribution of the light on the stage. The proper wattage and type of **lamp** are also indicated on the plot or hookup sheet, and it is the electrician's responsibility to ensure that the instruments are "lamped" as required. Additionally, the electricians also circuit and **patch** the instruments. The appropriate circuit and dimmer for each instrument are normally indicated on the light plot or instrument schedule, or the master electrician designates the appropriate circuit and dimmer during the hanging session. Finally, the electricians who are hanging the show also **gel** the instruments and, under the supervision of the lighting designer or assistant designer, focus the instruments.

The running crew is responsible for the operation of the lighting equipment during rehearsals and performances. Depending on the complexity of the production, as few as one or as many as five or more electricians are needed to run the lights for a production.

Although the electricians who operate the **light board** and specialty equipment during a performance have written instructions regarding the timed duration of each **cue,** they should be able to sense the rhythm of the play and integrate the various **fades** and other movements of the lights into the flow of the performance.

As previously mentioned, musicals and many other kinds of productions frequently require the use of a followspot. It is essential that the electrician who operates this instrument have a good sense of movement and timing as well as steady hands. Nothing is more distracting to an audience than a followspot that moves one way while the actor goes another. A followspot operator must master the mechanical intricacies of the instrument and follow the onstage action in a smooth, fluid, and unobtrusive manner.

In theatres with **patch panels,** it may be necessary for the running crew electricians to **repatch** during the performance. Occasionally, a circuit must be patched into or removed from a dimmer during a performance. In patch panel systems that don't have a large number of dimmers, repatching may occur frequently and indeed may be the norm more than the exception.

Running crew electricians are also normally responsible for replacing burned-out lamps and color media that deteriorate during the run of the production, as well as refocusing instruments that have been accidentally knocked out of focus. They also recircuit instruments, move booms, and take care of any other activities involving lighting equipment during rehearsals or performances.

Patch panel: An interconnecting device that allows you to connect any stage circuit into any dimmer.

Repatch: To remove one circuit from a dimmer and replace it with another during a performance.

PRODUCTION DESIGN TEAM

The lighting designer is a working member of the production design team. The composition of the team may vary slightly from organization to organization and even from production to production, but the positions of responsibility and the lines of communication among the various members of the team are the same. Close coordination among the producer; director; and scenic, costume, lighting, and sound designers cannot be overemphasized. If there is unity of thought, style, and direction among the various members of this team, then the chances are quite good that the production concept will also be unified.

The director is the artistic manager and inspirational leader of the production design team. As such, he or she usually makes the final decisions on all artistic aspects of the production. The lighting designer frequently meets with the director during the production meetings (see the box titled "Production Meeting"). Under ideal conditions, the production concept evolves during these meetings. If the members of the production design team cannot be assembled to jointly develop the production concept, then the director frequently takes a more authoritarian stance and develops the production concept alone. Either way, the lighting designer must meet with the director to learn of his or her thoughts regarding the production. If the director decides to change or adapt the script, the lighting designer has to know about it so that the lighting can be adjusted accordingly.

The lighting designer must work closely with the scenic designer because the work of one directly affects the work of the other. In many productions, the same person functions as both scenic and lighting designer. The form of the scenic design dictates, to a certain extent, the positions in which the lighting designer can place the lighting instru-

Mask: To block the audience's view—generally of backstage equipment and space.

ments. Obviously, if the set has a ceiling, the use of overhead or top lighting will be restricted, though not necessarily precluded. The scenic and lighting designers could decide, for example, to place beams on the ceiling. These beams could, in turn, **mask** slots cut on the upstage side of the beams, and instruments could be focused through those slots. Both the scenic and lighting designers will often have to compromise on their designs to achieve a compatible blend of the two.

Because even moderately saturated color can drastically alter the appearance of delicately colored costumes, the lighting designer must hold discussions with the costume designer to learn of the color palette being used for the costumes. It is the lighting designer's responsibility to see that the costume designer's palette remains unchanged when the costumes appear onstage under the lights.

The ultimate goal of the production design team is the creation of an atmosphere and environment that support the production concept. This goal can be achieved only when each member of the production design team openly communicates his or her concepts and plans to the other members of the team.

Communication among the members of the production design team, as well as effective and conscientious work by every member of the lighting production team, is critical to the successful realization of the entire production. Each member of every team is an important link in the chain, and a chain is only as strong as its weakest link.

ELECTRICAL
THEORY AND PRACTICE

I n the first edition of this book, I wrote, "A thorough understanding of electricity and the component elements of the electromotive force are not essential to a comprehension of basic stage lighting." At the time I wrote those words, the **preset light board** was the standard in the lighting industry; today the **computer board** is king. Control devices, for light boards as well as shop tools, that ten years ago were electromechanical are now electronic. Times have changed. It has become a pragmatic reality that students of technical theatre quite simply have to comprehend the function of electricity and electronics. The discussion that follows differentiates between the terms: electricity generally pertains to the use of the electromotive force to perform work—make lamps glow, motors run, and so on; electronics generally refers to the low-voltage circuits and devices used to control the flow of electricity.

ELECTRICITY—WHAT IS IT?

The study of electricity has to begin with a brief excursion into the not-so-mysterious realm of basic atomic theory. This is because some very fundamental laws of electricity are based on the laws of atomic structure. For this reason we need to know a little bit about the **atom.**

Preset light board: A lighting control console that uses electro-mechanical, variable resistance switches to control the output of the dimmers.

Computer board: A lighting control console that uses a computer to store and recall dimmer intensity levels and fade times for each cue; it also stores and recalls various other functions.

Atom: The smallest particle of a chemical element that retains the structural properties of that element.

The atom is the smallest complete building block in nature. But an atom is composed of even smaller particles: **protons, neutrons,** and **electrons.** The subatomic particles possess specific electrical properties. The proton has a positive charge, the neutron a neutral charge, and the electron a negative charge. The physical structure of any atom is very similar to the configuration of our solar system. In the same manner that the earth rotates around the sun (Figure 3.1A), electrons follow a slightly elliptical orbit as they whirl around the nucleus of an atom (Figure 3.1B).

In a stable atom the number of electrons in orbit around the nucleus is equaled by the number of protons in the nucleus. Hydrogen, the lightest and least complex atom, is a perfect example of this principle. Figure 3.2 shows the single electron of the hydrogen atom in orbit around the nucleus, which is composed of a single proton. Since the orbiting electron has a negative charge and the proton in the nucleus has a positive charge, an electrical attraction exists between them. The electron is prevented from being pulled into the nucleus by the centrifugal force of its orbital movement. At the same time the electron is restrained from breaking out of orbit and flying away by the attraction. This attraction is an important underlying principle of electricity and is the basis for the first important law of electricity, the Law of Charges: *like charges repel, and unlike charges attract.*

If it were physically possible to isolate two protons, they would defy all attempts to bring them together. The same results would occur if

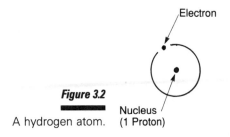

Figure 3.1

The structure of an atom is similar to the structure of the solar system.

Earth
Mercury
Sun
Venus
Mars

Electrons
Nucleus
Electrons

Figure 3.2

A hydrogen atom.

Electron
Nucleus
(1 Proton)

attempts were made to push two electrons together. But if an electron and a proton were placed in proximity, they would zip toward each other until they met. The Law of Charges is the "electrical glue" that actually holds the atom together.

In atoms that are more complex than hydrogen, such as oxygen (Figure 3.3), additional electrons orbit in several planes around the nucleus. These electrons are counterbalanced by an equal number of protons in the nucleus, so the atom remains in an electrically balanced, or stable, condition. These additional orbiting electrons occupy orderly spherical shells at specific distances from the nucleus. Each of these shells can hold only a certain number of electrons. When each shell is filled with its quota of electrons, a tight bonding takes place, and no additional electrons can be added. Although it is possible to dislodge an electron from one of these filled shells, it takes a relatively large amount of energy to do so.

As the structure and weight of the atom grow, the number of protons in the nucleus increases, as does the corresponding number of electrons orbiting around it. Since the electrons cannot force their way into the already filled shells, they must orbit at a greater distance. The increased distance between the orbiting electron and its counterbalancing proton in the nucleus decreases the attractive force that holds the electron in orbit.

An atom of copper has twenty-nine electrons in orbit around its nucleus. Because of copper's particular atomic structure, only a very weak force holds its outer electrons in orbit, and only a very weak force is needed to dislodge them from the outer shell, or **valence shell,** of the copper atom.

A strand of copper wire is composed of billions upon billions of copper atoms, all having the same characteristically weak valence electron. The atoms in the wire are in such close proximity to one another (most of them are intertwined with their neighbors) that the nuclei of adjacent atoms can actually exert the same or more attractive force on their neighbors' valence electrons than they do on their own.

Proton: A fundamental particle in the structure of the nucleus of an atom; possesses a positive charge.

Neutron: A fundamental particle in the structure of the nucleus of an atom; possesses a neutral charge.

Electron: A negatively charged fundamental particle that orbits around the nucleus of an atom.

Valence shell: The outermost plane of orbiting electrons in the structure of an atom.

Electrons

Nucleus

Figure 3.3

An oxygen atom.

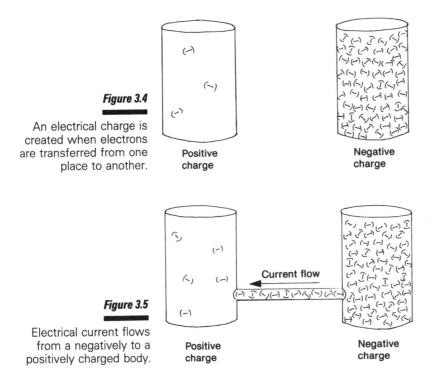

Figure 3.4

An electrical charge is created when electrons are transferred from one place to another.

Positive charge

Negative charge

Figure 3.5

Electrical current flows from a negatively to a positively charged body.

Positive charge

Current flow

Negative charge

Consequently, many of the valence electrons break away from their "home" atoms, momentarily attach themselves to other atoms, or simply float freely within the confines of the wire.

If this cloud of **free electrons** meandering in the wire could be organized to move in the same direction, an **electrical current** would be generated, simply because an electrical current is defined as the flow of electrons from one point to another. The unit of measurement for this electron flow is the **ampere.**

How can free electrons be motivated to move from one point to another? The answer lies in a practical application of the Law of Charges (like charges repel, and unlike charges attract). Since the electrons have a negative charge, they are attracted to a body that has a positive charge. However, it isn't possible to create a positive charge by itself. A negative charge is created simultaneously with the creation of a positive charge, because electrical charges are produced by the transfer of electrons from one point to another. Specifically, when electrons leave one point (creating a positive charge), they move to another point (creating a negative charge). (In the process, electrons are neither created nor destroyed but simply transferred.) Figure 3.4 simplistically illustrates the principle that the positive charge is created by the removal of electrons, and the negative charge is the result of an accumulation of electrons.

If two bodies of opposite charge are created, an electrical current could be generated if a conductor, such as a copper wire, were connected between them. Free electrons would flow from the negatively charged body to the positively charged body, as shown in Figure 3.5. The flow, or current, would continue as long as there was a difference in charge between the two bodies. This difference in the electrical charge between the bodies is called **potential** and is measured in **volts.**

The amount of voltage, or potential strength of the electrical system, is directly related to the difference in potential between the charged bodies. The greater the difference in potential between the charges, the greater that system's capacity to do work. A system with a rating of 220 volts has a greater potential capacity to do work than does a 117-volt system.

ELECTRICITY AT WORK

Every electrical system must have three parts: a **source,** a **load,** and a **circuit.** The source is a mechanism that provides a difference in potential, or voltage. The load is a device that uses the electricity to perform some function. The circuit is a pathway that the current follows as it flows from the negative to the positive terminal of the source. (A negative terminal is created by an excess of electrons; a positive terminal, by a dearth of electrons. In batteries this electron transfer happens through a chemical reaction.)

A practical demonstration of the interrelationship between the three elements of any electrical system is provided by the example of a very simple battery and lamp, as shown in Figure 3.6. The source of this system is an ordinary flashlight battery. The load is a small incandescent lamp. The circuit is composed of copper wire. When the wires are attached to the lamp and the terminals of the battery, electrons flow from the negative to the positive terminal of the battery. As the electrons pass through the filament of the lamp, resistance to their flow causes the filament to heat up and incandesce, or give off light. The current will continue as long as the circuit is intact and there is enough voltage left in the battery to overcome the resistance within the circuit and lamp filament. When the voltage is reduced to the point that it cannot overcome the circuit resistance, the current will stop, and the lamp will no longer glow.

Free electron: An electron that has broken away from its "home" atom to float free.

Electrical current: The flow or movement of electrons through a conductor.

Ampere: The unit of measurement of electrical current.

Potential: The difference in electrical charge between two bodies; measured in volts.

Volts: The unit of measurement of electrical potential.

Source: The origin of electrical potential, such as a battery or 120-volt wall outlet.

Load: A device that converts electrical energy into another form of energy: a lamp converts electrical energy to light and heat; an electrical motor converts electricity to mechanical energy.

Circuit: A conductive path through which electricity flows.

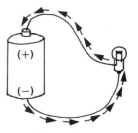

Current flow

Figure 3.6

A lamp will incandesce when current flows through it.

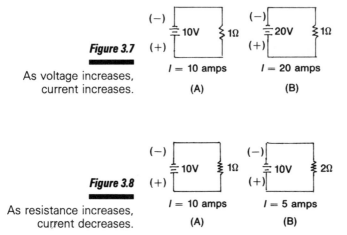

Figure 3.7

As voltage increases,
current increases.

$I = 10$ amps

(A)

$I = 20$ amps

(B)

Figure 3.8

As resistance increases,
current decreases.

$I = 10$ amps

(A)

$I = 5$ amps

(B)

Ohm's Law

Although it's interesting to know that electrons flow within a circuit, unless there is some way of determining how the various parts of the circuit affect one another, there is no real way to understand and predict what will happen in any electrical circuit. Fortunately, a German physicist, Georg Simon Ohm, discovered in the nineteenth century that some very basic rules apply to the functioning of electricity in a circuit. These relationships have been formalized as Ohm's Law, and they are the primary mathematical expressions used in determining electron action within a circuit. Ohm's Law states: *as voltage increases, current increases; as resistance increases, current decreases.*

The diagrams in Figures 3.7 and 3.8 will help illustrate these relationships. They show very simple schematic diagrams or drawings that substitute symbols for the various parts of the circuit. The ⏚ symbol represents a battery, and the ⏦ symbol represents a **resistance,** or load, within the circuit. Figure 3.7 illustrates the first portion of Ohm's Law. The voltage of the battery in Figure 3.7A is ten volts. With this voltage the 1-ohm resistance allows a current flow of 1 ampere. If the voltage is doubled to 20 volts, as shown in Figure 3.7B, and the resistance is not changed, the current will also double, to 2 amperes.

Figure 3.8 illustrates the second element of Ohm's Law. Figure 3.8A is a 10-volt system with a resistance, or load, of 1 ohm. This configuration allows a current flow of 10 amperes. In Figure 3.8B the voltage remains constant at 10 volts, but the resistance has been doubled to 2 ohms, which results in a reduction of the current to 5 amperes.

In both cases it is important to remember that the speed of the electron flow is constant. The increase or decrease in current flow is the result of an increase or decrease in the number of electrons flowing in the circuit.

Another way of looking at the relationships stated in Ohm's Law may help in understanding them. The voltage can be compared to the electrical pressure that causes the electrons to flow within the circuit. If more pressure (voltage) is applied, it would be logical for more electrons to flow. Since resistance is defined as opposition to the flow of electrons, any increase in the resistance would naturally cause the electron flow to decrease.

The relationships of Ohm's Law can be mathematically expressed as:

$$I = \frac{E}{R}$$

where I = current in amperes, E = voltage in volts, and R = resistance in ohms. This basic formula can be rearranged into two other forms. Each of these can be used to find the value of the other components of the relationship.

$$E = IR$$

$$R = \frac{E}{I}$$

These mathematical expressions of Ohm's Law are extremely valuable when working with low-voltage electronic systems such as those found in the control portion of electronic dimmers.

The Power Formula

Another formula, which is a derivation of Ohm's Law, is much more useful when dealing with higher voltage electricity. It is called the power formula. This formula is used when it is necessary to determine how much power will be consumed by an electrical circuit.

Household light bulbs, toasters, stage lamps, and electrical motors all convert electrical energy into mechanical energy, light, or heat in accomplishing their tasks. The amount of electrical energy converted, or consumed, is measured in watts. Usually the wattage figure is written on a label located somewhere on the device. Almost all household lamps have both the voltage and wattage printed on the top of the bulb. Toasters, electrical motors, and similar devices usually have a tag or label fixed on the bottom or back of the unit. The label states both the

Resistance: The opposition to electron flow within a conductor, measured in ohms; the amount of the resistance is dependent on the chemical makeup of the material through which the electricity is flowing.

CONDUCTORS, INSULATORS, GROUNDING, AND SHORTS

An electrical conductor is any material with an abundance of free electrons. Copper, aluminum, gold, and silver are all excellent conductors. Water is also a very good conductor. Conversely, an insulator is a material with few free electrons. The lack of free electrons effectively prevents the flow of electricity through an insulator. Air, glass, paper, rubber, and most plastics are good insulators. In electrical wire the conductor (usually copper) is surrounded by an insulator (normally rubber or plastic) to keep the electrical flow confined to the conductor and to prevent the conductor from making contact with anything else.

Safety dictates that all electrical equipment be grounded. This involves making a direct mechanical connection between the conductive housing of an electrical device and the earth. This connection is made through the gound pin on the electrical cord of the equipment. (The ground pin protrudes farther than the circuit connectors on all late-model plugs.) The ground pin makes contact with the ground wire, which, if you followed it back to the point where it enters the house or building, would be clamped to a metal rod driven five or more feet into the ground or to a metal water pipe. The purpose of the ground wire is to provide a low-resistance path for the electricity to follow in case of a short circuit between the power circuit and the device's metallic housing.

The difference between an overloaded circuit and a short circuit is really just a matter of degree. An overload occurs when the current flowing through a circuit is greater than the maximum current for which the system was designed. A short circuit is created when a very large surge of current in an overloaded circuit causes a portion of the wire, insulation, and anything else at the point of the short to explode.

An overload is created when a too-heavy load is placed on a circuit—as when a 3,000-watt load is placed on a circuit that was designed to safely carry a load of only 2,400 watts. A short circuit, or short, happens when a very-low-resistance alternative to the primary circuit is created. These alternate paths form when a wire breaks or comes loose from its terminal or when the insulation is worn away from the conductor, allowing it to touch another conductor or come into contact with the unit's metal housing.

If a short occurs in a grounded circuit, the very-low-resistance path between the circuit and the earth invites the surge of current to follow the ground circuit path. The high current flow activates a fuse or circuit breaker to shut off the electricity to the shorted equipment. If the circuit isn't grounded or if the ground circuit doesn't function (perhaps because someone has clipped off the ground pin from the plug), and you picked up the shorted device, you would be severely shocked, and possibly killed, because your body would act as the ground circuit to provide the path of least resistance between the shorted circuit and the earth.

You may find that some electrical hand tools do not have a grounding pin on the plug. The information plate attached to the tool's casing will probably carry the words *double insulated*. These tools don't need grounding, because the casing that you hold is actually a second, or outer, casing. These two layers of plastic insulators (casings) effectively isolate you from harm from any potential short.

voltage and wattage of the unit. Stage lighting lamps have this information printed on either the metal lamp base or the top of the lamp.

The power formula is usually referred to colloquially as either the "pie" or the "West Virginia" formula:

$$P = IE$$

where

P = power in watts
I = current in amperes
E = voltage in volts

$$W = VA$$

where

W = power in watts
V = voltage in volts
A = current in amperes

The power formula can be rearranged as Ohm's Law can:

$$P = IE$$
$$E = \frac{P}{I}$$
$$I = \frac{P}{E}$$

$$W = VA$$
$$A = \frac{W}{V}$$
$$V = \frac{W}{A}$$

With these three expressions of the power formula it is possible to find the unknown quantity in an electrical circuit if the other two factors are known.

An everyday example will help illustrate the point. You want to put a desk lamp on a table, but the power cord won't reach from the table to the wall outlet. You go to the hardware store to buy an extension cord, and the only information attached to the power cord indicates that it will safely carry 6 amperes of current. You know that the voltage in your apartment is 117 volts (standard household voltage in the United States). The lamp you plan to use is rated at 150 watts. To determine if the extension cord is safe to use, you will need to find out how many amperes of current the 150-watt lamp will create. To find the answer just plug the known information ($V = 117$, $W = 150$) into the appropriate variation of the power formula—the variation that has the unknown variable (in this case, A) located on the left side of the equal sign.

$$A = \frac{W}{V}$$
$$A = \frac{150}{117}$$
$$A = 1.28 \text{ amps}$$

The lamp creates a current of 1.28 amperes, so the extension cord, which can carry 6 amperes, will be safe to use.

Fuse: A device to protect a circuit from an overload; has a soft metal strip that melts, breaking circuit continuity.

Circuit breaker: A device to protect a circuit from an overload; has a magnetic device that trips open, breaking circuit continuity.

Practical Information

The output load voltage of dimming systems in the United States is 117–120 volts alternating current (VAC). The input voltage for most portable dimming systems is either 208 VAC (3 phase) or 220–240 VAC (single phase). (The figure 220 VAC is a generic term frequently, though often inaccurately, used to describe voltage in the 208–240 range. The specific voltage and phase are important for calculating purposes and vary from installation to installation.) The voltage figure that you will use in calculating the safe loading capacity for dimmers is the output voltage—117–120 VAC.

Electrical wires and cables are designed to carry specific current loads, as shown in Table 3.1.

Any electrical system is designed to work within certain limits. If those safe limits are exceeded, the system will do one of two things:

1. If adequate protective devices (**fuses, circuit breakers**) have been placed in the circuit, those units will break the continuity of the circuit and stop the flow of electricity.

OUTPUT AND INPUT VOLTAGE

Input voltage is the voltage that is fed into a device (amplifier, dimmer). The output voltage is the voltage that comes out of the same device. In stage lighting systems input voltage refers to the voltage that is fed to the dimmer pack (used with portable dimming systems) or rack (used with permanently installed systems). The input voltage (usually 208–240 volts) is broken down (reduced) inside the dimmer pack so that it can be used by the individual dimmers, which are designed to work at a maximum output voltage of 117–120 VAC.

Electronic dimmers have two voltage systems—a low-voltage control circuit and a high-voltage load circuit. The low-voltage control circuit (which varies between 8 and 28 VAC depending on the manufacturer) is used to regulate the output of the high-voltage (117–120 VAC) load circuit. This means that the intensity of the lighting instruments, which are connected to the load circuit, is controlled by the low-voltage control circuit.

TABLE 3.1   American Wire Gauge Current Capacity Chart

Gauge of wire	10	12	14	16	18
Capacity in amps	25	20	15	6	3

2. If there are no fuses or circuit breakers in the circuit, the various elements within the system will heat up. If the overload is sufficiently large, the elements within the system (dimmers, cables, plugs, and so on) will heat up to the point where they will either melt or burn up. If combustible material is in the immediate proximity of the overheated elements, it is very possible that a fire will start.

The following problems illustrate how the power formula can be used to calculate the safe electrical load limits of typical stage lighting situations.

Problem No. 1   The output voltage of a dimmer is 120 VAC. The dimmer can handle 20 amperes of current. What is the maximum safe load that can be placed on this dimmer?

$$\text{watts} = \text{volts times amperes } (W = VA)$$
$$W = 120 \times 20$$
$$W = 2{,}400 \text{ watts}$$

The dimmer can safely carry any load up to, but not exceeding, 2,400 watts.

Problem No. 2   The system voltage is 120 VAC. The dimmer can carry 2,400 watts (2.4 kilowatts, or KW). The 14-gauge cable connecting the dimmer to the lighting instruments can carry 15 amperes (see Table 3.1). How many 500-watt lighting instruments can be safely loaded onto the dimmer (Figure 3.9)?

We already know that the dimmer can handle 2.4 KW, but we need to determine the load that can be safely carried by the cable.

$$W = VA$$
$$W = 120 \times 15$$
$$W = 1{,}800 \text{ watts}$$

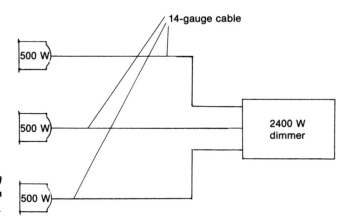

Figure 3.9

Problem No. 2.

The cable can carry a maximum load of 1,800 watts. To determine the number of 500-watt lighting instruments that can be carried by the cable, divide 1,800 by 500.

$$\frac{1,800}{500} = 3.6$$

Theoretically, the cable can safely carry 3.6 instruments. Pragmatically, it can safely carry three instruments. Even though the dimmer can safely carry four instruments, the single cable connecting the dimmer to the instruments can handle only the current flow generated by three 500-watt stage lighting instruments.

Electrical Circuits

Two primary types of circuits, series and parallel, are used to distribute electricity. A third type, known as a combination circuit, combines the principles of the two.

Series Circuit   In a series circuit all of the electricity flows through every element of the circuit, as shown in Figure 3.10. In a series circuit if any of the lamps burn out, the circuit will be broken, the electricity won't flow, and the remaining lamps will go out.

Parallel Circuit   In a parallel circuit only a portion of the electricity flows through each of the branches of the circuit. If one of the lamps shown in Figure 3.11 burns out, electricity will continue to flow in the rest of the circuit, and the other lamps will continue to glow.

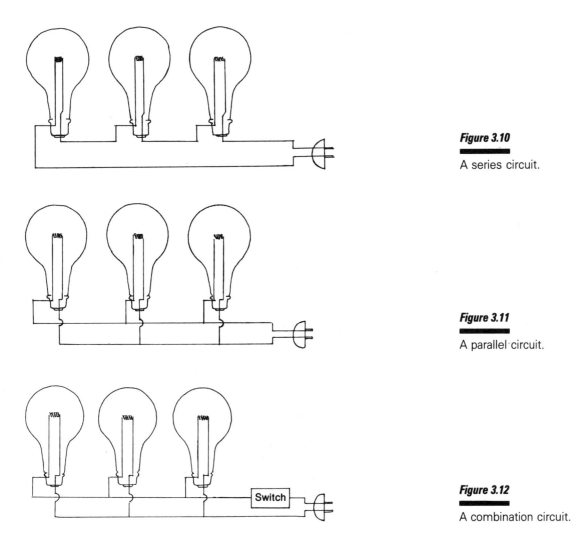

Figure 3.10

A series circuit.

Figure 3.11

A parallel circuit.

Figure 3.12

A combination circuit.

Combination Circuit   Any electrical circuit that uses a switch to control a light is a working example of a combination circuit. In a typical application of a combination circuit in stage lighting, a control device (switch, dimmer, fuse, circuit breaker) is used in series with the lamp load, and the lamps are wired in parallel, as shown in Figure 3.12. The series arrangement allows the switch or dimmer to exert control over the whole circuit, and the parallel wiring of the lamp outlets allows individual lamps to be inserted or removed from the circuit without affecting its operation.

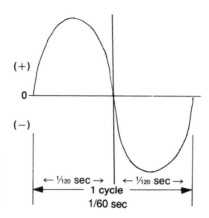

Figure 3.13

An alternating current (AC) cycle.

Electrical Current

There are two types of electrical current, direct and alternating.

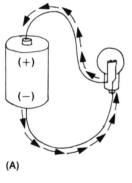

(A)

Direct Current   In direct current (DC) the electron flow is in one direction only. The battery demonstration discussed in a previous section is an example of direct current. The flow of the current is always from the negative terminal of a battery to its positive terminal. All batteries are examples of direct current sources.

Alternating Current   The overwhelming majority of electrical power generated by power stations throughout the world is alternating current (AC). The electron flow in AC is the same as in DC with one exception—the current flow periodically changes polarity, which causes the electron flow to change direction. In the United States alternating current changes polarity at the rate of sixty cycles per second (60 Hz). This means that the electricity changes polarity (direction) every 1/120th of a second, as shown in Figure 3.13.

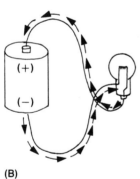

(B)

Figure 3.14

Current flow reverses direction when the circuit wires connected to the battery are reversed.

An example may help to explain this phenomenon. If the wires connected to the terminals of a battery, as shown in Figure 3.14A, were reversed (Figure 3.14B), the lamp would still emit light, but the current flow would have changed directions. Alternating current works like this example, except that the direction of current flow changes direction every 1/120th of a second.

The principal advantages of AC over DC are that AC is easier and cheaper to generate and that there is less voltage loss when the electricity is transmitted over a great distance.

This chapter has provided a brief glance at the nature and uses of electricity. Anyone who is thinking about a career in lighting design or any other area of theatrical design or production would be wise to take a course or two in practical electronics as well as make an intensive study of standard electrical wiring practice.

ELECTRICAL WIRING

Before beginning this discussion of electric power service, remember: these high-voltage distribution systems can kill; if you don't fully understand how the systems work, call a supervisor or licensed electrician.

A number of wiring configurations are used to distribute AC power. Figure A illustrates a typical 120-VAC service system. According to National Electrical Code (NEC) practice, in the United States the insulation of one wire is normally colored black. It is called the "hot" wire. The insulation on the other wire is white, and it is called the "neutral."

The ground wire is not included in any of these illustrations, because it should not be used as part of the electrical distribution system. However, it needs to be included in the wiring of the system, and, according to code, its color should be green.

Figure B illustrates a three-wire, single-phase 120/240-VAC system. The voltage between either of the two hot wires (normally black) and the neutral (white) will be 120 VAC. The voltage between the two hot wires will be 220–240 VAC. Electrical service is delivered to most houses with this three-wire

system. At the main service box (fuse box or circuit breaker panel) the 120 VAC is distributed to the various lamp and wall outlets, and the 240 VAC service is usually routed only to the electric range and clothes dryer.

Figure C shows a three-phase, or four-wire, 120/208-VAC service system. The voltage between the neutral (white) and any of the three hot lines (black) will be 120 VAC. Although the input voltage measured between any of the hot lines and ground will be 240 VAC, the voltage measured between any two of the hot lines (phases) will be 208 VAC.

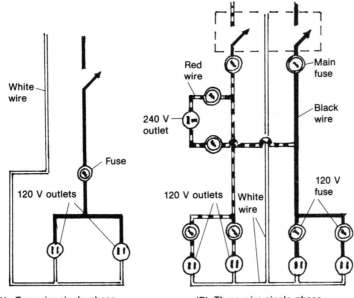

(A) Two-wire single-phase 120 VAC system

(B) Three-wire single-phase 120/240 VAC system

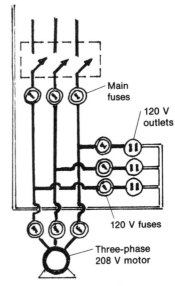

(C) Four-wire three-phase 120/208 VAC system

SAFETY TIP *ELECTRICAL HAZARDS*

Electricity is extremely dangerous. It can burn, maim, and kill. Any piece of equipment that is connected to an electrical outlet should always be handled with caution and common sense. If you follow the safety procedures and work habits outlined below, your work with electricity can be safe and productive.

1. If you don't know what you're doing, don't do it. Ask your supervisor, or consult a trained electrician.

2. Use tools that are covered with plastic or rubber insulation when working with electricity.

3. Use wooden or fiberglass ladders when working on elevated electrical jobs. Electricity will always take the path of least resistance, and a metal ladder (and your body) provides a very-low-resistance path. If metal ladders must be used, insulate them with high-quality rubber foot pads. Movable metal scaffolds or adjustable ladders should have lockable rubber casters.

4. Disconnect any device (lighting instrument, motor, amplifier) from the circuit before you work on it. Unplug any lighting instrument before changing the lamp.

5. Use common sense: Don't touch any bare wires. Don't work in damp locations or put a drink where it could spill on an electrical or electronic component. Don't intentionally overload a circuit. Don't try to bypass fuses or circuit breakers.

6. Maintain the integrity of all ground circuits. Don't clip the ground plug off of any extension cord or power cord. When necessary, use ground plug adapters.

7. Check cables and connectors periodically, and replace any items that show signs of cracking, chipping, or other deterioration. Cracks in the insulation of cables and connectors increase the chances of receiving a shock from the device.

8. Keep the cables and connectors clean. Remove any corrosion, paint, grease, dust, or other accumulations as soon as they become evident. These substances can act as insulation between the contacts of the connector, and–if flammable–they can pose a fire hazard.

9. When stage or microphone cables are not in use, coil them and hang them up. A cable will stay neatly coiled if the connectors are plugged together or if it is tied with light rope or fastened with a Velcro loop.

10. Always disconnect a plug by pulling on the body of the connector, not the cable. Pulling on the cable puts an unnecessary strain on the cable clamp and will eventually defeat the clamp. When the cable clamp no longer functions, pulling on the cable places the strain directly on the electrical connections.

11. Be sure that all elements of a cable are of the same electrical rating: 12-gauge cable (capable of carrying 20 amperes of current) should only have 20-ampere-rated connectors.

LENSES, LAMPS, AND LIGHTING INSTRUMENTS

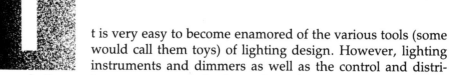

t is very easy to become enamored of the various tools (some would call them toys) of lighting design. However, lighting instruments and dimmers as well as the control and distribution systems are not ends in themselves; they are simply the metaphorical mallet and chisels that lighting designers use to create their sculptures in light. This chapter will explore the major lighting instruments used in the theatre.

LENSES

The lenses used with most stage lighting instruments control the angle of the beam of light emitted by those instruments. Lenses refract light, which means that they redirect, or deflect, light from its normally straight path. The amount of deflection depends on the angle of intersection between the light ray and the surface of the lens, as well as the density of the medium through which the light is passing.

When a light ray passes from one medium into another medium of greater density (for example, from air into glass), it bends away from its original direction of travel. The direction of the deflection depends on the angle of intersection of the light ray and the boundary between the two media. When it passes through the glass and reenters the air (from more to less dense), it bends back toward its original direction of travel. Figure 4.1 provides an illustration of these principles.

The more pronounced the curvature of the convex face of the lens, the more quickly the parallel light rays will converge, as shown in Figure 4.2. The distance that it takes the light to converge into a single point is referred to as the **focal length** of the lens.

The focal length of a lens affects the angle of the beam of light emitted by that lens. When considered in relationship to the diameter of the lens, the shorter the focal length, the wider the beam of light emitted by that lens, as shown in Figure 4.3. A standard stage lighting instrument—the ellipsoidal reflector spotlight (ERS)—can be used to demonstrate this principle. If it is equipped with a lens 6 inches in diameter that has a focal length of 9 inches (known as a 6 × 9), it will produce a wider beam of light than an instrument equipped with a 6 × 12 lens. Similarly a 6 × 12 ERS produces a wider beam of light than a 6 × 16 ERS.

Focal length: The distance from the lens at which the light rays converge into a point; for lenses used in stage lighting instruments the focal length is most frequently measured in even inches.

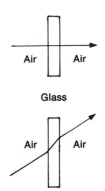

Figure 4.1
▬▬▬
Light rays are deflected when they pass through a lens.

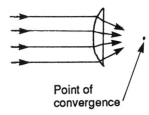

Figure 4.2
▬▬▬
The greater the curvature of the convex face of a lens, the greater the angle of deflection, and vice versa.

WHY SO MANY LENSES?

Theoretically, a single plano-convex lens would work very nicely in stage lighting instruments, but several practical considerations preclude the use of these lenses. To be optically effective, a single lens would need a severe curvature on its convex side, which would result in a thick lens; and a thick lens has two disadvantages. First, thick lenses are susceptible to heat fracture. During the manufacture of the lens, molten glass is poured into a mold. In the cooling process the outside of the lens cools faster than its inside, setting up stresses inside the lens that can cause it to crack. The internal stresses can be controlled by slow cooling in a special oven that carefully lowers the temperature over a period of hours. In practical theatre applications, however, lenses are quickly heated by the lamps, and there is no controlled heating or cooling. As a result, thick lenses almost always crack. Second, a certain amount of light passing through any lens is absorbed by the glass: the thicker the glass, the more light it absorbs. In reality, double plano-convex lens trains, step lenses, and Fresnel lenses all absorb less light than does a single thicker lens of the same focal length.

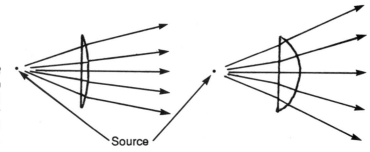

Figure 4.3

The shorter the focal length of a lens, the wider the beam of light emitted by that lens.

Figure 4.4

Double plano-convex lens train.

The specific focal length of a **plano-convex lens** is determined by the curvature of the convex face of the lens. The greater the curvature, the shorter the focal length.

Three primary types of lens systems, all based on the plano-convex lens, are used with theatrical lighting instruments: the double plano-convex lens train, the step lens, and the Fresnel lens.

Double Plano-Convex Lens Train

The double plano-convex lens train consists of two plano-convex lenses placed with their convex surfaces toward each other, as shown in Figure 4.4. This double configuration provides the same optical properties as a single lens of greater thickness and curvature, and the total thickness of the two lenses is less than the thickness of the optically comparable

(A)

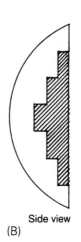

Side view

(B)

Plano-convex lens: A lens with one flat and one outward curving face.

Figure 4.5

Step lens. The shaded area in (B) is eliminated from the lens.

single lens. The single lens with short focal length is not used in lighting instruments, because its thickness makes it very susceptible to heat fracture. The thicker single lens also transmits less light than does its thinner optical equivalent in the double plano-convex lens system.

Step Lens

A step lens retains the optical characteristics and shape of a plano-convex lens, but the glass on the flat side is cut away in steps, as shown in Figure 4.5. The stepping process gives the lens the optical properties of a thick, short-focal-length, plano-convex lens while eliminating its negative characteristics.

An inherent property of step lenses is the prismatic effect caused by the steps themselves. Light passing through the steps at a shallow angle tends to create a spectral flare in the same manner that a prism breaks white light into a rainbow. Finishing the edges of the steps with a flat-black ceramic coating eliminates the spectral breakdown in most step lenses and does not interfere with the light passing through the rest of the lens (Figure 4.6).

Fresnel Lens

Originally intended for use in lighthouses by its inventor, Augustin Fresnel, the Fresnel lens is a type of step lens with the glass cut away from the convex face of the lens instead of its plano side, as shown in Figure 4.7. The advantages of the Fresnel lens are the same as for the step lens; reduction of the thickness of the lens allows more light transmission and lessens the chances of heat fracture.

Black ceramic coating

Figure 4.6

A black ceramic coating prevents spectral breakdown.

Figure 4.7

Fresnel lens. The shaded
area in (B) is eliminated
from the lens.

(A)   (B)

Side view

Fresnel lenses are used with both ERS and Fresnel spotlights. However, there are optically significant differences between the finishing of the two types of lens. Fresnel lenses for use with ERS's have black ceramic coating applied to the vertical faces of the steps to eliminate spectral flare. Fresnel lenses for use in many Fresnel spotlights do not have such a coating (although some do), and the plano side of the lens is finished with a surface treatment to **diffuse** light. The diffusing treatment generally makes the plano side of the lens appear as though it has been sandblasted, or it may be finished with a series of small rectangular indentations. Regardless of the appearance of the treatment, its purpose is to soften the light to create the characteristically soft, luminescent light of the Fresnel spotlight.

LAMPS

Since many stage lighting instruments are designed to use lamps of specific shapes and characteristics, it makes sense to study about lamps before we discuss lighting instruments.

The two primary sources used for stage lighting instruments are the standard incandescent lamp and the tungsten-halogen lamp.

Incandescent Lamp

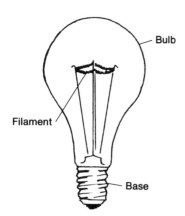

Bulb

Filament

Base

Figure 4.8

A standard incandescent
lamp.

The standard incandescent lamp contains a tungsten **filament** that is placed in an inert gas environment inside the lamp **bulb,** as shown in Figure 4.8. The inert gas within the bulb is not pure and contains some oxygen. As an electrical current passes through the filament, heating it to incandescence, particles of tungsten are released. These particles are deposited to form the dark coating frequently found on the inside of older bulbs or envelopes. Eventually the filament weakens sufficiently to cause it to break. The average life expectancy of a regular incandescent lamp designed for use in stage lighting instruments ranges anywhere from 50 to approximately 200 hours. The life rating for a lamp does not mean that the light will burn out in the rated time. It means that the original output of the lamp will be reduced by 40 percent by the buildup on the inside of the bulb. Most lamps continue to burn long after their rated life, but at a significantly reduced output.

Tungsten-Halogen Lamp

Although it looks rather different from its cousin, the tungsten-halogen (T-H) lamp (Figure 4.9) is primarily the same as the standard incandescent lamp in all respects but one: the atmosphere inside the bulb of the T-H lamp is a halogen, or chemically active, gas instead of an inert gas. As the bits of tungsten are released from the tungsten filament, they unite with the halogen gas to form a compound that is attracted back to the filament. The tungsten reunites with the filament, and the halogen gas is released to repeat this chemical action. Because of the halogen cycle, tungsten is not deposited on the inside of the bulb, and the filament of the T-H lamp is constantly being replenished. This results in a significantly longer life expectancy for the T-H lamp. Many T-H lamps designed for stage lighting instruments are rated from 150 to 2,000 hours, as shown in Figure 4.10.

The halogen cycle becomes active only in a high-temperature environment. To achieve this goal the T-H filament is encased within a small, highly heat-resistant synthetic quartz envelope. The heat generated by the filament is confined within the small space, and the resultant temperatures are much higher than if a larger bulb were used.

Arc Sources

An electric arc that produces a brilliantly blue-white light is created when an electric current jumps the air gap between two electrodes. An **open arc** is used as the source on some followspots.

When an arc is struck in an oxygen-rich environment such as air, the electrodes are consumed in the same way that a welding rod deteriorates during arc welding. If the arc is encapsulated in a noncorrosive atmosphere, however, the electrodes deteriorate extremely slowly. Encapsulated arcs such as the xenon and HMI (metal halide)

Diffuse: To soften the appearance of light by using a translucent filtering element to scatter the rays.

Filament: The light-producing element of a lamp; usually made of tungsten wire.

Bulb: The Pyrex glass or synthetic quartz container for a lamp filament and gaseous environment.

Open arc: A light source in which the two electrodes operate in the open air.

Figure 4.9

A tungsten-halogen incandescent lamp.

Sylvania Tungsten Halogen Lamps

MEDIUM PREFOCUS – 3½" LCL – REPLACEMENT*

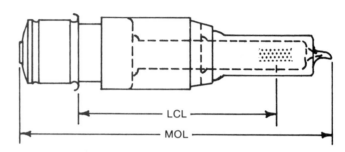

Figure 4.10

The rated life of tungsten-halogen lamps varies according to their color temperature and output (lumens). Generally, the higher the output, the higher the color temperature and the shorter the life (and conversely). (Courtesy of Sylvania Lighting Products.)

ANSI Code	Watts	Volts	Bulb	Fila-ment	Base	Lumens	Color Temp. (°K)	Avg. Rated Life (Hrs.)	LCL In.	mm	MOL In.	mm
EGC/EGD	500	120	T-4	CC8	Med. Pf.	13,000	3200	150	3½	88.9	5½	139.7
EGE	500	120	T-4	CC8	Med. Pf.	10,000	3000	2000	3½	88.9	5½	139.7
EGF	750	120	T-4	CC8	Med. Pf.	20,000	3200	250	3½	88.9	5½	139.7
EGG	750	120	T-5	CC8	Med. Pf.	15,000	3000	2000	3½	88.9	5½	139.7
DNT/FMD	750	120	—	—	Med. Pf.	17,000	3050	500	3½	88.9	6⅛	155.6
EGJ	1000	120	T-6	CC8	Med. Pf.	25,500	3200	400	3½	88.9	5¾	146.0
EGK	1000	120	T-6†	CC8	Med. Pf.	24,500	3200	400	—	—	5¾	146.0
DNV/FME	1000	120	—	—	Med. Pf.	27,500	3200	200	3½	88.9	6⅛	155.6

*Family of lamps which are replacements for existing incandescent T12 types primarily utilized in ellipsoidal reflector spotlights.
†Frosted

lamps are frequently used in followspots. Neither arc nor encapsulated arc sources can be dimmed, so they are not used in "regular" stage lighting instruments.

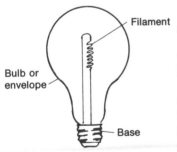

Figure 4.11

Lamp structure.

Lamp Structure

All lamps, regardless of shape or type, are composed of three basic parts: bulb, base, and filament, as shown in Figure 4.11.

Bulb   The bulb is the Pyrex or synthetic quartz envelope that encases the filament and acts as a container for the gas-filled atmosphere of the lamp. The shape and size of the bulb is determined by the position and shape of the filament, the burning position of the lamp within the lighting instrument, and the heat dissipation requirements of the lamp. Figure 4.12 illustrates common incandescent bulb shapes. Bulb sizes vary, depending on individual lamp requirements.

COLOR TEMPERATURE

All the standard light sources appear to be white. They are actually a variety of colors, however, and these colors can be identified by using the color temperature scale.

The color temperature scale was originally determined by heating a device known as a blackbody radiator. As the blackbody was heated, its color was read at specific temperatures by a spectrometer (a device for measuring specific wavelengths of light). The color temperature scale, measured in degrees Kelvin (K), was the result of this experiment. The following table shows the color temperature of a number of standard sources.

Color Temperature of Some Common Sources

Color Temperature	Light Source
6500	An overcast day
6000	Xenon
5500	HMI (halide metal incandescent)
5000	Sunshine on a clear day
4500	Fluorescent (cool white)
4000	
3500	
3000	Theatrical Incandescent (standard and tungsten-halogen)
2500	Household lamps
2000	

There is a loose, but fairly constant, correlation among color temperature, light output, and lamp life. Generally speaking, the higher the light output of a lamp (which is measured in lumens), the higher its color temperature and the shorter its rated life. A comparison of the specifications for similar lamps such as the EGC/EGD and the EGE (the American National Standards Institute codes for two commonly used theatrical lamps) illustrates this relationship (Figure 4.10).

Although it isn't essential that the color temperature of all lamps used to light a production be the same, the instruments that are going to be gelled with color media of a specific hue are generally equipped with lamps of the same color temperature so that the color of the resultant light will be uniform.

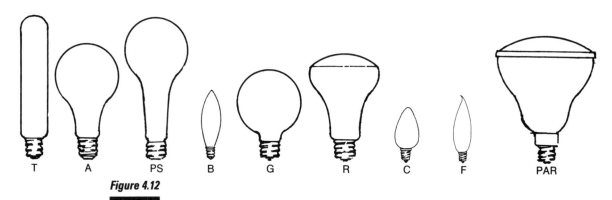

Figure 4.12

Common incandescent
lamp shapes.

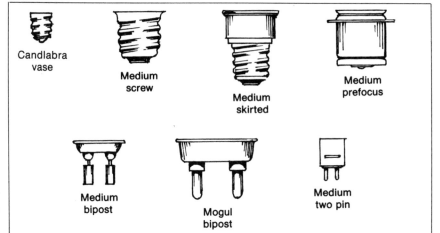

Figure 4.13

Typical lamp bases.

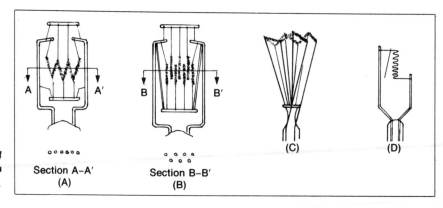

Figure 4.14

Filament styles.

TABLE 4.1   Comparison of Same Wattage/Different Output Lamps

Watts	Sylvania Ordering Abbreviation	Other Designation	NAED Code	Standard Case Quantity	Volts	Color Temperature (°K)	Nominal Lumens	Average Rated Life (hrs.)	Filament Class	Fused Silica Bulb Finish	Lighted Length (in.)
1000	DXN	—	53993	12	120	3400	33500	30	CC-8	Clear	11/16
1000	DXW	—	53997	12	120	3200	28000	150	CC-8	Clear	13/16
1000	FBY	Frosted DXW	53996	12	120	3200	26000	150	CC-8	Frosted	—
1000	FBZ	Frosted DXN	53999	12	120	3400	31500	30	CC-8	Frosted	—
1000	BRH	—	54563	12	120	3350	30000	75	CC-8	Clear	—

Source: Sylvania Lighting Handbook, 7th ed.

Base   The lamp base secures the lamp in the socket and provides the electrical contact points between the socket and the filament. There are several styles of lamp base, as illustrated in Figure 4.13. Generally, large, high-wattage incandescent lamps have the larger bases. Figure 4.13 shows not only the different bases but also the relative size relationship that each base has to the others. The candelabra base is approximately ½ inch in diameter, the medium-size bases are approximately 1 inch in diameter, and the mogul bases are about 1½ inches across.

The prefocus, bipost, and two-pin bases are used for instruments that need the filament in a specific location in relationship to the reflector—such as the ERS or Fresnel spotlight discussed later in this chapter.

Filament   Various lamp filaments are available, each designed to perform a particular function. All filaments for stage lighting instrument lamps are made of tungsten wire, usually tightly coiled, and strung in one of the general configurations shown in Figure 4.14.

Light Output of Lamps

The output of an incandescent lamp, while related to the lamp wattage, is primarily a function of the size and composition of the filament. This output is measured in lumens. Generally speaking, if two lamps have the same wattage but one has a smaller filament, the smaller-filament lamp will have a higher lumen output but a shorter life expectancy, as shown in Table 4.1.

LAMP MAINTENANCE

Although it is a good idea to keep all lamps clean and free from dirt and grease, it is particularly important to handle tungsten-halogen lamps with extreme care. The bulb of the T-H lamp must be kept free of all fingerprints, grease, or any other foreign substance that could cause a change in the heat-dissipation characteristics of the bulb. Because a T-H lamp reaches a high temperature, any change in its heat dissipation characteristics could cause the lamp to break or explode.

When installing lamps, grasp the lamp by the base rather than the bulb. If this is not practical, a soft cloth or glove should be used to handle the glass envelope. This practice will protect both your hands and the lamp bulb.

Although it is not as important to keep a regular incandescent lamp as scrupulously clean as a T-H bulb, it is good practice to wipe the bulb with a soft cloth after handling.

Lamp bases should be kept free of any corrosive buildup or insulating deposits that could interfere with the electrical contact between the socket and base.

LIGHTING INSTRUMENTS

Various lighting instruments are used in the theatre, but the ellipsoidal reflector spotlight and the Fresnel spotlight are the real workhorses for the lighting designer.

Ellipsoidal Reflector Spotlight

The light produced by an ellipsoidal reflector spotlight (ERS) has a relatively narrow beam width and is capable of traveling long distances. The quality of the light produced by this instrument, also known by the trade names Leko and Klieglight, can be characterized as generally hard edged with little diffusion. The shape of the beam is controlled by internally mounted shutters. The spill light from an ERS (that is, any light that escapes past the edge of the beam) is minimal. Because of all these characteristics, ERS's are the primary lighting tool of the designer. Several manufacturers' versions of the ERS are shown in Figure 4.15.

Figure 4.15

Ellipsoidal reflector
spotlights. (Courtesy of
Kliegl Bros., Colortran, and
Strand Century.)

General Operating Principles The reflector of an ERS is a truncated conical ellipse, which has properties that are uniquely suited to focusing light. The conical elliptical reflector shown in Figure 4.16A has two focal points, F1 and F2. Light emitted by a light source at F1 will reflect off the walls of the conical ellipse and pass through F2. If half of the elliptical reflector were removed (Figure 4.16B), light emitted from the source at F1 would again pass through F2, although some of the light would pass out of the open end of the reflector and be lost.

The ERS operates on this basic principle of gathering light from one focal point (F1) and focusing it on the second focal point (F2). Some ERS's have a kickback reflector placed at the open end of the conical ellipse to redirect any spill light back into the reflector, as shown in Figure 4.16C. The shutters, made of stainless steel or some other highly heat-resistant metal, are located in a plane close to the second focal point to shape the light.

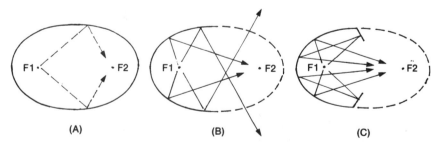

(A) (B) (C)

Figure 4.16

Optical properties of a
conical ellipse reflector.

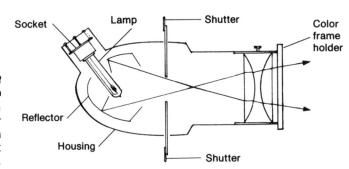

Figure 4.17
─────

Cutaway view of an
axial-mount ellipsoidal
reflector spotlight.

Figure 4.18
─────

Cutaway view of an
ellipsoidal reflector
spotlight designed for a
T-shaped incandescent
lamp.

Figure 4.19
─────

A continuously
variable-focal-length
ellipsoidal reflector
spotlight. (Courtesy of
Strand Century.)

Figure 4.17 shows a cross section of an axial-mount ERS, so called because the lamp is placed on the optical, or center-line, axis of the instrument. This configuration was made possible by the development of the tungsten-halogen lamp. Compare the position of the lamp in the axial-mount instrument (Figure 4.17) with the instrument shown in Figure 4.18, an ERS designed for the larger incandescent T-shaped lamp, which predates the T-H lamp. Note how the lamp filament is still located at the focal point of the ellipsoidal reflector even though the lamp is mounted in a different position.

The lens is placed at a point in front of the shutters to focus the light into the desired field angle, as shown in Figures 4.17 and 4.18. ERS's are equipped with one of three lens systems: a double plano-convex lens train; a step lens; or, on some older models, a Fresnel lens. Although there may be slight differences in light output and quality, the three types work equally well.

The **zoom ellipse,** more officially known as the variable-focal-length ERS (Figure 4.19), is an extremely versatile instrument. This variation of the standard ERS has lenses that can slide forward or backward to change the focal length of the instrument. Changing the

TABLE 4.2   Beam and Field Angles for Typical ERS's*

Instrument Type	Beam Angle	Field Angle	Maximum Effective Range†
6 × 9	16°	37°	35 feet
6 × 12	11°	26°	50 feet
6 × 16	9°	18°	65 feet
20°	10°	20°	65 feet
30°	12°	30°	60 feet
40°	15°	40°	55 feet

*All data are approximate but typical. Specifics vary with manufacturer.
† Determined by point at which output diminishes to 50 footcandles.

Zoom ellipse: An ellipsoidal reflector spotlight with movable lenses that allow the focal length to be changed.

Color frame: A lightweight metal holder for color media that fits in a holder at the front of a lighting instrument.

Gobo: A thin metal template inserted into an ellipsoidal reflector spotlight to project a shadow pattern of light.

focal length affects the beam angles and field angles of the instrument, with those angles widening as the focal length becomes shorter. The field angle of most zoom ellipses can be varied between approximately 20 and 45 degrees.

Figure 4.20 illustrates another type of variable-focal-length ERS. Its lenses can be moved between slots in the housing to change the field angle in 10-degree increments between 20 and 50 degrees.

Table 4.2 lists the beam and field angles in degrees of arc for several varieties of 6-inch ERS's. The beam angle (Figure 4.21) is that point where the intensity of the cone of light emitted by the instrument diminishes to 50 percent of its intensity as compared with the center of the beam. The field angle is that point where the light diminishes to 10 percent of the output of the center of the beam. An explanation of how this information is used is given in Chapter 13, "Using the Lighting Key to Draw the Light Plot."

Accessories   The most basic accessory designed for use with an ERS is the **color frame** (Figure 4.22), a lightweight-metal or heat-resistant-fiber holder for plastic colored media. The color frame is inserted into the holder on the front of the ERS to color the light.

The **gobo** (Figure 4.23), also known as a pattern, template, or cookie, is a lightweight metal cutout that turns the ERS into a pattern projector. Most ERS's are equipped with a built-in pattern slot located adjacent to the shutter plane. A wide variety of commercially designed gobos, usually made of stainless steel, are available from scenic and lighting supply houses. Gobos can be constructed from metal offset printing sheets or from heavyweight disposable aluminum cookware

Figure 4.20

A variable-focal-length ellipsoidal reflector spotlight. (Courtesy of Colortran.)

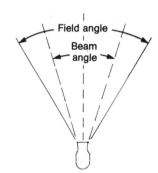

Figure 4.21

Beam and field angles.

Dremel tool: A hand-held router similar to a dentist's drill, which can be equipped with a number of bits for grinding, cutting, or carving of wood, plastic, and metal.

Iris: A device with movable overlapping metal plates, used with an ellipsoidal reflector spotlight to change the size of the circular pattern of light.

(roasting pans, pie plates), as shown in Figure 4.24. Offset printing sheets are thin, flexible aluminum sheets, which can usually be obtained from local newspaper publishers at low cost. They can withstand the heat generated by an ERS, are stiff enough to prevent flexing or buckling, and can be worked quite easily with scissors, chisels, or a **Dremel tool.** The disposable aluminum pie plates are very satisfactory for making cloud gobos and similar patterns that have little intricate detail. The aluminum used in these products is about one-third as thick as the offset printing sheets and will vaporize under the high heat generated by the instrument lamp if the pattern is too detailed. It is much better to make intricately designed gobos from the offset printing sheets or from stainless steel.

Another useful accessory for an ERS is the iris (Figure 4.25). The iris varies the size of the circular pattern produced by an ERS. It is mounted in the shutter plane, and the size of the aperture is controlled by an external handle.

Fresnel Spotlight

The Fresnel spotlight produces a soft, diffused, luminescent light. Examples are shown in Figure 4.26. When the instrument is focused on narrow beam, or spot, as shown in Figure 4.27A, it produces a beam with a central hot spot that rapidly loses intensity toward the edge. When the instrument is focused on wide beam, or flood (Figure 4.27B), it produces a smooth wash of light.

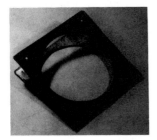

Figure 4.22

A color frame.

Figure 4.23

(A) A gobo, and (B) the pattern that the gobo projects.

(A)

(B)

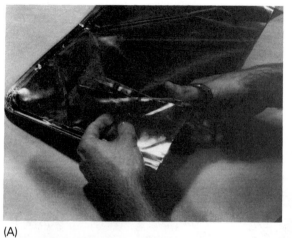

(A)

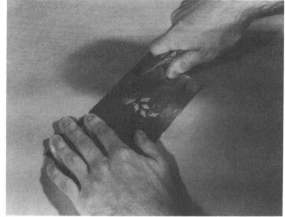

(B)

(C)

(D)

Figure 4.24

Gobos can be built in the shop by cutting the pattern out of disposable aluminum cookware (A,B,C) using scissors or from offset printing sheets using a Dremel tool (D).

Figure 4.25

An ellipsoidal reflector spotlight equipped with an iris.

Figure 4.26

Fresnel spotlights.
(Courtesy of Kliegl Bros.
and Colortran.)

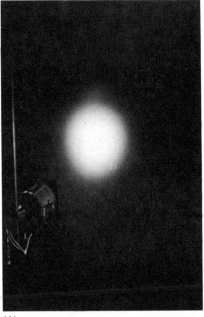

Figure 4.27

The Fresnel spotlight can
be focused on spot (A) or
flood (B).   (A)   (B)

The lens of a standard Fresnel spotlight has a diffusing treatment on its plano face that produces a soft, circular beam of light. The oval-beam Fresnel lens (Figure 4.28) has the same luminescent and optical qualities as its round-beam counterpart but produces an oval, instead of round, beam of light.

General Operating Principles The Fresnel spotlight is simple. The instrument housing holds the lens and provides a mounting platform for the socket, lamp, and small reflector assembly, which are mounted on a small sled that moves closer to or farther from the lens during focusing, as shown in Figure 4.29. Figure 4.30A shows the instrument on spot focus with the socket and reflector assembly moved toward the back of the instrument housing. In this position most of the light is concentrated into a hot spot in the center of the beam. Figure 4.30B shows the instrument on flood focus, with the socket and reflector assembly moved all the way forward. This creates a relatively smooth wash of light from edge to edge, with only a small, almost undetectable, hot spot in the center of the beam.

Accessories The primary, and almost indispensable, accessory for the Fresnel spotlight is the **barn door** (Figure 4.31). Its flippers are movable and can be swung into the beam of light until they cut off as much light as desired.

Barn door: An accessory for a Fresnel spotlight whose movable flippers are swung into the beam to control it.

LAMP COMPARISON CHART

Although the specific lamp that is used with any instrument depends on the design of the instrument, some fairly standard wattages are used with various families of instruments.

Instrument	Standard Lamp Wattage Range
4-inch ERS	250–600
6-inch ERS	500–1,000
8-inch ERS	1,000–2,000
6-inch Fresnel	250–750
8-inch Fresnel	750–1,000
Scoop	350–1,500
Striplight	150–500
Followspot (incandescent)	1,000–2,000

Figure 4.28

An oval-beam lens for a Fresnel spotlight.

Funnel: An accessory for a Fresnel spotlight that masks the beam to create a circular pattern; also called a snoot or a top hat.

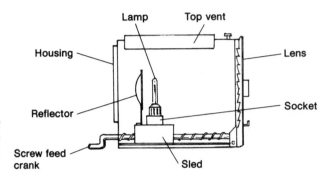

Figure 4.29

A cutaway view of a Fresnel spotlight.

Figure 4.30

The sled holding the lamp/reflector assembly is (A) moved backward to produce a hot spot in the middle of the beam, or (B) moved forward to produce a relatively smooth wash of light.

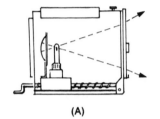
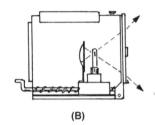

(A)   (B)

Another accessory is the **funnel** (Figure 4.32). The funnel, like the barn door, fits into the color frame slot on the front of the instrument. The circular pattern of light that it creates is dependent on the diameter of the funnel's cone.

Striplight

The striplight is used to create a smooth wash of light. It resembles a long trough with a series of lamps inside, as shown in Figure 4.33. Striplights are available in a variety of lengths and configurations, but they are most often between 6 and 10 feet in length.

The individual lights within the instrument are wired in parallel to form three or four circuits, as shown in the block diagram of Figure 4.34. This type of configuration provides designers with the opportunity to mix and blend color if they gel all the lamps of each circuit with a separate color. By placing each circuit of the striplight on a separate dimmer, designers can manipulate the intensities of the individual colors to mix the desired resultant hue. To create the maximum potential for color mixing, the individual circuits of a three-circuit striplight are

Figure 4.31

A four-flipper barn door.

Figure 4.32
━━━
Funnels are used to
create small circular
patterns of light with a
Fresnel spotlight.

Figure 4.33
━━━
Striplight. (Courtesy of
Colortran.)

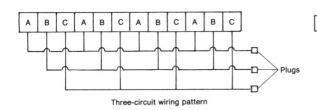

Three-circuit wiring pattern

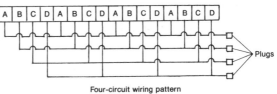

Four-circuit wiring pattern

Figure 4.34
━━━
Circulating pattern for
striplights.

Roundel: A glass color medium for use with striplights; frequently has diffusing properties.

frequently colored with the primary colors in light (red, blue, and green). If a four-circuit striplight is used, the fourth circuit is frequently gelled with amber. It is not mandatory that striplights be colored with red, blue, and green; if the designer knows that he or she will be working in a relatively narrow color spectrum, it is usually preferable to color the individual circuits in the appropriate hues.

Striplights are used primarily to light background drops and cycloramas, although they can be used in any position wherever a diffused, general wash of light is desired. Striplights are equipped to hold plastic color media as well as **roundels** (Figure 4.35), which are glass color media that have diffusing properties to help blend the light. Roundels are available in the primary colors as well as amber, frosted, and clear.

Cyc Light

The cyc light (Figure 4.36) is superior to the striplight for creating a smooth wash of light over the expanse of a cyclorama or drop. This relatively new type of fixture uses an eccentric reflector to create such a wash from only 7 or 8 feet away. The cyc light emits a much smoother light than does the striplight, and it is equipped with a color frame holder so the light can be colored as desired.

Ellipsoidal Reflector Floodlight

The ellipsoidal reflector floodlight (Figure 4.37), also known as the scoop, is used primarily to light drops and cycloramas. It is a lensless instrument that has the light-focusing characteristics of a conical ellip-

Figure 4.35

Roundels are glass filters used with striplights.

Figure 4.36

A cyc light. (Far Cyc courtesy of Colortran.)

Figure 4.37

An ellipsoidal reflector floodlight. (Courtesy of Kliegl Bros.)

TABLE 4.3   Beam and Field Angles for Various PAR 64 Configurations

PAR 64 Lamp	Beam Angle (In Degrees) (Height × Width)	Field Angle (In Degrees) (Height × Width)
Very Narrow	6 × 12	10 × 24
Narrow	7 × 14	14 × 26
Medium	12 × 28	21 × 44
Wide	24 × 48	45 × 71

Figure 4.38

A beam projector. (Courtesy of Kliegl Bros.)

soidal reflector, which provides a wide, smooth wash of light. It is equipped with a large color frame holder that, in many cases, has wire restraining lines crisscrossed over the circular opening to prevent the color medium from falling out. The scoop is available in a variety of sizes, but in the theatre the 14-, 16-, and 18-inch diameters are most commonly used.

Beam Projector

The **beam projector** (Figure 4.38) is a lensless instrument with a parabolic primary reflector and a spherical secondary reflector. It produces a very intense shaft of light that has little diffusion and cannot be easily controlled or modified.

The parabolic reflector focuses the light into parallel rays, and the spherical reflector redirects the light emitted from the front of the lamp back through the filament to the parabolic reflector. The beam projector's characteristically hard-edged, intense beam of light makes it desirable for creating shafts of sunlight and similar illusions.

PAR Can

The parabolic aluminized reflector, or PAR, is a sealed-beam lamp similar to the headlight of an automobile. The lamp housing, known as a PAR can (Figure 4.39), performs no function other than safely holding the lamp and its color media.

The most widely used size of PAR can is designed to hold the PAR 64, a 1,000-watt lamp about 8 inches in diameter. The PAR 64 lamp is available in a variety of beam shapes, as shown in Table 4.3. The PAR

Figure 4.39

A PAR can. (Courtesy of Strand Century.)

Figure 4.40

A followspot. (Courtesy of
Strong International.)

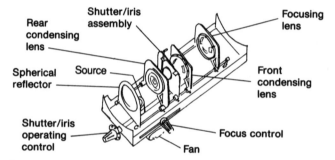

Figure 4.41

Cutaway drawing of a
followspot.

64 produces a powerfully intense punch of light, yet it has a soft edge. It
is used extensively in rock-concert lighting and is finding increased
usage in dance lighting because of its relatively low cost, portability,
durability, and light weight.

Followspot

The followspot is used when a high-intensity, hard-edged beam of light
is required to follow a moving performer. Followspots are manufactured
in a variety of sizes and styles (see Figure 4.40). The smallest followspot
is an incandescent model capable of a useful light throw of about 35 feet.
The larger models use high-intensity xenon, HMI, or unencapsulated
arc lamp sources and have a useful light throw of up to 300 to 400 feet.

All followspots function on the same general principles, illustrated
in Figure 4.41. They have an illumination source—either incandescent,
tungsten-halogen, HMI, xenon, or arc. Many have a forced-air cooling
system that helps to dissipate the heat generated by the light source.

INSTRUMENT MAINTENANCE

To function effectively, the various instruments discussed in this chapter must be maintained in good working order, and, as with any delicate piece of equipment, they must be handled with care.

The position of the lamp filament and the reflector must be kept in alignment, particularly in an ellipsoidal reflector spotlight. If this relationship is disturbed, the light output from the instrument will be greatly reduced, and the hot spot will be moved from the center of the beam. One of the significant advantages of the PAR 64 is that the filament and reflector are permanently aligned during the manufacturing process, so when the lamp in a PAR can is changed, there is no need to check the relationship.

The lenses and reflectors need to be kept clean and free from dust and fingerprints, and all nuts and bolts on the housing, yoke, and pipe clamp should be maintained so that the instrument can be locked securely into place.

When not in use, instruments should be hung on pipes or on rolling racks, as shown in the photo, so they won't be knocked over. If the theatre does not have an instrument storage cage, the instruments can be stored on a counterweight batten above the stage.

Ellipsoidal reflector spotlights should be stored with the shutters pushed all the way in to prevent them from being accidentally bent. When the instruments are in storage, care should be taken that the electrical pigtails are not pinched between the yoke and the instrument housing. The electrical plug and pigtail must be kept in good working order.

Followspots are mounted on a yoke and swivel-stand base that must move smoothly to follow the action of a performer. The base and yoke need to be properly lubricated, usually with graphite rather than oil or grease, and all nuts and bolts must be properly tightened.

Instrument storage

Shutter: A lever-actuated device used to control the height of the top and bottom edges of a followspot beam; also called a chopper.

Douser: A mechanical dimming device used in followspots.

Transformer: A device that changes the voltage in an electrical system; the output voltage of a step-down transformer is less than its source; a step-up transformer increases it.

The iris and **shutter** are internal control devices used to shape the beam of light. By manipulating them simultaneously, the operator can create a variety of beam edge patterns.

All followspots have some type of lens or reflecting system to gather and shape the light. Portions of the system can be adjusted to focus the light and adjust the crispness of the edge of the beam.

Some followspots are equipped with a dimming device called a **douser.** Since the intensity of some of the light sources used in followspots (unencapsulated arc, xenon, HMI) cannot be adjusted, the douser provides the only way of smoothly dimming those sources. The douser can also be used to achieve a slow fade-in or fade-out of the light. Followspots are also equipped with a color boomerang, which holds five or six color filters that can be easily inserted into the beam of light to control its color.

SPECIALTY INSTRUMENTS

There are several lighting instruments that do not fall conveniently into other categories.

Low-Voltage Sources

A number of specialty lamps use a voltage lower than the 120 output volts of most stage dimmers. The output of these low-voltage lamps is frequently as high as that of their 120-volt cousins. Aircraft landing lights (ACL's) have a very high output and high color temperature, and the parabolic reflector provides a very narrow beam spread. Automobile headlights provide another narrow-beam, low-voltage source.

A primary advantage of lower-voltage lamps is that their filaments are generally much smaller than their higher-voltage counterparts. The smaller filament can be used effectively in some types of scenic projectors discussed in Chapter 7, "Projections."

These low-voltage lamps require a **transformer** to decrease the 120-volt source voltage before it reaches the lamp, as shown in Figure 4.42. A step-down transformer of appropriate voltage and capacity to match almost any lamp can be purchased at any electrical supply store. For 12-volt lamps a heavy-duty automotive battery charger can be used as long as the current created by the wattage of the lamp does not exceed the rated capacity of the battery charger or its leads.

A number of lighting instruments and projectors have been designed to take advantage of the properties (small filament size, low heat output) of low-voltage lamps such as the MR16. These instruments normally have the required step-down transformer mounted inside of the instrument housing.

Automated Lighting Instruments

Devices have been introduced to automate certain functions on a lighting instrument. The Varimot (Figure 4.43A) is a motor-driven system that allows the operator to **pan, tilt,** manipulate the shutters, and focus the lens of the ellipsoidal reflector spotlight with a remote control device. The Vari-Lite (Figure 4.43B) is a computerized lighting system that lets the operator control the pan, tilt, beam size, color, and intensity of the instrument. A computer can be used to control a number of units simultaneously. A remote control color changer is another type of automated lighting instrument. It usually can be loaded with up to 12 colors, and the system operator can change the color as needed.

Pan: To rotate an object, such as an ERS, about its vertical axis.

Tilt: To rotate an object about its horizontal axis; to pan vertically.

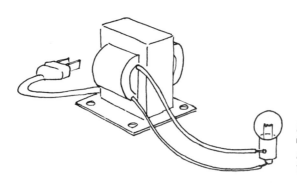

Figure 4.42

A low-voltage lamp and transformer.

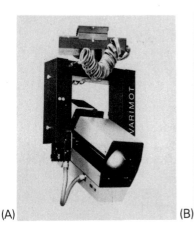

(A)

(B)

Figure 4.43

Automated lighting systems. (A) Varimot type HZM zoom followspot; (B) Vari-Lite. [(A) Courtesy of Emil Niethammer GMBH; (B) Courtesy of Vari-Lite.]

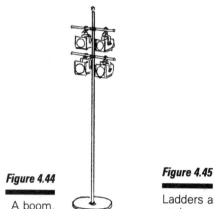

Figure 4.44

A boom.

Figure 4.45

Ladders are typically hung at the end of pipes.

With the increased use of computer control, the introduction of more remote focusing and color changing systems can be anticipated. Within 10 years we can expect to find some theatres fully equipped with computer systems for remotely focusing and coloring their instruments. In these systems the only real job of the hanging crew will be to relamp the instruments and change the color media when they are burned out.

Booms and Ladders

There are two pieces of equipment that aren't really lighting instruments, but they don't readily fall into any other organizational category either. Booms and ladders are typically shop-built equipment used to hold lighting instruments. A boom (Figure 4.44) is a vertical pipe with a heavy base. Typically made from 1¼- or 1½-inch pipe, booms are generally between 14 and 16 feet tall and have adjustable crossbars or side arms on which the instruments are hung. A ladder is similar to a boom in that it is another auxiliary hanging position for lighting instruments; however, the ladder is designed to hang on the end of an onstage electric pipe as shown in Figure 4.45.

In **proscenium** theatres booms are typically used when a design calls for the use of sidelight or when a backstage light needs to be put in a place where there is no permanent hanging position. Ladders are frequently substituted for booms if the placement of the boom might interfere with the movement of large rolling scenic pieces or if the instruments need to be placed higher than about 16 feet. Booms and ladders can be used in conjunction with each other if the design concept calls for the heavy use of sidelight (typical of some types of musicals and dance).

Booms aren't typically used in **thrust** and **arena** theatres because the vertical pipe might interfere with the audience's view of the stage. Ladders can be suspended from the lighting grid whenever there is a need to lower the angle of a particular instrument. However, a temporary lighting pipe can be constructed using two booms to support a cross pipe, as shown in Figure 4.46. If the cross pipe will be longer than about 10 feet or will be holding more than 8 to 10 instruments, a properly engineered truss should be used because the weight of the instruments and cable could bend the pipe. In any case, this type of temporary structure should always be well anchored with aircraft cable so that it won't tip over.

Proscenium stage: A stage configuration in which the spectators watch the action through a rectangular opening (the proscenium arch) that resembles a picture frame.

Thrust stage: A stage projecting into, and surrounded on three sides by, the audience.

Arena stage: A stage completely surrounded by the audience.

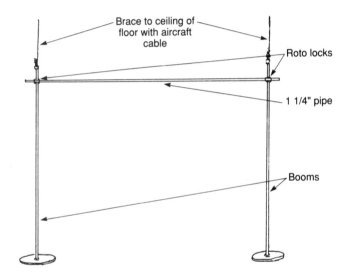

Brace to ceiling of floor with aircraft cable

Roto locks

1 1/4" pipe

Booms

Figure 4.46

A temporary lighting position can be made from two booms and a pipe.

CABLES AND CONNECTORS

n stage lighting, a flexible system for distributing electricity to the lighting instruments is necessary. This chapter discusses the types of cables and connectors that constitute this flexible distribution system, as well as several methods of circuiting, or connecting, the lighting instruments to the dimmers.

ELECTRICAL CABLE FOR STAGE USE

Almost all electrical wires or cables are made up of two basic components: a conductor and an insulator. Basically, a conductor is any material composed of atoms that have many free electrons. With its many free electrons, copper is used extensively in the construction of wires and cables for stage use. In addition to being an excellent conductor, it is also flexible and reasonable in cost. Brass, an alloy of copper, zinc, and other elements, possesses the good conductive properties of copper and can be formed into rigid shapes such as **plugs** and **receptacles.** Silver and gold are also excellent conductors, but their cost prohibits their use in all but the most sensitive of electronic applications. Although aluminum is a good conductor, it is not used in the types of cable approved by the National Electrical Code (NEC) for temporary stage use.

Insulators are materials that have few free electrons, making it all but impossible for electricity to flow through them. Since it is normal to have several conductors within one cable (see Figure 5.1), each conductor is covered with an insulator to isolate it from the other conductors within the cable; furthermore, all the conductors are encased inside an insulating jacket of—usually—the same material. Rubber is a good insulator and also cushions the wire or cable. Some types of thermoplastics are also good insulators, but thermoplastic insulation is usually thin and won't stand up to the physical abuse that rubber insulation can take. Fiber and paper are also good insulators and are frequently used as cushioning material inside multiconductor wire such the cable shown in Figure 5.1.

There are two basic types of electrical conductors: solid wire and stranded-wire cable (Figure 5.2). Solid wire, which is used in permanent installations such as in-wall house wiring, is semirigid and will break if subjected to repeated flexing. Stranded-wire cable is made up of a number of small wires grouped together to form a large single conductor. This structure is more flexible than solid wire because the individual strands that make up the conductor are very limber. Even when a number of these wires are encased inside an insulator, the resultant conductor is still quite flexible.

The NEC stipulates that the only electrical cables approved for temporary stage wiring are types S, SO, ST, and STO. These cables have stranded copper conductors and are insulated with rubber (S and SO) or thermoplastic (ST and STO). S and SO cables are more commonly used than ST and STO, because their thick rubber jacket can withstand more physical abuse than can the thin, heat-resistant thermoplastic insulation of the ST and STO cable. Type S is generally used for stage lighting, because SO costs more (its only advantage is that it is impervious to oil and gasoline).

Plug: The male portion of a connecting device.
Receptacle: The female portion of a connecting device.

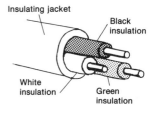

Figure 5.1

An electrical wire.

Wire Gauge

The American Wire Gauge (AWG) system rates wire according to the amount of current that a conductor of a particular size and composition can safely carry. As Chapter 3 explained, the rated current capacity for any given gauge should never be exceeded. Most cables have the gauge and wire type imprinted every foot or so on the insulating jacket.

The amount of current that can be safely carried varies greatly, as shown in Table 5.1. There is no standard size of cable for theatre use, because load requirements differ—often significantly—from one theatre to another. However, the NEC stipulates that receptacles used to supply

Figure 5.2

Solid wire (left) and stranded wire cable.

TABLE 5.1   American Wire Gauge Current Capacity Chart

Gauge of wire	10	12	14	16	18
Capacity in amps	25	20	15	6	3

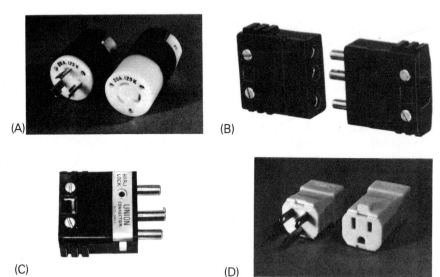

(A)

(B)

(C)

(D)

Figure 5.3

(A) Male and female twist-lock connectors; (B) grounded pin connector; (C) locking grounded pin connector; (D) grounded parallel blade (Edison) connectors. [(B) and (C) courtesy of Union Connector Co.]

incandescent lamps on stage must be rated at not less than 20 amperes and must be supplied by wires of not less than 12 gauge. Practical or decorative lamps are the only exception to this rule. These lamps may be wired with cable of smaller capacity as long as the lamp load does not exceed the rated capacity of the cable. This means that you can use 18-gauge wire (also known as lamp or zip cord) as long as the lamp load doesn't exceed 360 watts (assuming the system voltage is 120 volts: $W = VA; 360 = 120 \times 3$).

Connecting Devices

Lighting instruments are almost always moved between productions. An instrument that is hung in the **first ante-proscenium cut** for one production may be hung on the **third pipe** for the next. Because of this required flexibility, the electrical cables for both instruments and circuits normally terminate in connecting devices that are quick and easy to connect (or disconnect).

Several different styles of connector are used in stage lighting (Figure 5.3). Twist-lock connectors (Figure 5.3A) are considered by many people to be the best type of stage connector. The male portion, or plug, fits into the female portion, or receptacle, and is twisted to lock the two halves together. This locking action prevents most accidental disconnections of the circuit.

Pin connectors are probably more widely used than twist-lock connectors, primarily because they have been in existence longer. Older

Third pipe: When lighting instruments are hung on a batten over the stage, the terminology changes and the batten becomes a pipe. The third pipe is the third batten upstage of the proscenium arch that holds lighting instruments.

ATTACHING CABLES TO CONNECTORS

Several methods are used to attach cables to connectors. Many newer plugs have internal conductor grips, which simply require that you strip the insulation back until about ½ inch of wire is exposed, push the wire into the appropriate hole (black insulation to brass screw; white insulation to silver screw; green insulation, or ground, to green screw) and tighten the screw. The screw tightens a small clamp that firmly connects the conductor to its appropriate terminal.

If you are using an older, exposed-contact connector, the safest method of attachment is to use a closed-end solderless terminal (Figure A). This device is crimped onto the end of the stripped conductor with a plier-like tool called a crimper (Figure B). The seating screw of the plug is inserted through the hole in the solderless terminal and then firmly seated in the plug or receptacle. If you think that you might want to take the plug off the cable at some time in the future, then you might

want to use an open-end, or spade-lug, terminal (Figure C).

Another, slightly less safe, method is to twist the conductor into a hook shape and tin the wires by heating the conductor with a soldering gun and applying a small amount of rosin core solder to the wire. By binding the small wires into a solid unit, tinning improves the electrical connection between the conductor and connector. The hook is attached to the plug or receptacle by placing the wire around the screw in the direction of the twist of the screw, as shown in Figure D. This will draw the wire toward the shaft of the screw when the screw is tightened.

The least-acceptable method of attachment is to twist the wires into a hook, omitting the tinning process. When you try to tighten the screw, the wires tend to splay away from the terminal and come in contact with other elements in the connector, thereby creating the potential for a short circuit.

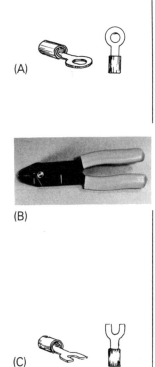

(A)

(B)

(C)

(D)

3 TINNED PORTION

DIRECTION OF ROTATION OF THE SCREW

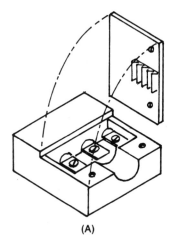

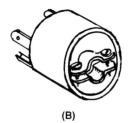

Figure 5.4

(A) Internal and (B)
external cable clamps.
            (A)   **(B)**

models of pin connectors (Figure 5.3B) have three distinct disadvantages: (1) they can be easily disconnected by accident; (2) the pins of the plug do not always make a good electrical connection with the receptacle; and (3) if the cable is connected to a live power source, it is very easy to be shocked, because the metal conductors in the receptacle are not deeply recessed. Newer models of the grounded pin connector (Figure 5.3C) overcome these disadvantages. The new designs, which also meet the NEC guidelines, have an excellent locking device that prevents accidental disconnections; and the metal contacts within the receptacle are recessed quite deeply into the insulating body of the connector.

The Edison, or parallel blade, plug (Figure 5.3D), should be used only on decorative lamps or devices that carry a similarly small load.

All connectors, regardless of style, are designed to carry a specific amount of current. The maximum load is usually printed somewhere on the plug, and that limit should be strictly obeyed.

The NEC stipulates that each plug should be equipped with an effective cable-clamping device (see Figure 5.4). The purpose of the cable clamp is to secure the connector to the jacket of the cable. This clamping action transfers any physical strain from the plug casing directly to the cable jacket, which effectively eliminates any strain on the electrical connections inside of the plug.

Extension Cables

Extension cables can be purchased, or made in the theatre's electrical shop, in any reasonable length. As noted, they are generally made of type S cable, although types SO, ST, or STO can also be used. Different theatres present differing requirements; but, in general, if a theatre has a permanent lighting system, an inventory of cables 5, 10, and 20 feet long should meet the needs of most operations.

A **two-fer** is used to connect two instruments to the same circuit. When using two-fers (Figure 5.5) or any other device that can increase the electrical load on a circuit, take particular care not to exceed the maximum current rating of any element (cable, plug, dimmer, and so on) in that circuit.

Two-fer: An electrical Y that has female receptacles at the top of the Y and a male plug at the bottom leg of the Y; used to connect two instruments to the same circuit.

CIRCUITING

The distribution of electricity from dimmers to lighting instruments creates a complex system. Any complex system is built on compromise, simply because the maximum amount of efficiency that can be built into any system is finite. The compromises on which stage lighting systems are predicated are speed and ease of hanging and circuiting versus flexibility of hanging position. The following methods of stage circuiting demonstrate the effects of tinkering with the variables of this complex equation.

Permanent Wiring

The simplest method of circuiting is to permanently wire the instruments to the dimmers. In this system a few ellipsoidal reflector

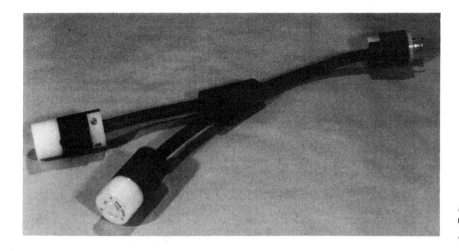

Figure 5.5

A Y or two-fer.

Work light: A lighting fixture, frequently a scoop, PAR, or other wide-field-angle instrument, hung over the stage to facilitate work; generally not used to light a production.

Drop box: A small connecting strip, containing four to eight circuits, that can be clamped to a pipe or boom.

Floor pocket: A connecting box, usually containing three to six circuits, the top of which is mounted flush with the stage floor.

Wall pocket: A connecting box similar to a floor pocket but mounted on the wall.

spotlights are usually hung somewhere on the ceiling of the auditorium, and some striplights or **work lights** over the stage. These instruments are permanently wired to specific dimmers. To operate the system you just turn on the dimmers. The only possible changes or adjustments within the system are changing the color or area of focus for each instrument.

Although this method is certainly the easiest to operate, it provides very little flexibility and just about eliminates any chance for creatively designing with light. Permanently wired lighting systems appear with great frequency in high school auditoriums, music halls, and other facilities where the lighting installation has been guided by criteria other than the needs and requirements of the creative use of designed light.

Spidering

Spidering, also known as direct cabling, involves running a cable from each lighting instrument directly to the dimmer to which it is assigned. It gets its name from the tangled web of cables created by circuiting a production in this manner.

Spidering is used extensively in Broadway theatres and on touring shows. It provides the greatest flexibility, because it allows the designer to put an instrument wherever it is needed. On the negative side, spidering requires an extensive inventory of electrical cable; this method also takes a relatively long time to hang unless the hanging crew is very experienced and the designer or master electrician has carefully planned the cabling requirements for the production.

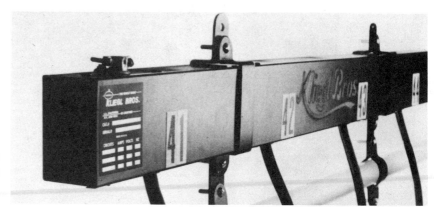

Figure 5.6

A connecting strip. (Courtesy of Kliegl Bros.)

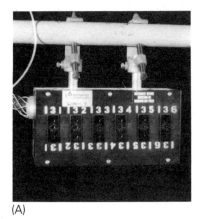

(A)

(B)

(C)

Figure 5.7

(A) Drop box; (B) floor pocket; (C) wall pocket.

Connecting Strips and Patch Panels

An electrical distribution system that utilizes connecting strips and a patch panel provides two advantages in a theatre that has an extensive production program: (1) the light plot can be hung and circuited quite rapidly and (2) the system provides a great deal of flexibility by allowing any circuit to be patched into any dimmer.

Two principal parts make up this system: the stage circuits and a patch panel. Most of the stage circuits are contained in connecting strips, which are sections of wireway, or electrical gutter, that contain a number of circuits (Figure 5.6).

The connecting strips are hung in a variety of positions about the stage and auditorium—counterweighted battens over the stage; various front-of-house positions (ante-proscenium cuts or slots, beamports, coves, boxes); and various locations on the walls of the stage house. Each circuit terminates in a receptacle that is usually mounted at the end of a 2- to 3-foot pigtail, although the receptacles are sometimes mounted flush on the gutter itself.

Additional stage circuit outlets are often contained in **drop boxes, floor pockets,** and **wall pockets** (Figure 5.7). Drop boxes are small connecting strips fed by cables that are attached to the grid above the stage. They usually contain four to eight circuits and are equipped with one or two pipe clamps so they can be easily attached to pipes or booms. Floor and wall pockets are recessed into the floor or wall and usually contain three to six circuits.

All of the circuits contained in connecting strips, drop boxes, and floor or wall pockets have certain properties in common. Each circuit is a

Patch panel

Connecting
strip

Stage circuit

Figure 5.8

In a patch panel system
the stage circuit runs
from the female
receptacle on the stage
outlet to a male plug at
the patch panel.

Receptacle

Plug

Figure 5.9

Patch panels. (Courtesy of
Colortran.)

rather long extension cable that, at the stage end, terminates in a female receptacle. Some connecting strips are designed to provide two receptacles for each circuit. In the patch panel system, the other end of the circuit terminates at the patch panel in a male plug, as shown in Figure 5.8.

The second part of the distribution system is the patch panel, or patch bay. It is an interconnecting device that provides the system with the capability of connecting, or patching, any stage circuit into any dimmer. Patch panels (Figure 5.9) are manufactured in a variety of styles and configurations.

Figure 5.10 illustrates the basic operational design of a patch panel. The lighting instrument is connected into a stage circuit, which terminates at the patch panel in a male plug. The dimmer, which is usually located in another part of the theatre, is permanently wired to a receptacle on the face of the patch panel. To enable the electricity to flow from the dimmer to the lighting instrument it will be necessary to complete the circuit. This is done by patching the circuit into the appropriate receptacle for the dimmer.

The patch panel is actually very simple to operate. What makes it seem so complex is that it contains many more than the one circuit and one dimmer cited in this example. In fact, a patch panel usually contains between sixty and several hundred stage circuits, and from forty to several hundred dimmers. In addition, each dimmer is usually provided with several receptacles on the face of the patch panel, so that more than one circuit can be patched into each dimmer.

Patch panels usually have some type of electrical overload protection for both the stage circuit and the dimmer circuit. The circuit breaker automatically breaks the continuity of the circuit when an unsafe amount of current is passed through the line. Each stage circuit

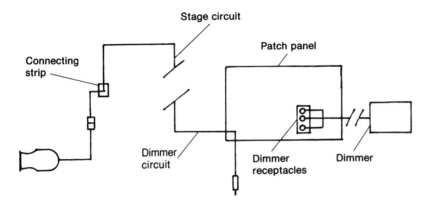

Figure 5.10

The patch panel allows you to plug more than one circuit into a single dimmer.

FUSES AND CIRCUIT BREAKERS

Fuses and circuit breakers are devices that protect an electrical circuit from an overload. When either device senses an overload, it breaks the continuity of the circuit (creates an actual open space in the circuit), which effectively shuts off the circuit. The only difference between the two is the way they accomplish this task.

The operative element of a fuse (Figures A and B) is actually a thin piece of soft metal. When too much current is present in the circuit, the piece of metal, a fusable link, actually melts, breaking the continuity or opening the circuit. When a fuse "blows," or melts, it must be replaced with an identical fuse of the same rating. You'll find the specifications written (engraved) somewhere on the body of the fuse. Never replace one fuse with another of a higher rating. To do so will allow the circuit to be overloaded, which may start a fire.

A circuit breaker is actually a type of magnetic trip switch. When too much current is present in the circuit, the magnetic switch pops open, breaking the continuity of the circuit. The advantage of the circuit breaker is that when it trips open, you only have to reset the switch (turn the circuit breaker back on) to create continuity in the circuit again. However, be sure that you locate and repair the original problem before you replace the fuse or reset the circuit breaker.

(A)

Figure

Fuses and circuit breakers protect electrical circuits from overloads: (A) plug fuse, (B) cartridge fuse.

(B)

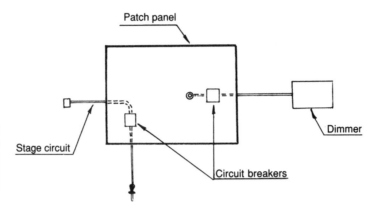

Figure 5.11

Circuit breakers provide
overload protection for
both the stage circuits and
the dimmer circuits.

has a circuit breaker, as shown in Figure 5.11, that provides overload
protection. Another circuit breaker is usually located either in the line
connecting the patch panel to the dimmer or in the dimmer itself. This
circuit breaker protects the dimmer circuit and dimmer from an
overload.

Dimmer Per Circuit

The dimmer-per-circuit configuration is probably the most efficient
electrical distribution system for stage lighting. It combines the efficiency in hanging and circuiting of the connecting strip with the ease of
operation of the permanently wired system.

As in the connecting strip and patch panel system, the onstage end
of each circuit terminates in an outlet on a connecting strip, floor pocket,
or similar location. The other end of the circuit is directly wired to a
dimmer instead of terminating in a male plug at the patch panel.

Before the introduction of the computer-assisted lighting control
board it required a very large and unwieldy control system and three to
six—or more—electricians to run all the dimmers required by this type
of system. But the computer board (see Chapter 6, "Intensity Control")
makes control of the large number of dimmers associated with this type
of system a relatively simple task for one person. The dimmer-per-circuit
configuration, when combined with a computer-assisted light board,
provides what is probably the most efficient electrical system for stage
lighting available at this time.

CABLE AND CONNECTOR MAINTENANCE   SAFETY TIP

The following steps are suggested to keep cables and connectors in good operating condition and in compliance with NEC and federal regulations.

1. When a cable is not in use, coil it and hang it on the wall of the lighting storage room. The cable will stay neatly coiled if the connectors are plugged together or if it is tied with heavy twine or narrow rope.

2. Check cables and connectors periodically, and replace any items that show signs of cracking, chipping, or other deterioration. Cracks in the insulation of cables and connectors increase the chances of someone's receiving a shock from the device. Also, dust can accumulate in the crack and may cause an electrical fire.

3. Always disconnect a plug by pulling on the body of the connector, not the cable. Pulling on the cable puts an unnecessary strain on the cable clamp and will eventually defeat the clamp. When the cable clamp no longer functions, pulling on the cable places the strain directly on the electrical connections.

4. Keep the connectors clean. Remove any corrosion, paint, grease, or other accumulations as soon as they become evident. These substances can act as insulation between the contacts of the connector and, if flammable, pose a fire hazard.

5. All elements of a cable should be of the same electrical rating; for example, twelve-gauge (AWG) cable (capable of carrying 20 amperes of current) should have only 20-ampere-rated connectors, and so forth.

Cable storage.

INTENSITY CONTROL

You're sitting in the auditorium of your favorite regional professional theatre company watching the lights fade out after the final curtain call of a wonderful musical. A number of random thoughts run through your mind—the leads' voices were beautiful, the scenery and costumes were stunning, everybody got whom, or what, they wanted. Probably the last thing that you'd think about at this time, if you'd think about it at all, would be the fact that it took between 60 and 200 dimmers, all working in unison, to achieve the smooth fade-out that you'd just witnessed.

Every lighting system, regardless of size or complexity, is composed of three basic elements: an electrical distribution system, dimmers, and dimmer control. Chapter 5 covered electrical distribution systems; this chapter deals with dimmers and the various systems and methods used to control them.

DIMMERS

The relatively brief history of electrical stage lighting has seen many different kinds of dimmers used to control the intensity of instruments. Some of the older dimmers, such as the salt water, saturable core,

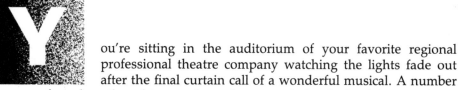

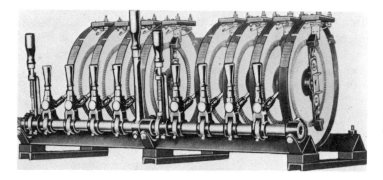

Figure 6.1
___

Some dimmers require a
mechanical control
technique.

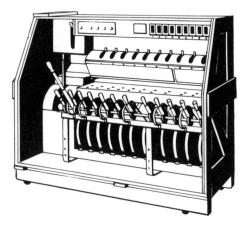

Figure 6.2
___

A resistance board.

thyratron tube, and resistance dimmer, have dropped by the way-side. Other older dimmers, such as the autotransformer, have continued in use.

Dimmer Control Techniques

Dimmers can be divided into two groups, based on the type of control used to regulate the current flow through them, mechanical or electronic.

Mechanical Control   Older types such as the resistance and auto-transformer dimmers require direct mechanical manipulation of an axle running through the central core of the dimmer to adjust the intensity of a lamp, as shown in Figure 6.1. This method of dimmer control is awkward. When a number of dimmers are linked, as shown in the illustration of an archaic resistance board (Figure 6.2), the resultant

Figure 6.3

A motorized
autotransformer dimmer.

dimmer board is noisy, is difficult to operate, and requires at least several rather muscular electricians to run even a moderately complex production. You can imagine that a certain delicacy of touch and smoothness of operation are lost when you have to control one dimmer with each hand and try to operate another one with your foot.

Electronic Control   The methods and operating principles vary according to the specific type of dimmer, but all electronically controlled dimmers use a low-voltage control current to regulate the high-voltage load current. The process of controlling the output of the dimmer by electronic rather than mechanical means lets the control console be located some distance away from the dimmers. Additionally, the low-voltage, low-amperage current of the control circuit allows all parts of this electronic circuit to be miniaturized.

Autotransformer Dimmer

Autotransformer dimmers increase or decrease lamp intensity by varying the voltage within the circuit. Although this type of dimmer is only rarely used to control stage lights, houselights in some theatres are controlled by a motorized autotransformer dimmer, as shown in Figure 6.3. A control switch, usually located in the light booth, is used to activate a motor, which runs a mechanical linkage that controls the dimmer and enables it to raise or lower the intensity of the houselights. The only drawback to the motorized autotransformer dimmer occurs when the motor runs at a single speed, so the fade time for the houselights cannot be varied.

Silicon Controlled Rectifier Dimmer

The silicon controlled rectifier (SCR) dimmer (Figure 6.4) is the most reliable and efficient unit that has been developed for stage lighting. The SCR dimmer operates on a gating principle (see box titled "Gating Principle") which is simply a rapid switching on and off of the power.

The SCR is a solid-state power transistor, which means that it has no moving parts and no filaments to burn out. The electronic circuitry necessary to switch the SCR to a conducting state is also relatively simple. These properties result in a dimmer that is rugged, long lived, compact, relatively lightweight, moderate in cost, and reasonably quiet in operation.

ARCHAIC DIMMERS

Although the dimmers described in this box are no longer installed in theatres, they do have historical significance in the progress of stage lighting.

Salt Water Dimmer

The oldest type of dimmer was a frightening contraption. The primary component of this death trap was a bucket of salt water. Metal plates were attached to one leg of the circuit, and one of these plates was completely immersed in the bucket. The current passing through the circuit varied with the depth of immersion of the second plate.

Saturable Core Dimmer

Another old dimmer worked by using a small DC current to magnetize an iron core. The AC load current passed through this iron core. As the level of magnetism was increased, the conductivity of the core also increased, and the lights connected to the dimmer came on.

Magnetic Amplifier Dimmer

A more efficient version of the saturable core dimmer, the magnetic amplifier was introduced in the 1950s but was soon relegated to obscurity by the development of the silicon controlled rectifier dimmer.

Thyratron Tube Dimmer

The thyratron tube dimmer was the first electronically controlled dimmer, and the first to use the gating principle—a rapid switching on and off of the load current. However, thyratron vacuum tubes were large, had to warm up before they worked, didn't last very long, and were somewhat expensive.

Resistance Dimmer

The resistance dimmer functioned as a large variable capacity resistor. When lights connected to it were turned off, it converted all the electrical energy flowing to it into heat. As it was turned on, its resistance decreased, and current reached the lamps.

GATING PRINCIPLE

If, in a given period of time, you turn a lamp on, then off, then on, off, on, and off, you effectively control the amount of light it puts out for that specific amount of time. If the lamp is turned on, and left on, for 1 second, it burns at full intensity for that 1-second period. If you turn the lamp on for ½ second and turn it off for ½ second, it burns at half intensity for the 1-second span. If you turn the lamp on for ¾ of a second and off for ¼ of a second, it burns at three-quarters intensity for the 1-second span. In each of these cases you will obviously see the lamp being switched on and off. But if the time span for the on-off cycle is reduced to 1/120th of a second, you perceive the on-off sequence as being a continuous level of illumination—an average of the on-off cycle ratio.

The SCR dimmer operates on this principle. The SCR is actually an electronic switch. The switch, or gate, opens and allows current to pass through the load circuit when it receives the proper electronic command. The gate stays open until the power is turned off. Sixty-cycle alternating current (AC), the standard current in the United States, alternates its polarity 120 times a second, or twice in each cycle, as illustrated in Figure A. Each time that it alternates its polarity, or crosses the zero point on the graph, there is actually no voltage. The effective result of this "no voltage" situation is that the electricity is turned off. If a command is fed to the SCR to start conduction at the beginning of the cycle, point A in Figure B, the SCR will conduct for the full half cycle, or until the electricity is turned off when it changes polarity at point B. Similarly, if the command specifies that the SCR is to begin conducting halfway through the cycle (Figure C), the transistor conducts for only half the cycle, or half as long.

By varying the time that the SCR is able to conduct electricity, you vary the intensity of any lamp load connected to it. This means that if the SCR conducts for a full half cycle, the lamp will glow at full intensity for the duration of that half cycle. If it conducts for only half of the half cycle, the lamp will be perceived to be glowing at half intensity. Similarly, a quarter-cycle electrical conduction means the lamp will appear to be glowing only one-fourth as brightly. Since each SCR conducts for only half a cycle, two SCRs, one for each half cycle, are necessary to make an effective dimmer.

The gating principle.

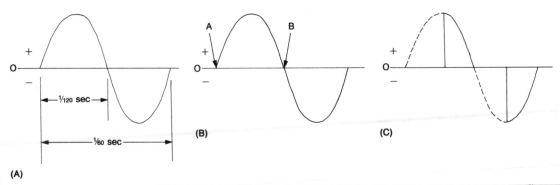

CONTROL CONSOLES

The design and style of any control console are dictated by the type of dimmer that will be used with the system. Because the mechanically controlled dimmers are for the most part outdated, their control consoles will not be discussed here. However, the types and designs of the electronic control consoles are predicated on the principles that were developed and refined with mechanically controlled dimmers. Electronic control consoles are divided into four main categories: (1) group master, (2) preset, (3) combination, and (4) computer-assisted memory.

Group Master

The group master console design is a direct carryover from the control board configurations used with mechanically controlled dimmers. Individual dimmers are controlled by a submaster, which is subsequently controlled by a grand master, as shown in Figure 6.5.

DIMMER MAINTENANCE   **SAFETY TIP**

The greatest enemy of an electronic dimmer such as the SCR is heat. To dissipate heat, some dimmers are equipped with large heat sinks. Heat sinks are metal—usually aluminum—structures that absorb the heat generated by an SCR and radiate it to the atmosphere. Other dimmer packs are equipped with fans.

It is vital for the longevity of dimmers that they have plenty of air circulating around them. Don't pile anything on top of a dimmer. If you are working with portable dimmers, be sure that the dimmer pack is raised off the ground so air can circulate under, as well as over, the case.

If your dimmer system is equipped with fans, be sure that they are running smoothly. The dimmers will frequently function for several hours even if the fan isn't working, but the heat buildup will cause a relatively rapid deterioration of the electronic equipment that will usually lead to premature dimmer failure.

Almost all SCR dimmers need to be adjusted periodically so they will smoothly increase or decrease their lamp loads. The specific methods vary from manufacturer to manufacturer, but they all involve an adjustment of the low-, middle-, and high-output voltage of the dimmer. These adjustments should be made by a qualified electrician at least annually.

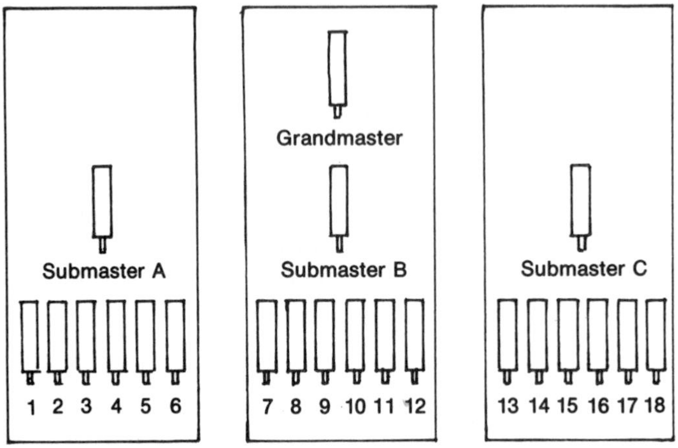

Figure 6.5

Dimmers 1 through 6 are controlled by submaster A; dimmers 7 through 12 by submaster B; dimmers 13 through 18 by submaster C. The grand master acts as a master control for all submasters.

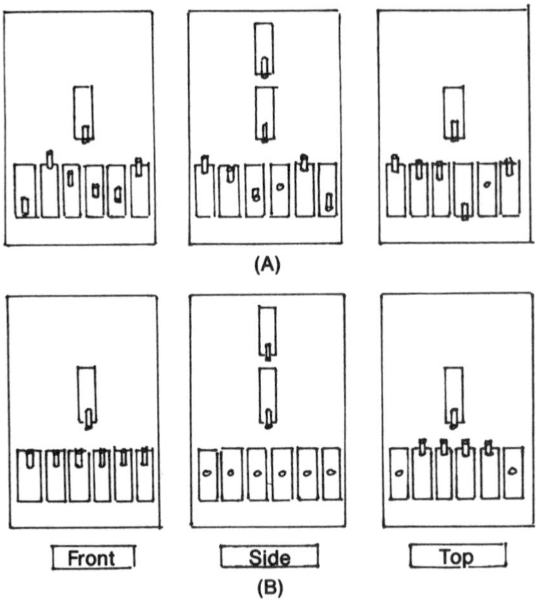

Grandmaster

Submaster A   Submaster B   Submaster C

1 2 3 4 5 6   7 8 9 10 11 12   13 14 15 16 17 18

(A)

Figure 6.6

Group master operating principles.

Front   Side   Top
(B)

Two general operating techniques are used with group master consoles. The first is to set individual dimmer intensity levels on a group of dimmers that are assigned to one particular submaster, as shown in Figure 6.6A. When the submaster is activated, the dimmers will fade up to the previously set levels. This technique is particularly useful when a designer wants to change the color blend of the lighting. For example, group A could be assigned all of the lights that are colored red; group B, blue; and group C, green. The color of the onstage light can be changed by varying the intensity of the submaster control for each color group.

The second operating technique involves using the dimmers of one group to control the lighting instruments from a particular direction or location, as shown in Figure 6.6B. For example, group A might control all **front-of-house** instruments; group B, side lights; and group C, the top lights.

Preset

The primary advantage of a preset control console is that it allows you to keep ahead of the onstage action by presetting the intensity levels for each dimmer before it will be needed. Figure 6.7 is an example of a three-scene lighting control console. Although there may not actually be a control console that works like this one, all preset lighting boards work on the same basic principles being discussed for this hypothetical board.

The controls for dimmers 1 through 6 are repeated three times in the blocks of dimmer controls labeled Preset Scenes I, II, and III. In this simplistic example we will assume that the intensity levels of the lighting for the first cue will be preset on Preset Scene I, the second cue will be assigned to Preset Scene II, and the third cue will be set on Preset Scene III. After the board operator sets the appropriate intensity levels for each dimmer on the three preset scenes, he or she assigns control of Preset Scene I to **fader** A by pushing the button marked I next to fader

Front-of-house: Describing lights that are hung on the audience side of the proscenium arch.

Fader: A device, usually electronic, that effects a gradual changeover from one circuit to another; in lighting it gradually changes the intensity of one or more dimmer circuits.

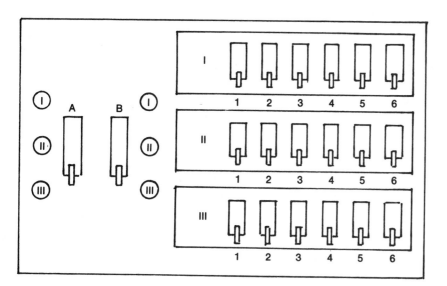

Figure 6.7

Preset board operating principles.

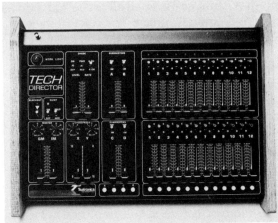

Figure 6.8

Combination boards. (Courtesy of Kliegl Bros. and Teatronics, Inc.)

A. When the cue is called by the stage manager, the operator brings up fader A, which automatically raises the intensity of the lights to the levels that had been preset on the dimmer controls of Preset Scene I. The second cue, preset on Scene II, is assigned to fader B. When the cue is called, the operator simultaneously moves fader B up and fader A down, which results in a cross-fade between the lights preset on Preset Scenes I and II. Similarly, before the third cue being called, the operator assigns control of Preset Scene III to fader A. When the cue is called, the operator cross-fades between faders A and B, which results in activation of the dimmer intensity levels associated with Preset Scene III.

To preset the intensity levels for the fourth cue, the operator presets the appropriate intensity levels on Preset Scene I as soon as he or she had cross-faded into the second cue. To run the remaining cues in the show the process of presetting intensity levels on open, or nonactive, preset scenes is repeated as often as necessary. Many preset control consoles have mechanically or electronically interlocked faders, so when either fader A or B fades up, the other fader automatically dims down.

Combination

A fusion of the principles of preset and group master control provides an extremely flexible lighting control system. In the combination console (Figure 6.8) each dimmer channel has an associated switch capable of assigning the dimmer to preset, group master, or independent control. The combination control console provides an operator with more creative choices in controlling dimmer intensities, because it enables him or her to choose the control best suited to each individual production situation.

Computer-Assisted Memory

Computer-assisted memory control for stage lighting has become the standard for the industry. These systems offer much greater control flexibility than does any other method of lighting control, and they are less expensive to manufacture than a preset control console for a comparably sized system.

All "computer boards" (Figure 6.9) function in fundamentally the same way: a computer electronically stores the intensity levels of all dimmers for each cue. The computer memory replaces the cumbersome preset board and eliminates the chance of human error in the setting of intensity levels during a show. Even the most basic computer boards have a minimum of about 100 memories for cue storage. More expensive boards have sufficient storage capacity for up to 1,000 cues.

Since most computers will lose their memory when the power is turned off, these systems frequently have some type of battery backup that provides enough power so the system can retain its memory for a reasonable length of time. This period varies from several hours to several weeks, depending on the manufacturer.

Because of the **volatility** and relatively limited storage capacity of the memories used in most systems, almost all but the lowest-priced computer boards have some method of storing the cuing and programming information. This additional storage capability is generally referred

Volatility:
Nonpermanence; in computers, a volatile memory will be lost if the computer loses its power supply.

Figure 6.9

Computer boards. (Courtesy of Kliegl Bros. and Strand Lighting.)

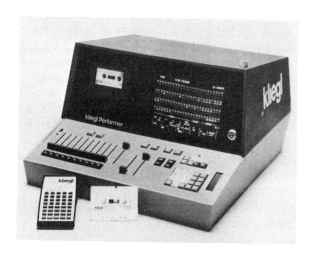

Floppy disk: A thin piece of plastic coated with metal oxide, used to record the information stored in a computer's memory.

Cassette tape: Audio recorder tape, used in computer storage.

Microcassette tape: A tape cassette approximately 1¼ by 2 inches, used in computer storage; identical to microcassette audio tape.

Micro-floppy disk: A floppy disk 3½ inches in diameter.

to as library storage. The most common methods used for library storage are the 3½-inch **micro-floppy disk,** the **floppy disk,** the **cassette tape,** and the **microcassette tape.**

Computer boards have functions in addition to cue or preset memory capability. Almost all systems memorize the timed duration for each cue or preset. Most systems have two or more faders, so a cue can be assigned to each fader to allow two or more lighting actions to occur at the same time.

Whenever a system has an automatic, or timed, fader, it usually has a manual override feature that enables the electrician to interrupt the timed fade to increase, decrease, stop, or reverse the rate of fade. Almost all computer boards except very-low-priced ones have one or more video screens to display information about the various memory functions.

Someone once said that the only thing constant is change. So it is in the field of lighting-intensity control. At the present time the SCR dimmer is state of the art. But we can be assured that it will be

---

SAFETY TIP   *CONTROL SYSTEM MAINTENANCE*

The operating voltage for most electronic lighting control systems is relatively low—normally, between 8 and 24 volts. Because of the low voltage and the miniaturization of the electronic components, the systems need to be kept scrupulously clean and free from dust, dirt, and grease. For this reason smoking and eating should not be permitted in the lighting control booth. The tar from tobacco smoke can settle on the printed circuit boards and actually change the resistance within the electronic circuits. Even a small change in resistance can cause some elements of the system to malfunction. The obviously disastrous results of spilling a soft drink on a control board don't need further elaboration.

The floppy disks that are used for library storage in many computer systems need to be handled carefully. They should be stored vertically in a dust-free environment away from power lines and electric motors. (The power lines and motors generate magnetic fields that can scramble or erase the information stored on a disk.) Cassette and microcassette library storage tapes should always be replaced in their protective cases and stored in a manner similar to floppy disks. Use only a soft-tip marker to write on the floppy disk label. Pencils and ballpoint pens can dent the recording surface of the disk, and the graphite and ink can interfere with the reading head.

supplanted by an even better dimmer at some time in the not-too-distant future. The computer-assisted memory control console—the computer board—is similarly state of the art. But new developments in computer science will quickly be applied to the lighting industry, and the current state-of-the-art systems, which do more than we could have imagined just 5 years ago, will quickly be outmoded by systems that can do more, in less time, and for less cost.

COMPUTER BOARDS: A COMPARISON OF FEATURES

Smaller Systems

1. memory for up to several hundred cues
2. capability of controlling 100–150 dimmers
3. maximum of one video screen for displaying various system functions
4. a timed fader
5. some type of group or sub-master control
6. control of dimmer intensity by individual sliders
7. keypad for addressing memory and functions
8. limited backup system in case of main computer malfunction

These smaller, less expensive systems work well in theatres that have modest production demands.

Larger Systems

1. memory for approximately 1,000 cues
2. control of 1,000 or more dimmers
3. expanded functions
   a. two or more video screens to display more functions simultaneously
   b. advanced backup systems
   c. sophisticated group or sub-mastering
   d. more control functions to permit simultaneous cues at different fade rates
4. dimmer and other functions addressed through a keypad
5. remote keypad
6. hard-copy printer for printing data about the lighting design
7. self-diagnostic program to identify malfunctioning component in case of breakdown

These larger and more expensive systems work well in facilities that have extensive production programs.

PROJECTIONS

rojections enhance the visual texture of a design immeasurably. They can provide the stage with seemingly unlimited depth or create an aura of surrealism as one image dissolves into another. They can be used to replace or complement other visual elements of the setting, or they can be used as an accent.

However, projections aren't a universal panacea. They are simply another tool for the designer to use in the never-ending quest for an evocative visual expression of the production concept.

Both lens and lensless projectors are used in the theatre.

LENSLESS PROJECTORS

If you've ever made shadow pictures by holding your hands in the beam of a slide or movie projector, you understand the principle of lensless projection. As shown in Figure 7.1, a shadow image can be projected when an opaque object is placed in the path of a light source. If the object casting the shadow is colored and transparent rather than opaque, a colored image is projected instead of a shadow.

Several factors determine the sharpness of the projected image, but the primary one is the size of the projection source. Although an arc can provide a very small point source, it isn't particularly practical because

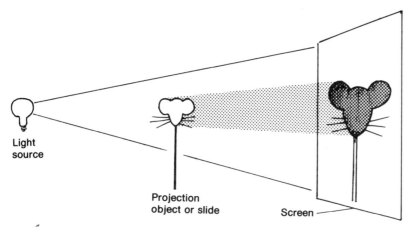

Light source

Projection object or slide

Screen

Figure 7.1

Principles of lensless projection.

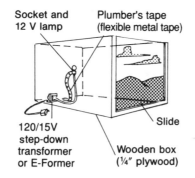

Socket and 12 V lamp

Plumber's tape (flexible metal tape)

120/15V step-down transformer or E-Former

Wooden box (¼" plywood)

Slide

Figure 7.2

A low-voltage lamp can provide a high-intensity, small-sized source for a lensless projector.

its intensity can't be varied through the use of a dimmer. There are two practical lamp sources for lensless projectors:

1. For large-scale projections a 500-, 750-, or 1,000-watt, 120-volt, tungsten-halogen lamp normally used in an ellipsoidal reflector spotlight works well. When selecting a specific lamp, remember that the smaller the filament, the sharper the image.

2. For small-scale projections—under 6 feet wide—a single-filament 12-volt lamp (used for automotive brake and turning lights) can provide a high-intensity, small-filament source. For the lamp to provide enough output it must be run at about 15 volts. This voltage is supplied to the lamp through a 15-volt wire-wound step-down transformer, as shown in Figure 7.2. The transformer may not work properly, however, and the intensity of the 12-volt lamp will probably flutter, or simply switch off, if you try to dim

Aerial perspective: An optical phenomenon in which objects that are farther away appear less sharply in focus and less fully saturated in color.

the unit with an SCR dimmer. A smooth fade of a load attached to a wire-wound transformer can be achieved only if the transformer is dimmed with an autotransformer or resistance dimmer. However, a recent technological development, the dimmable electronic transformer (E-Former, manufactured by Luminance, Inc.) has made it possible to smoothly dim low-voltage lamps with electronic dimmers such as the SCR. To do so, simply substitute an E-Former of appropriate output voltage for the wire-wound transformer.

Another important factor in determining image sharpness with a lensless projector is the distance between the slide and the projection surface. The closer the slide is to the screen, the sharper the image. Having the slide closer to the screen does not necessarily mean that the projector is closer to the screen. A relatively long, somewhat skinny projector, as shown in Figure 7.3A, can be built in the shop. If the ratio of the distance between the projection surface and the slide and the distance between the slide and the lamp of this somewhat bizarre projector can be kept at approximately 1:1, an acceptably sharp image can be produced. The multiplane lensless projector (Figure 7.3B) is a natural adaptation of this development. As slides are placed closer to the lamp, the image they project becomes less focused. This phenomenon can be used to good advantage to create **aerial perspective.** In the projection of a landscape, the clouds and distant objects could be painted on one slide and placed relatively close to the lamp to create a

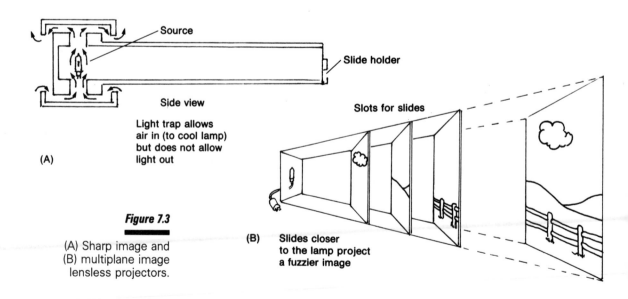

Figure 7.3

(A) Sharp image and (B) multiplane image lensless projectors.

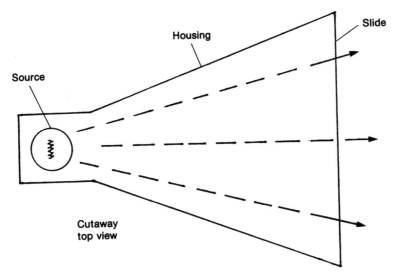

Figure 7.4

Principles of operation of a Linnebach projector.

soft-edged image. Middle-distance objects, such as hills and a forest, might be painted on a second slide and placed farther from the lamp so that the image they project is more clearly defined. A third slide, with perhaps a fence row and the branch from an overhanging tree, could be painted on a third slide and placed farther away from the lamp so that its image is the sharpest of the three.

Although the multiplane projector might seem to be an ideal solution, there is one very basic problem: slide size. You will remember that for a slide to project a relatively sharp image it needs to be approximately the same distance from the screen as it is from the lamp. If you wanted to project an image 20 feet wide, the sharp-image slide would have to be 10 feet wide! However, if you are only trying to project on a relatively small area (5 feet wide or less), the multiplane projector can provide you with a very realistic aerial perspective effect.

A multiplane projector can be built in the shop using the techniques described later in this chapter for making Linnebach projectors. A 750- or 1,000-watt tungsten-halogen lamp from an ellipsoidal reflector spotlight will usually provide a more-than-adequate light for projections less than 5 feet wide, and the slides can be painted on ⅛-inch Plexiglas with transparent acetate inks.

Linnebach Projector

The primary lensless projector used in the theatre was developed by Adolph Linnebach. All lensless projectors are based on its principles of operation, which are illustrated in Figure 7.4. The metal housing holds

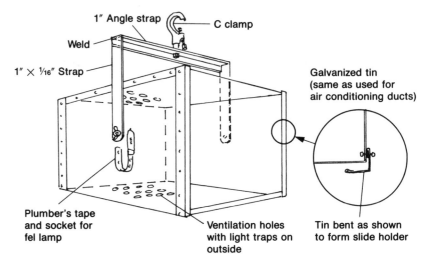

Figure 7.5
———
Shop-built Linnebach
projector.

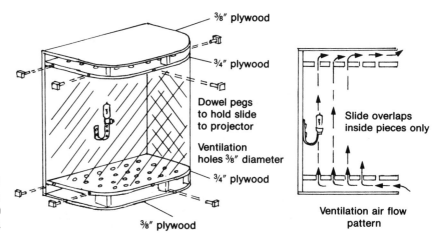

Figure 7.6
———
Curved-image Linnebach
projector.

the lamp at a fixed distance from the open front of the projector, which is designed to securely hold a removable glass slide. The design is painted on the slide with transparent inks.

Projectors that work on the Linnebach principles can easily be made in the theatre shop using galvanized tin and a **pop riveter.** They can also be fabricated using plywood (Figure 7.5), but the inside of the back and top sides of the plywood box must be lined with tin or some other heat-reflecting or -absorbing material.

Linnebach projectors for use with curved cycs can also be shop-built, as shown in Figure 7.6. These projectors, while using only a

1,000-watt FEL lamp, can project a patterned wash of pastel color over a full semicircular cyc. Slides for the curved-front Linnebach are made from 20-mil acetate. These slides are fitted to the curved edge of the projector, and the image is painted on the slide using transparent acetate inks. Dr. Martin's Watercolors, when supplemented with a commercial additive that allows the paint to adhere to plastic, work extremely well for this purpose.

Other Lensless Projectors

Small lensless projectors can be made by removing the lens from Fresnel or plano-convex spotlights and inserting a slide (painted or photographic transparency) in the instrument's color frame holder. Although these makeshift projectors won't cover a large surface, they are handy for making relatively soft projections on small surfaces.

LENS PROJECTORS

The second basic type of projector uses a lens to control the focus and size of the image on the projection surface. Two primary types of lens projector are used in the theatre, the **scenic projector** and the **slide projector**.

Scenic Projector

The scenic projector is composed of three basic parts: the lamp housing, the optical train, and the slide, as shown in Figure 7.7A.

Lamp Housing A lamp of high intensity is a prime requisite of a good scenic projector. Incandescent lamps of 1,000 to 2,000 watts are fairly

Pop riveter: A tool used to secure rivets in thin metal.

Scenic projector: A high-wattage instrument used for projecting large-format slides or moving images.

Slide projector: A reasonably high-output instrument capable of projecting standard 35-mm slides.

SLIDE TECHNIQUES FOR LENSLESS PROJECTORS

A number of systems based on mathematical principles can be used to lay out the slides for lensless, or Linnebach, projectors. However, the fastest and most accurate method is also the easiest. Put a slide into the projector, and place it and the projection screen (usually a cyc or sky tab) in the onstage positions that they will occupy during the production. Turn the projector on, and draw or paint the projection on the slide while watching the projection grow across the screen.

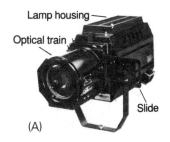

Lamp housing

Optical train

Slide

(A)

Figure 7.7

(A) A scenic projector is composed of a lamp housing, the optical train, and the slide. (Courtesy The Great American Market.) (B) Scenic projector. (Courtesy Kliegl Bros.) (C) Slide projector. (Courtesy George R. Snell Associates.)

(B)

(C)

typical, and some extremely expensive scenic projectors are designed for xenon or HMI lamps. The housings are frequently equipped with blowers that help dissipate the substantial heat that these powerful sources generate. Unfortunately, these fans are almost always noisy, so the scenic projector usually needs to be placed in some location that will mask the fan noise.

Optical Train   The optical train, shown in Figure 7.8, is composed of several parts that perform specific functions. The reflector (usually ellipsoidal or spherical) and collector lens gather and concentrate the light. Some scenic projectors utilize a **heat filter,** which is a special type of glass that filters out a substantial portion of the infrared (heat) segment of the electromagnetic spectrum emitted by the lamp. The **condensing lenses** focus the light onto the **slide plane aperture,** which is the point where the slide or moving projection effect is placed. The **objective lens** is used to focus the material in the aperture onto the projection surface.

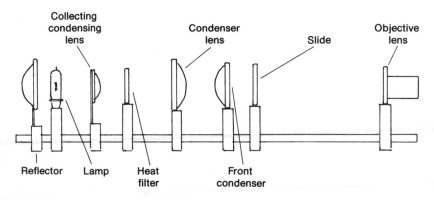

Figure 7.8

A typical scenic projector optical train.

Collecting condensing lens · Condenser lens · Slide · Objective lens

Reflector · Lamp · Heat filter · Front condenser

The reflector, lamp, collector lens, and aperture are normally mounted in fixed positions within the lamp housing unit. In contrast, the relative positions of the condensing lens and objective lens are variable on some models of scenic projector to allow the size of the projected image to be changed. Other scenic projectors are available with several **heads,** which hold the condensing and objective lenses in fixed positions to control the image size.

Rosco Labs has recently introduced a motion effects machine designed to be used in conjunction with a standard ERS. The system consists of several pieces: a fixed- or variable-speed motor that fits into the instrument's color frame holder and rotates one of several large, patterned, stainless steel disks mounted in front of the instrument lens; a gobo rotator that rotates a gobo in the gate of the instrument; and a gobo yo-yo that moves a gobo back and forth in the gate. By varying the combination of system elements you can achieve a variety of motion effects such as waves, flickering flames, rain, and abstract movement patterns that normally require a scenic projector.

Slide   Glass slides are frequently used with scenic projectors to project still images. The image can be painted on a single glass slide, or a photographic transparency can be sandwiched between two glass slides. The longevity of a painted or photographic image on the slide can be increased if a heat filter is placed between the collector lens and the slide.

A variety of moving effects can be created through the use of **effects heads.** These motorized devices are attached to the lamp housing in place of the slide holder. Effects heads move images in front of the aperture gate to create abstract or realistic moving images such as the

Heat filter: A glass medium that removes much of the infrared spectrum from light.

Condensing lens: A device that condenses the direct and reflected light from a source and concentrates it on the slide plane aperture of a projector.

Slide plane aperture: The point in a projection system where a slide or other effect is placed.

Objective lens: A device to focus a projected image on a screen or other surface.

Head: A housing that holds scenic projector lenses in fixed positions to project images of a specific size.

Effects head: A motor-driven unit capable of producing relatively crude moving images with a scenic projector.

CAROUSEL PROJECTOR TIPS

1. Use the slide tray that holds 80 slides rather than its larger-capacity (140-slide) cousin, because the greater space allocated to each slide in the 80-count tray significantly reduces the chances of the slides becoming stuck in the tray.
2. Mount the slides in plastic, rather than pasteboard, slide holders. The plastic holders are slicker and slightly heavier, which makes it easier for them to be fed into the projector.
3. For the best image use the highest-wattage lamp designed for the specific model with which you are working.
4. Select a lens that will permit you to place the projector as close to the projection surface as possible.

lighted windows of a passing train on the projection surface. The speed of the control motor is usually variable, so the speed of the projected effect can be adjusted to suit the design need. Depending on the specific model, effects heads use either rotating disks or bands to create the specific effect desired. Most scenic effects projectors are equipped to use either Plexiglas or metal disks or plastic bands.

KEYSTONING

Unless the projector is placed on a perpendicular axis to the projection screen, some linear distortion will be introduced to the projected image. This phenomenon is known as keystoning, because the distortion generally resembles the shape of a keystone.

Keystoning results when the light from one side of the projected image (slide) has to travel farther than the light from the other side of the slide, as illustrated in Figures A and B. Keystoning can be corrected in one of two ways: (1) the screen can be tilted (Figure C) so the projection axis is perpendicular to the screen, or (2) a distortion can be introduced to the slide that counteracts the effects of the projection distortion. To do this, determine the angle of intersection between the projection axis and the screen. To introduce the counterdistortion to the slide, place the camera at the same angle, but on the opposite side, when you are taking the picture of the slide material (Figure D).

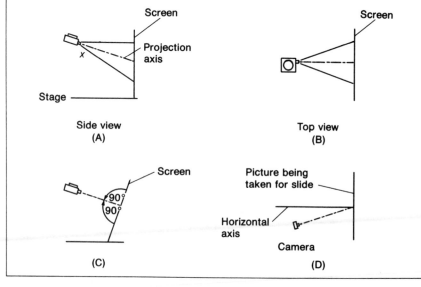

Slide Projector

Projectors using 35-mm (2-by-2-inch) slides provide another excellent system for producing scenic projections. The challenge of using these projectors, which are designed for audiovisual, not theatrical, purposes, is that the lamp output is frequently not so bright as that of a scenic projector. If you work within the limitations that the lower lamp output imposes, however, the slide projector can be an extremely useful tool.

The Kodak Carousel equipped with a 300-watt lamp provides sufficient light to create a readable image if the slide is of normal contrast and the maximum dimension of the projected image is kept at about 6 to 8 feet.

Adaptations of the basic audiovisual (Ektagraphic) line of Kodak Carousel projectors provide higher-wattage lamps and a number of other interesting features. Although the 300-watt lamp available on the basic models will work adequately, by all means acquire the higher-output models if your budget can afford them. The image can be significantly brighter.

Other types of 35-mm slide projector can be used, but the carousel types generally offer specific qualities that make them preferable for theatrical projection work: dependable and versatile slide-feeding capabilities, adequate light output, and interchangeable lenses.

Until recently the Buhl Optical Company manufactured a modification of a basic Kodak Ektagraphic Carousel projector that provided a high-output (1200-watt) lamp. Unfortunately, citing reasons of modification to the basic Kodak projector model, Buhl has suspended production of the Hi-Lite.

PROJECTION SCREENS

Actors' bodies, painted scenery, dust motes, smoke, and fog have all been used as projection surfaces. However, they don't work nearly so well as scenic elements that have been specifically designed as front and rear projection screens.

Front-Screen Material

Front-screen projection materials are those surfaces that are designed to reflect light. The best front-projection materials are slide or movie screens. They are white and highly reflective, and the surface is often designed to focus the reflected light in a specific angular pattern. Unless you want a large, glaringly white screen sitting in the middle of the

Hue: The qualities that differentiate one color from another.

Saturation: The relative purity of a particular hue.

Value: The relative lightness or darkness of an object.

Texture: The relative roughness or smoothness of the finish of an object.

Heat welding: The use of a heat gun (a high-temperature air gun, visually similar to a hand-held hair dryer) to fuse two pieces of plastic.

Hot spot: An intense circle of light created when a projector lens is seen through a rear screen.

stage, however, it is essential that the screen be lit with either a projection or color wash at all times.

A smooth, white, painted surface (muslin, Masonite, and the like) provides a low-cost alternative to the commercial projection screen. Although the reflected image won't be so crisp as that from the projection screen, it will be more than adequate for most theatrical purposes. When the projections or color washes are turned off, however, the challenge of what to do with the "great white blob" continues.

Unless you are planning on using continuous projections or removing the screen from the set, it is frequently desirable to have the projection screen blend into the surrounding scenic elements until it is time to use it. In these cases the vertical or horizontal surfaces of the set itself can be used instead of a projection screen. When you are projecting on scenery, the sharpness and brightness of the reflected image will be directly related to the **hue, value,** and **texture** of the paint job used on the scenery. Surfaces with low **saturation,** high value, and little texture provide the best reflective surfaces for projected images.

Rear-Screen Material

A major challenge of front-screen projection—actor shadows on the projection surface—is eliminated through the use of rear-screen projection. In this technique, illustrated in Figure 7.9, the projector is placed behind the screen, and the image is transmitted through the screen to the audience.

A significant challenge of rear-screen projection is created by the **hot spot.** If the projector is located within the audience's sight line, as illustrated in Figure 7.10, a small, intensely bright circle of light will appear on the screen. This bright circle is caused by seeing the actual lens of the projector through the screen material. The hot spot can be

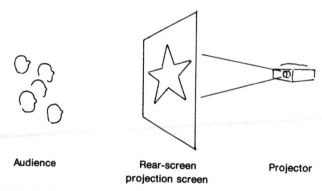

Figure 7.9

A typical rear-screen projection setup.

Audience   Rear-screen   Projector
                    projection screen

eliminated either by positioning the projector so that the hot spot is out of the audience's sight line or by using a screen material that eliminates the hot spot.

Commercial rear-screen materials transmit clear, crisp images while diffusing or eliminating the hot spot. Rosco Labs and Gerriets International offer several types of reasonably priced flexible plastic rear-screen material in rolls 55 inches wide. Wider screens, with invisible seams, can be made by butting strips of the material edge to edge and taping the joints with No. 200 Scotch transparent plastic tape. Unless the atmosphere in your locale is of relatively low humidity, however, the tape seams are only a temporary solution. **Heat welding** of the seams will provide a permanent bond.

If the projector can be placed in a position that will eliminate the hot spot, a variety of translucent materials can be used to receive the projected image. Scenic muslin and other fabrics of similar weight and weave transmit light quite well. The muslin (which will present a crisper image if it is primed with a starch solution—one cup of starch per gallon of hot water) can be painted with dye if it is necessary or desirable for the screen to blend into the set. When using this technique be sure to use dye, not paint. Dye is transparent and won't interrupt the transmission of the image.

Plain white shower curtains provide another effective, low-cost rear-screen material. The plastic transmits light well, the larger-sized shower curtains are big enough for many scenic uses, and some of the plastics actually diffuse the hot spot.

White (not clear) polyethylene plastic sheeting, sold as plastic drop cloths in paint stores, is also an effective rear-screen material.

Figure 7.10

A hot spot, caused by seeing the lens of the projector through the screen, will result unless special rear-screen projection material is used.

SLIDE PREPARATION

Slides for the various types of commercial and shop-built Linnebachs are generally made from ⅛-inch clear Plexiglas. Slides for the curved-image Linnebach can be made from .020-inch acetate. Although still quite flexible, the .020 thickness provides enough stiffness so that these slides don't bend or flop when secured to the projector.

The slide image can be painted on the acetate with a variety of materials. Transparent acetate inks, available in a wide range of colors, are a standard type of slide paint. If an additive, which makes the water-based dyes adhere to the plastic, is used, Dr. Martin's Watercolors are an excellent choice. As a last resort, the bottles of Magic Marker refill inks can also be used. Although the Magic Marker inks remain slightly tacky, they don't smear easily; however, they do attract a great deal of dust.

Scenic projectors can use both photographic and painted slides. To be used in a scenic projector, photographic transparencies should be sandwiched between sheets of projection-grade glass. This type of glass is usually available from photography stores. This "sandwich" accomplishes two things: it keeps the heat of the lamp from crinkling or melting the slide, and it keeps the slide in a vertical plane. Painted scenic projector slides are also usually sandwiched for heat protection. The image is painted on a glass slide, and either that slide is sandwiched between two other clear slides or the painted surface is simply covered with a second slide. The transparent inks mentioned above will also work on glass. Additionally, silhouettes can be created by using opaque acetate inks. However, you must take care when using opaque inks, simply because they absorb more heat than do transparent ones. The additional heat may crack the glass or cause a deterioration of the other inks.

Thirty-five-millimeter slides shouldn't be used in the cardboard mounts in which they are placed by the film processors. These mounts don't really have enough weight to drop the slide into the projector if the projector is mounted at anything other than a perfectly horizontal angle. At a minimum, the slides should be remounted in plastic slide mounts, and ideally you will sandwich them between two layers of slide glass. (The plastic mounts and 35-mm glass mounts are available at photography stores.)

OTHER PROJECTORS

Figure 7.11

An overhead projector. (Courtesy of George R. Snell Associates.)

A wide variety of other projectors can be used for special situations in the theatre. However, two of them, the overhead projector (Figure 7.11) and the opaque projector, are arguably the most useful.

A relatively large transparent slide (most overhead projectors will accept slides up to 11 by 14 inches) is placed on the light table of the overhead projector. A high-output lamp shines through the slide, and the image is redirected and focused on the screen by a mirror mounted in an optical head located a short distance above the light table. The luminance level of this projector is fairly low, but it can work well in short-throw, low-light situations.

The opaque projector works in generally the same fashion, except that the slide is opaque and the lamp is located above the slide so that the light can be reflected, rather than directly transmitted, to the mirror and optical head. The output of the opaque projector is generally less than that of the overhead projector, because some of the lamp output is lost to absorption and scattering during the reflection process.

| 257 | ★315 | 542 | ★535 |
| CLOUD 9 | REVERSED TREES | PAISLEY BREAKUP | ELIZABETHAN WINDOW |

GOBOS

Ellipsoidal reflector spotlights equipped with gobos are very effective projection tools available to the lighting designer. Numerous commercially available gobos can be purchased to provide very specific shadow patterns (Figure 7.12). These patterns are generally etched in thin stainless steel. Shop-built gobos can be made from offset printing sheets or disposable aluminum cookware (see Chapter 4 for specific techniques). These "homemade" gobos are frequently as effective as their commercial counterparts in creating abstract patterns such as the medium breakup pattern illustrated in Figure 7.13. Medium breakup patterns can be used in a variety of ways. If they are placed in the top lights, they can project an interesting highlight/shadow pattern on the stage floor. Depending on the color used in the "goboed" instruments and the direction, intensity, and color of the other lights, the breakup design can be interpreted as dappled sunlight, moonlight, or simply an irregular, abstract texture.

The Artifex Corporation has recently introduced a halftone projection pattern that can be used in place of a gobo. At the present time these projections are available only in black and white, and the contrast range between the highlight and shadow areas is not very dynamic; but it is the first time that a slide image capable of withstanding the extreme heat of the gate of an ellipsoidal reflector spotlight has been made commercially available.

A new product, the Slide-Pak by Soft-17, Inc., is an adapter that mounts in the color frame holder of ellipsoidal reflector spotlights, Fresnels, and PAR cans to convert those instruments into large-format image projectors. The company also makes full-color heat-resistant transparencies from your artwork for use as slides. If an available heat

Figure 7.12
—

Commercial template patterns. (Courtesy of Great American Market. Designs are copyrighted by the Great American Market.)

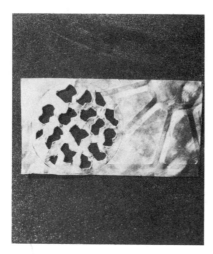 

Figure 7.13

A shop-built medium breakup gobo (left) and the pattern it projects.

filter is inserted into the unit, normal 35-mm slides can also be projected. There is some fuzziness and a little distortion at the edge of the projected image, but the center of the image is quite sharp. The cost of the unit is relatively low, and the cost of the slides is quite reasonable.

GENERAL PROJECTION TECHNIQUES AND HINTS

It is prudent to test the characteristics of any projection system, technique, or material (commercial or noncommercial) under actual stage conditions before you launch into a design concept that depends on projections. You will frequently discover that your vision of how the projections should look is at odds with the physical reality of how they actually appear onstage. Some general hints and guidelines may help you in working with projections.

1. To prevent the projected images from being washed out, keep ambient light off of the screen. Be sure that the stage lights for the acting areas in the vicinity of the screen(s) are placed at angles that minimize their effect (direct and reflected) on the screen.

2. To reduce the effects of ambient light and to keep the actors from blocking the spectators' view of the projected image, try to place the screen so that its bottom edge will be no lower than 5 to 7 feet above the stage floor.

3. To maximize the brightness of the image when working with an audiovisual slide projector:

    a. Keep the size of the projection as small as possible.
    b. Use a lens with a low f-stop (3.5 or less).
    c. Use a short-focal-length lens, and place the projector as close to the screen as possible.

4. Rear-screen projection is affected by ambient light less than front-screen projection is, so try to work with rear-screen techniques whenever possible.

5. Become thoroughly familiar with the equipment that you will be using well before technical rehearsals begin. Shoot your slides early, so that you will have time to shoot and process additional slides if it becomes necessary.

PRACTICALS AND EFFECTS

hile the lighting designer creates the lighting that simulates whatever—sun, moon, fireplace, table lights, and so forth— is supposed to be the light source for a scene, very frequently those sources are specified by the scene designer or director. However, it is the responsibility of the lighting designer and lighting crew to see that all of these **practicals** and **effects** are electrically wired and work as they were intended.

Practicals and effects can provide the audience with a wealth of visual information about the time, season, and mood of a play. If a table or floor lamp is turned on, the audience will normally assume that the scene is set in the late afternoon or night. If it's turned off, they'll think it's day. If a fire cheerfully glows in the corner of a brightly lit room, the audience will believe that it's cold in the outside world of the play. If the room lights are dim or off, the mood evoked by that same cheerfully glowing fireplace would probably be interpreted as romantic or sinister depending on the context of the scene. Flickering torches or candles can also be used to create dynamic visual moods.

Regardless of the type of practical or effect that is used, its physical appearance should be appropriate to the period of the play. The shapes, styles, and designs of lamps, lanterns, candles, and fireplaces have all changed through the years. If, in your production situation, the electrical shop is responsible for obtaining or making the practicals and effects as well as wiring them, be sure that you properly research the style of each practical and check its appearance with the scenic and property designers.

One of the lighting shop's more interesting challenges is to create practicals and effects that will look like the source that they are simulating. However, a note of caution and a disclaimer are needed before we launch into a discussion of the various techniques used to achieve these effects.

Creating practicals and effects is fun. However, you need to keep everything in perspective. Remember that the audience came to see the play, not the effects. Just like the rest of the lighting, the best practicals and effects will tread that very narrow line between being so dynamic that they divert the audience's attention and being obviously fake. The best compliment that you could possibly receive would be that they "looked just like the real thing."

While the following suggestions aren't exhaustive, they do provide you with a good beginning reference point for producing realistic practicals and effects.

Practical: An onstage working light source such as a table lamp, wall sconce, or oil lamp.

Effect: A specialty device designed to give the appearance of being a light source such as a fire effect, candle, torch, or lightning.

LIGHTING FIXTURES

When you are producing a contemporary production, it isn't particularly difficult to wire table and floor lamps, wall sconces, and chandeliers so that they will work. Run some cable from the fixture to the nearest stage outlet, patch the circuit into a dimmer, and turn it on. The only problem you might have is if the fixture is equipped with a switch. In that case tape the switch in the "on" position and have the crew check it before each rehearsal or performance.

Lighting designers almost never use lamps of "normal" wattage in these onstage light fixtures because the fixture should be bright enough to look like it's working, but not bright enough to call attention to itself. It is common practice to put in lamps of very low wattage and then further dim them—especially with bare-bulb fixtures such as chandeliers.

When you want or need to see the light output of the fixture, such as when you want to see a splash of light on the wall or floor from a table or floor lamp, you can use a higher wattage lamp and line the inside of the shade with one or more layers of brown kraft paper.

A greater challenge to your ingenuity comes from trying to re-create realistic-appearing gas, oil lamp, or candle sources.

GAS LAMPS

Gas lamps of the type used for room lighting were almost always housed within glass chimneys. These chimneys were frequently globular in shape and frosted. The gas jet itself had a small flame—between ½ inch and 2 inches tall—that flickered non-rhythmically. A specialty lamp, called a flicker bulb, available from most home lighting stores, provides a very realistic-appearing "gas jet" light. This 4-watt, F-shaped lamp with a candelabra base uses two flame-shaped, metallic screen electrodes as the igniters for the neon gas inside the lamp. The resulting yellow-orange light flickers as if it really were a gas flame.

CANDLES

Obviously the most realistic-looking candle flame is obtained by simply lighting a candle. However, in many localities fire codes don't allow the use of open flames. Be sure to check with the local fire-safety inspector before using any flames onstage. If candles can be used onstage, be sure to set them away from flammable materials. While they may look beautiful gracing the mantel above a fireplace, don't put them there because they might set fire to the flat behind them. In fact, candle flames flicker and dance in the slightest breeze and can be very distracting for

---

SAFETY TIP

Never use lamps that burn any type of liquid fuel onstage. Their use violates all fire codes and would probably void any insurance coverage your producing organization might have.

SAFETY TIP

When wiring practicals and effects, be sure to follow the safe wiring procedures outlined in Chapter 5. Try to run all wires in places with the least amount of traffic. To avoid tripping anyone, try to run all wires and cables under rugs (both onstage and offstage) whenever possible. If they have to be run across the bare floor, tape them in place.

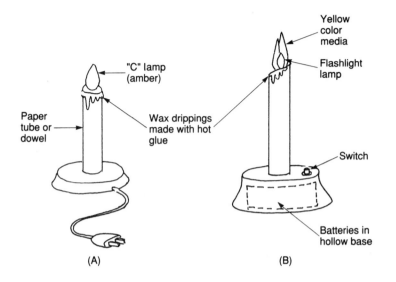

Ghost load: To connect an offstage, unseen load to the dimmer. An instrument, usually a 500- to 1,000-watt Fresnel, is two-fered with the small onstage load to provide sufficient wattage for the dimmer to operate properly.

Figure 8.1

(A) 120-volt candle;
(B) battery-powered candle.

the audience. Electric candles that use either 120-volt electricity or batteries can be made in the shop. If the candles are going to be stationary, then a 120-volt "C" (Christmas tree) lamp can be hot-glued to the end of a dowel or paper tube (see Figure 8.1A). This lamp can be connected to a stage circuit, and the whole unit can be controlled by a dimmer. Because of the very small wattage of these lamps it will probably be necessary to **ghost load** the dimmer in order to keep the lamp from flickering when it is turned on or off.

If the candle is going to be handled or moved, then batteries can be hidden in the base or in the candle itself, and a flashlight lamp of appropriate wattage, painted with amber acetate ink, can be used for the flame (Figure 8.1B). A scrap of flame-shaped yellow gel, lightly sandpapered until it is partially translucent, can be hot-glued to the tip of the candle, around the bulb, to simulate a flame. It's also easy to hide an inconspicuous switch somewhere on the candle base.

SAFETY TIP

If it is permissible to use open flames onstage in your locality, be sure that you never place candles or torches where their flames will come near anything flammable such as scenery, drapes, or costumes.

LANTERNS

The techniques outlined for candles are equally applicable to most types of lanterns. The candle or battery-and-lamp assembly is hidden in the base of the lantern. The plastic or glass windows can be treated with spray paint so that they appear translucent and smoked around the edges and top.

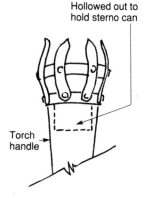

Hollowed out to hold sterno can

Torch handle

Figure 8.2

Sterno torch.

TORCHES

The same provisos regarding the use of open flames should be applied to the use of torches. Nothing simulates an open flame better than an open flame. If fire regulations permit it (as in some outdoor theatres) and the torches won't be placed anywhere where they might catch scenery, drapes, or costumes on fire, a can of Sterno securely fastened to a torch (Figure 8.2) will create an appropriate flame. Under no circumstances should liquid fuels of any type be substituted for the Sterno. To get the flame of period torches to burn with a yellow flame rather than the blue flame of Sterno, sprinkle a little table salt into the can of Sterno.

If real flames can't be used and the torches are going to be stationary (for example, the torches lining the walls of a medieval castle hallway), then 120-volt electricity can be used. A single lamp that glows steadily doesn't look like a torch flame; however, a variation of the flickering gas-light effect can provide a fairly realistic torch light. Instead of using a single bulb, closely bunch three of the flicker bulbs together at the tip of the torch (Figure 8.3). If the resultant light output is too "flickery," substitute a clear 3- or 4-watt 120-volt "C" (Christmas tree) lamp for one of the flicker lamps. This "always-on" lamp (which should be painted with yellow or amber transparent acetate inks or lamp dip) will minimize the apparent flicker of the torch. After the desired rate and light output are attained, hot-glue individual pieces of flame-shaped plastic color media between, outside, and over the lamps. Use various tints of yellow/orange/amber, some lightly sanded to make them translucent, some clear, some half and half. The flickering lamps shining through the multiple colors will create a fairly realistic flame. An effective variation on this theme can be achieved by substituting flame-colored chiffon or extremely lightweight silk for some of the plastic color media and blowing the material with a concealed fan. The reasonably silent medium-volume fans used to cool electronic equipment—frequently sold in electronics stores as "stereo fans"— work well in these applications.

If the torch is going to be hand-carried it will have to be battery-powered. The challenge here is again to get the torch to flicker

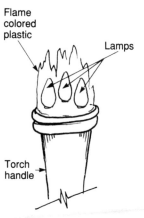

Flame colored plastic

Lamps

Torch handle

Figure 8.3

120-volt torch.

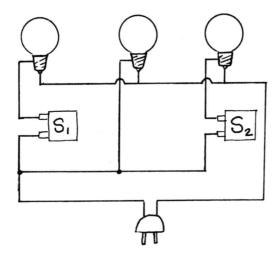

S_1 and S_2 are fluorescent starters

Figure 8.4
━━━━━
Wiring diagram for a
random-flicker fire effect.

realistically. However, if you consult almost any "Basic Electronic Projects" book, it will describe a battery-powered, variable-rate lamp flasher based on the 3909 IC (integrated-circuit) chip. Unfortunately, these flashers have a regular periodic rhythm rather than the erratic pulsing of a flame. However, if you use three of these flashers, all set at different rates, and one "always-on" circuit, a fairly realistic flickering effect can be achieved. Be sure that each flasher circuit is set at a slightly different intensity. Some of these circuits make provisions for varying the intensity. If the one you use doesn't, try using flashlight lamps of slightly differing voltage in each circuit. Keep experimenting until the desired results are achieved. A four-D-cell battery holder or the body of a four-battery flashlight can be hidden in the handle of the torch to provide the battery power for the torch. The switch can be concealed in any number of places. Like the 120-volt version, the lamps should be painted with varying tints of flame-colored transparent acetate inks or lamp dips, and they should be surrounded with simulated flames.

FIRE EFFECTS

Traditionally, fire effects have been made by building a prop fire of logs and hiding lights of varying colors behind the logs. The resulting steady glow of light isn't realistic. A variation on this theme included a motor-driven, slowly rotating cylinder of crumpled aluminum to reflect the light, which was more realistic but still didn't have the random flicker of a real fire. Figure 8.4 illustrates the wiring diagram for a

Variegated gel: A multicolored gel made in the shop from strips of color media of differing hues.

random-flicker fire effect that can be quite realistic. The random flicker of this system is provided by the starters used with fluorescent-light fixtures. Starters are wired in series with two of the three branches of this 120-volt parallel circuit. There are a number of different-sized starters (FS-2, FS-5, FS-25, and so forth), and they all have differing flicker rates. Additionally, the starters are load sensitive, so you can vary the flicker rate (and light output) by changing the wattage of the lamps. Use ''A'' lamps (regular household) of differing wattages (15, 25, 40, 60, and so forth) to create the specific effect you're looking for. Again, you'll need to paint the lamps with transparent acetate inks or lamp dip to achieve the color appropriate to the type of fire effect you're designing.

A device that reinforces the effect of a flickering fire can be constructed easily with a 6-inch Fresnel, a small fan, and some strips of flame-colored lightweight silk, as shown in Figure 8.5. A flame-colored **variegated gel** can be used in the Fresnel, and the silk strips are also dyed red and orange. The wavering movements of the silk, caused by the fan, create a realistically flickering light. The unit is normally placed in a hidden corner of the fireplace so that the light will strike anyone approaching the hearth.

MOON EFFECTS

The moon can be re-created in a couple of ways. Traditionally used (and still effective) is the moon box, which is illustrated in Figure 8.6. This wooden box has the silhouette of the desired phase of the moon cut out of the front of the box. The inner face of this cutout is covered with

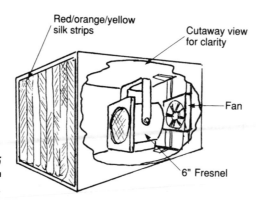

Figure 8.5

Fire reinforcement effect.

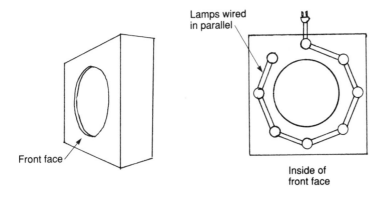

Lamps wired
in parallel

Front face

Inside of
front face

Figure 8.6

Moon box.

muslin (to diffuse the light), and the cutout is surrounded with between six and eight 25-to-40-watt lamps wired in parallel. (If you use fewer than six lamps it may be possible to see hot spots from the individual lamps.) The completed moon box is suspended *in back of* the cyc or sky tab and connected to a dimmer, and the intensity is adjusted accordingly. The moon box can also be rigged to move, and so it is possible to have a "rising" or "setting" moon.

Gobos or projections, described in Chapters 4 and 7, can also be used to create the moon. Both gobos and projections can be rear- or front-projected depending on the design and materials from which the set is constructed.

STAR EFFECTS

Stars can be re-created in several ways. Gobos made with lots of very tiny pinpricks, used in an ERS with a wide field angle (such as a 50-degree or 4½-by-6½-inch instrument) and thrown a fairly short distance, create reasonably realistic star effects.

Grain-of-wheat lamps or white LED lamps (which can usually be purchased at well-equipped lighting, electronics, or hobby stores) can be sewn or hot-glued onto a black cyc or skytab. These are low-voltage lamps, so an appropriate transformer will have to be used. (See the discussion of the E-Former in Chapter 7 for a transformer that can be dimmed with an electronic dimmer.) Strings of the tiny, clear Christmas tree lights also make very effective, if somewhat larger, stars. Just be sure that the strings are wired in parallel rather than series, so the whole starlit vista won't disappear if one lamp burns out.

Momentary-on switch: A push-button switch without a locking feature. The circuit remains on only as long as the button switch is depressed.

Flash pot: A device used to detonate flash powder.

Thin strands of fiber-optic material can be used to create another very effective star effect. Fiber-optic materials, such as Lucite or Plexiglas, act like a light tunnel to conduct light in the same way that wire conducts electricity. If you shine a strong light in one end of the fiber-optic strand, a strong light will shine out of the other end regardless of the length of the strand. Light loss in transmission is negligible. To make a "star curtain," hundreds of individual strands are attached to the back of a black drop. One end of each strand is pushed through the fabric to create a pinpoint of light on the audience side, while all the other ends are bundled together and rigidly mounted directly in front of a small, high-intensity light source such as a 1½-inch Fresnel or 3½-inch ERS. The only drawback to the use of fiber optics is the substantial expense of the materials.

LIGHTNING

Fortunately, bolts of lightning are rarely called for in the theatre. If they are, any number of the projection techniques outlined in Chapter 7 can be used. More frequently, lightning will be seen through the windows of the set as intense, erratic bursts of high intensity light. There are several ways to achieve this effect.

The traditional, and most dangerous, way of creating lightning is by rapidly striking and breaking the contacts of an arc. While this method is effective, it is also very dangerous because an arc of sufficient intensity will use 220-volt electricity; and the brilliance (and ultraviolet emissions) of the arc can severely damage the retina of the operator or anyone looking at the contact zone when the arc is made.

Single-flash heavy-duty strobe lights provide a brilliant flash of light. These units can be placed where needed and then remotely triggered by an effects operator. Because these units frequently require a "reset" time before they can be fired again, several units may be required to create the erratic, multiple-flash illumination characteristic of lightning. Large-size flashbulbs, which provide about the same amount of light as a strobe, can also be used.

Any source that has a fast rise time (time that it takes the filament to heat to full incandescence) is a good candidate as a lightning source. The lamps used in most theatrical instruments have fairly large, heavy filaments with resulting slow rise times. However, 200-watt household lamps have fast rise times and reasonably high light output. Several of these lamps mounted inside the reflector of a scoop (ellipsoidal reflector floodlight), each lamp circuited separately with a **momentary-on switch,** can be used to create a relatively realistic lightning effect.

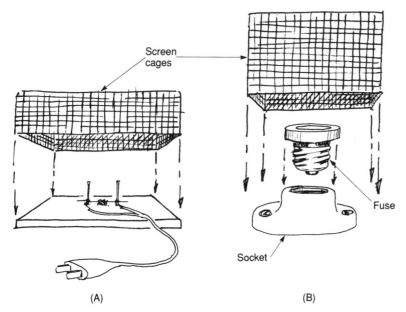

Screen cages

Fuse

Socket

(A)

(B)

Figure 8.7

(A) Wire-detonator flash pot; (B) plug fuse detonator flash pot.

EXPLOSIONS AND FLASHES

While the strobes, flashbulbs, and fast-rise-time lamps suggested for lightning can also be used for explosions and flashes, other devices may also be used to create the proper effect.

A **flash pot** is traditionally made by stringing a piece of very thin wire (a single strand from a piece of multistrand cable such as 18-gauge lamp cord) between two contacts, as illustrated in Figure 8.7A. About ½ teaspoon of flash powder is sprinkled onto the wire. When the switch is turned on, the wire instantly heats to incandescence and ignites the powder.

TO SMOKE OR NOT TO SMOKE

When using your flash pot, if you want just a flash of light, but no smoke, then flash powder is what you need. If, however, you want to have a flash *and* smoke, then you can either add a little sal ammoniac to the flash powder, or you can substitute black powder for the flash powder.

Another type of flash pot (Figure 8.7B) uses a low-amperage (2 to 5 amps) plug fuse as the detonator. The small plastic window of the plug fuse can be cut out, or the entire metal top and glass removed. One-half teaspoon or less of powder is loosely poured into the cavity in the fuse, and a ⅛-inch-mesh hardware cloth or metal window-screen cover is placed over the unit. To operate this unit, the fuse is screwed into a porcelain socket, the unit is plugged into a switched circuit, and the switch is closed when the effect is desired.

There are numerous companies that advertise pyrotechnic devices and switching controls in trade magazines such as *Theatre Crafts* and *Lighting Dimensions*. In general these devices are safer to use than are their shop-built counterparts.

SAFETY TIP   ***WORKING WITH PYROTECHNIC DEVICES***

Flash pots, explosion simulation, and other pyrotechnic devices are extremely dangerous. They can burn, maim, blind, and kill.

If you choose to build the switching mechanisms for these devices in your electrical shop rather than purchase commercially available units, be sure to add a warning lamp in-line with the power feed so that anyone who sees the box will know that the power is on.

If you adhere to the following commonsense safety guidelines, your use of these devices should be relatively safe.

1. Always disconnect the power before loading or reloading a flash pot. Do not assume that since the unit is switched off, the power won't reach the detonator. Always unplug the power cord.

2. Never load more than about ½ teaspoon of powder into a flash pot. If you do, the device may explode.

3. Never tamp down the powder. This *will probably* cause an explosion when the device is detonated and *may* cause an explosion *while you are tamping*.

4. Never place any cap or wadding on top of the flash pot. This will probably cause the device to explode.

5. Never place a flash pot directly under or adjacent to any flammable materials.

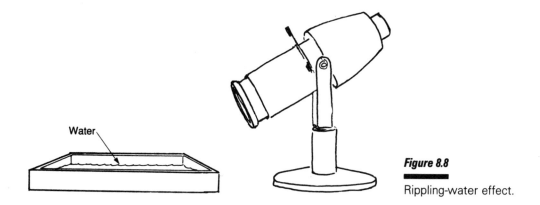

Water

Figure 8.8

Rippling-water effect.

WATER EFFECTS

Occasionally a production calls for a rippling- or sparkling-water effect. Probably the best way to achieve such an effect is to shine an ERS into a shallow container of water (Figure 8.8) and let the rippling highlights play across the scene. The container has to have a highly reflective bottom, or you can use a glass dish such as a rectangular Pyrex cake pan and set it on top of a mirror, aluminized mylar, or similar highly reflective surface. The real challenge in this effect is to make the water move, and it can be done in a number of ways. A crew member can jiggle the dish, or you can set up a fan (be sure it's quiet) to blow into the dish, or you can construct a motorized Rube Goldberg-like machine to rock or jiggle the water dish.

The secret to constructing any practical or effect is to understand the appearance of the desired result. When you know what you're looking for, it is usually just a matter of piecing together various elements from known techniques, such as those outlined in this chapter and elsewhere in this book, to create the "look" that is needed.

THE DESIGN PROCESS

esign is not itself an art, but rather a process, a series of steps through which we pursue the goal of creating what we hope will be a work of art—a lighting design. The design process is a method for finding answers to questions. Although the examples and terms used in this chapter will direct your thinking toward lighting design and production, the principles of the design process can be applied with equally productive results to other theatrical design areas, acting, directing, and—for that matter—life in general. These principles and techniques can help you discover an appropriate and creative solution to almost any design problem. This problem-solving model consists of seven distinct phases: (1) commitment, (2) analysis, (3) research, (4) incubation, (5) selection, (6) implementation, and (7) evaluation.

Unfortunately, the design process isn't a simple, linear progression. As you move from step to step, you must check back on your previous steps to make sure that you are headed in the right direction with your proposed solution. Figure 9.1 shows the back-and-forth movement that occurs as you move through the various stages of the design process. Although Satchel Paige, the wise old pitcher, once advised, "Don't look back; something may be gaining on you," you would do well to look back during your progression through the design process, because the thing that might be gaining on you could be a new thought, a better mousetrap.

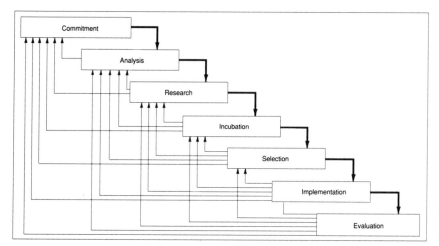

Figure 9.1

The design process is not simply a linear progression. As you move through the steps of the design process, you monitor your progress by continually checking back to see where you have been.

COMMITMENT

Commitment is probably the most important step in the whole design process. If you wholeheartedly *commit* your energies to an assignment, you are promising yourself that you will do the best work you can possibly do.

A very simple semantic game may help you commit yourself to an assignment. Use the word *problem* as infrequently as possible—it has a negative connotation—and substitute the word *challenge*. Everybody likes a challenge: the word itself hints at fun, games, and competition. When your problem has been transformed into a challenge, it automatically becomes more interesting and manageable.

ANALYSIS

The analysis step in the design process has two objectives: (1) gathering information that will help clarify and refine the definition of the challenge you are facing and (2) identifying areas that will require further research. Analysis in theatrical production is primarily a search for information and an objective evaluation of the data you discover. Prime sources of this information are members of the production design team—the producer, director, and your fellow designers. In your discussions with them you need to examine everything—production style, concepts, budgets, schedules—that is relevant to your design

Stream-of-consciousness questioning: Asking whatever relevant questions pop into your mind in the course of a discussion.

project. "*Who* is producing the play? *What* is the production budget? *Where* is the play being produced? *When* is the design due? *Why* are we doing this play? *How* is the lighting equipment we're renting being moved to the theatre?" The answers to these questions will provide you with information that will further define and clarify your challenge. Each answer should also raise another question or two in your mind. Ask them. This **stream-of-consciousness questioning** can provide you with invaluable information about your challenge.

Carry a small notebook with you. Whenever a thought or idea pops into your mind, regardless of how inconsequential it seems, put it into your notebook. These thoughts can be anything relevant to the design challenge. A thought about a character's texture—"He is rough like burlap"—is an idea that should be noted. An impression that the atmosphere of the play is hot, heavy, and sticky is important. Your sense that the play is soft and curved, not sharp and hard, should also be noted.

The Questioning Process

Questioning is one of the keys to creativity. Your drive to create is based, to a great extent, on your perceived need for change, or your creative discontent with the status quo. If you are satisfied with everything in your world, you will see no need to change, modify, or create anything.

To analyze effectively it is necessary to shed fear—fear of criticism, fear of making mistakes, fear of seeming less than brilliant, fear of being thought a fool or somehow different. Fear inhibits thinking and makes us afraid to ask questions. All too frequently I hear students in my classes say, "I don't want to ask a dumb question, but . . ." As far as I am concerned, the only dumb question is one that isn't asked.

Analyze the script, question the director, question the other members of the production design team, and question the producer. Learn what they are thinking, feeling, and planning for the production. Analyze what they say. See how it fits in with your reactions and plans. The more information you receive, the more source material you will have to draw on when you finally begin to design.

RESEARCH

As you gather information, you will discover small pockets of knowledge in which your personal experience and background are weak. List them in your notebook as the areas in which research is necessary. You will be doing both background research and conceptual research.

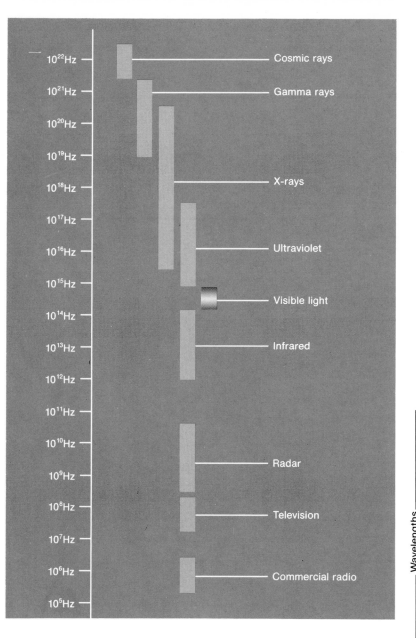

10^{22}Hz	Cosmic rays
10^{21}Hz	Gamma rays
10^{20}Hz	
10^{19}Hz	
10^{18}Hz	X-rays
10^{17}Hz	
10^{16}Hz	Ultraviolet
10^{15}Hz	
10^{14}Hz	Visible light
10^{13}Hz	Infrared
10^{12}Hz	
10^{11}Hz	
10^{10}Hz	
10^{9}Hz	Radar
10^{8}Hz	Television
10^{7}Hz	
10^{6}Hz	Commercial radio
10^{5}Hz	

Color Plate 1

The frequency range of
selected energy forms
contained in the electro-
magnetic radiation spectrum.

Color Plate 2

The frequency range of
visible light.

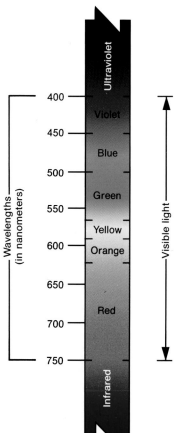

Wavelengths
(in nanometers)

Ultraviolet

400
Violet
450
Blue
500
Green
550
Yellow
600
Orange
650
Red
700
750

Infrared

Visible light

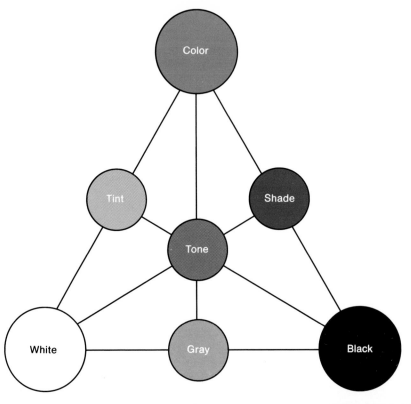

Color Plate 3

The color triangle is a visual representation of the relationships that exist between color, shade, tint, and tone.

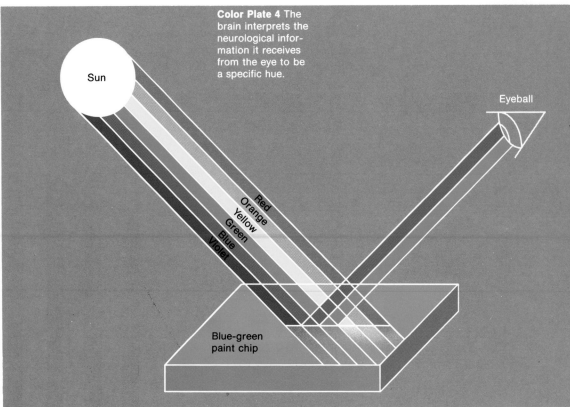

Color Plate 4 The brain interprets the neurological information it receives from the eye to be a specific hue.

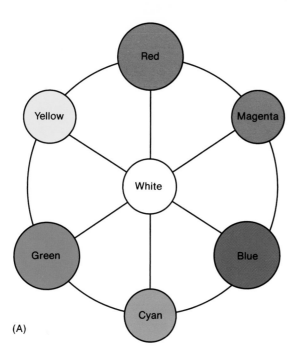

(A)

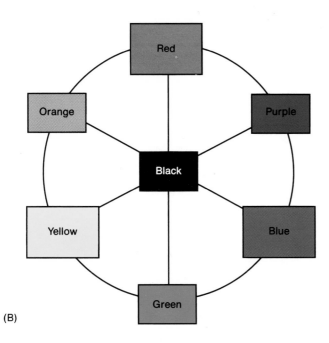

(B)

Color Plate 5

Color wheels for (A) light and (B) pigment.

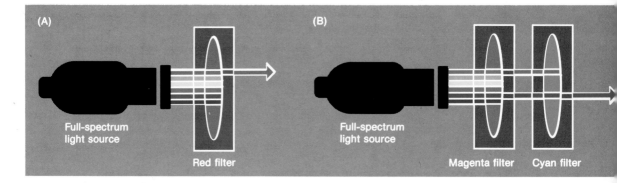

(A)

Full-spectrum
light source

Red filter

(B)

Full-spectrum
light source

Magenta filter   Cyan filter

Color Plate 6

Subtractive color mixing in
light. A colored filter will allow
its own color to pass but will
absorb all others.

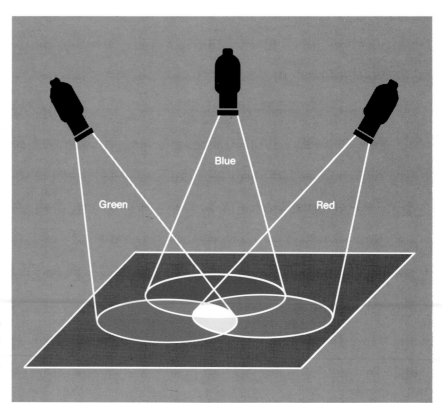

Blue

Green

Red

Color Plate 7

Additive color mixing in light.
The eye sees each separate
color; the brain interprets the
ratio of the color mix to be a
specific hue.

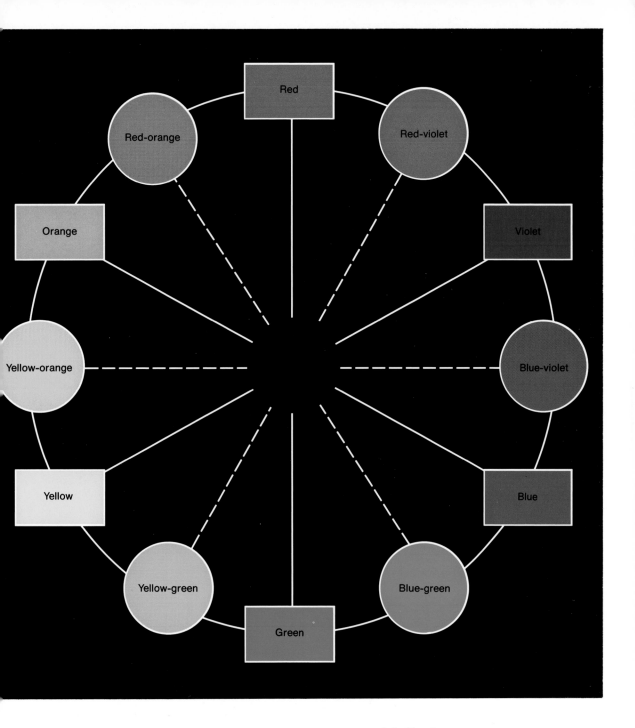

——————— = **Light**

——————————— = **Pigment**

Color Plate 8

Integrated color wheel. This
device is used to help clarify
the relationships that exist
between the primary and
secondary hues in both
pigment and light.

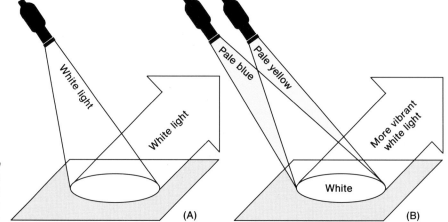

Color Plate 9

The use of an additive mix of complementary tints results in a more lively, vibrant light.

White light

White light

(A)

Pale blue

Pale yellow

More vibrant white light

White

(B)

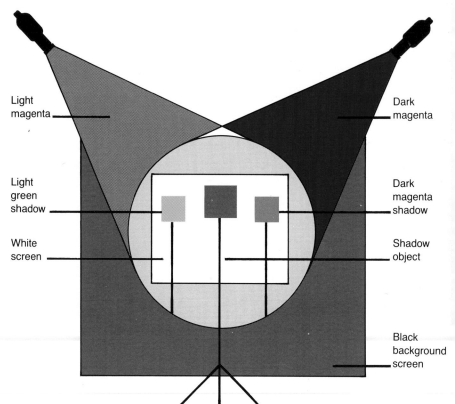

Light magenta

Light green shadow

White screen

Color Plate 10

Color shadowing produces the perception of complementary hues.

Dark magenta

Dark magenta shadow

Shadow object

Black background screen

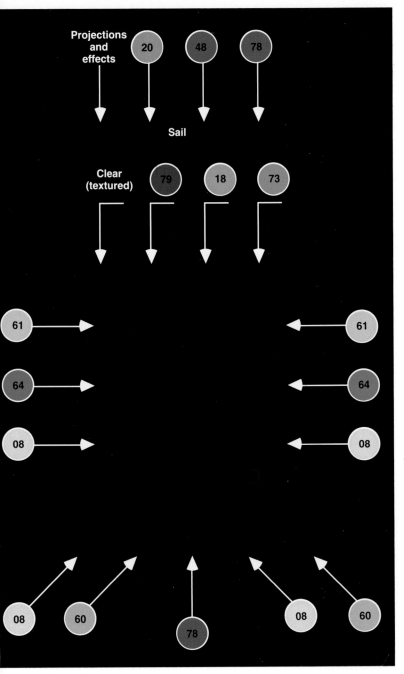

Projections and effects

Sail

Clear (textured)

Analysis of the Lighting Design for Terra Nova

Director: Harold Dixon; scenic and lighting design: J. Michael Gillette; costume design: Jerry D. Allen; property design: Peter Wexler—the properties were designed and constructed for the original production of *Terra Nova* at the Mark Taper forum in Los Angeles, produced by the Center Theatre Group.

An audience can only see objects as a result of reflected or emitted light. Since almost all objects onstage reflect rather than emit light, a look at the color and texture used in the lighting design provides an effective analysis of the color design for the whole production.

The entire set for the University of Arizona's production of Ted Tally's *Terra Nova*, from the representational ice floe in the foreground to the abstracted ship's sail in the background, was finished in an off-white hue. The palette chosen for the lighting (Color Plate 11) on this neutral, highly reflective surface provided the primary color element in the visual design for the production. With this in mind, specific colors were chosen to create psychological keys in support of the emotional content of various scenes in the play. Color Plates 12 and 13 illustrate the blending of various design elements (scenic, costume, properties, lighting) to create the color impact of the production design.

The scenes in Antarctica (Color Plate 12) were lit with almost painfully brilliant white light, while the memory scenes (Color Plate 13) were lit with textured top lights and color washes selected for their psychological impact.

The use of low-saturation complementary colors to light the acting areas from the front and sides significantly reduced the color-shifting effects of the stage lights on costumes and skin tones. The clear, textured top lights, when used in conjunction with the heavily saturated top washes, created significant changes in the visual appearance of the set. These elements working together created a subtly effective color design that worked for the support of the production.

Color Plate 11

The lighting key. The arrows indicate the direction from which the light is traveling toward the stage. The horizontal flags on the arrows in the upper part of the illustration indicate that those lights are coming from above, rather than behind the actors. Note that numbers indicate Roscolux color numbers.

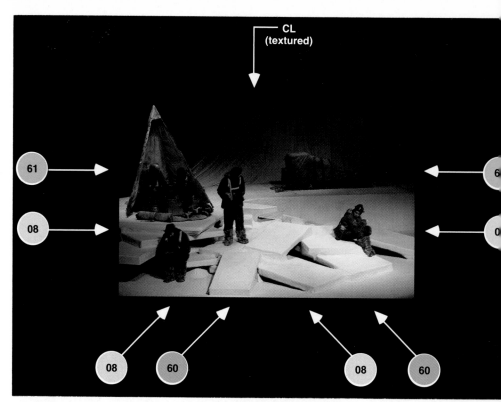

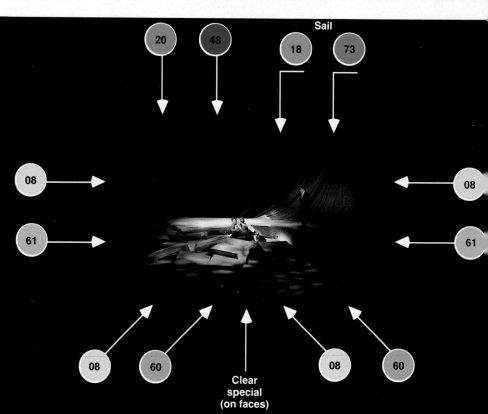

Background Research

Designers have to study the historical background of each production they design. This type of research involves searching the library for books, catalogs, paintings, periodicals, and other sources of information about the era.

Your historical research should include reading about previous productions of the play and may include looking at photos and sketches of those prior productions. Don't fall prey, however, to the temptation

---

TALK IT OVER

The most unified production concepts are developed as a result of talking. In a production of *Cabaret* at the University of Arizona, the production design team began preliminary concept discussions in early January for a production that was to open on April 25.

The director indicated at the first meeting that he wanted to stress the decadence of Berlin society. Our initial informal discussions centered on what this decadence should look like. Someone said that the cabaret should appear to be below ground level (to subliminally support the idea of descending into the hell that was about to engulf Germany). Another person mentioned that it could be useful to have four towers onstage with followspots on top, because the audience might make a connection between them and the guard towers in a concentration camp. The

director said he wanted to have the cabaret audience watching the onstage action (cabaret and noncabaret scenes) at all times. He thought that this device would add an appropriately voyeuristic quality. Ideas just seemed to pop up as we all became more excited about the project.

Within a month we developed the production concept through our discussions at these once-a-week meetings. We all brought rough sketches, photos, and ideas to every meeting. We discussed everything— acting style, acting areas, color, visual motifs, atmosphere, history. When the deadline for final designs arrived, we all knew what everyone else was thinking and doing.

This example shows what can happen when the production design team, under the leadership and coordination of the director, works

together to evolve the production concept. For a variety of reasons, however, it frequently isn't possible for the director and designers to sit around a table and work together to develop the production concept. When this happens, a good director usually adopts a more authoritarian posture in the development of the production concept. He or she develops a primary production concept and discusses it in individual meetings with the designers. The designers then work toward this concept.

The two methods work equally well. Quality productions can be achieved with either method. The common denominator is communication. A good production concept can evolve only if the director and designers talk to one another and share their ideas, thoughts, and imagination.

Pigment: Material that imparts color to a substance such as paint or dye.

to simply duplicate someone else's design. That practice squelches your creativity and, more pragmatically, it is illegal in most states.

Additional background research in the field of color will also be necessary. A thorough understanding of this extremely important area will enable the designer to match and blend colors in **pigment** and light. Furthermore, by studying the psychology of color, you will be able to select colors for the lights that will help establish the mood and atmosphere of the production. Color is discussed in detail in Chapter 10.

HOW DOES IT REALLY LOOK?

Several years ago I designed the sets for a production of Somerset Maugham's venerable play *Rain* at the University of Arizona. One of my graduate students was doing the lighting design. The play is set in an old hotel on the tropical Pacific island of Pago Pago. Everything to do with this production was rushed, and we didn't take much time for production meetings. When the student lighting designer asked me what kind of atmosphere the lights should suggest, I told him that it should be hot, oppressively hot. When we got to the lighting rehearsal the set looked hot, but it was a dry desert heat, not the sticky closeness of the tropics. After talking with the lighting designer, I discovered that he had never been out of Arizona, and so he had no firsthand experience with the wet heat of the tropics.

The moral of this story is that lighting designers need to do research. You need to know about the climate and color of the sunlight in the locale of the play. Ideally, you would be able to experience the locale firsthand; but since most production budgets don't include travel money for the lighting designer to do research, you'll have to accomplish it in other ways. The excellent photos that accompany *National Geographic* stories about various locales provide a wealth of information about the quality and color of light as well as the density of the air (humidity). Look at other picture magazines. Study any and all sources that can tell you what it *looks like* in the locale of the play.

You can also make reasonable comparisons between different geographic areas. With any lighting design you're trying to create the psychological impression of an atmosphere in the audience's mind. You're not trying to replicate the climate of an actual place. If you're designing a show set in Pago Pago and you've never been there, think of where you've been that is similar. Florida during the summer is humid and tropical. If you've been there, try to remember the quality of the light and use that as a base. Chances are very good you've never been to the upper reaches of the Himalayas. So what do you do if you have to design *K-2*? Anyone who's been to the Rockies has seen the clarity and crisp brilliance of sunlight in mountain air. If you've experienced January in one of our northern states, you know what cold looks and feels like. Translate those experiences.

When designing lights you have to do research and then imaginatively translate that research to create a new reality that will exist on the stage.

Conceptual Research

Conceptual research involves devising multiple solutions to specific design challenges. In reading a script, for example, you may discover that the first act takes place in a seedy apartment at night. The second act occurs in the same apartment the following morning. Through conceptual research you would resolve this challenge in as many ways as possible.

Unfortunately, we all seem to have difficulty conceiving of any more than two or three possible solutions to any given challenge. Too often our brains go numb and refuse to dream up new ideas. Psychologists refer to this type of nonthinking state as a perceptual block. If the perceptual block can be eliminated, our ability to devise, or create, additional solutions to any given problem greatly improves. In other words, removing perceptual blocks significantly increases our personal creative ability.

INCUBATION

How many times have you left an examination room and then suddenly remembered the answer to a question that eluded you while you were writing the test? How many times have you come up with the solution to a problem after having "slept on it"? In both cases the information necessary to answer the questions was locked in your subconscious and only needed time and a little stress reduction to allow the answer to float into your conscious mind.

Incubation provides you with time to let ideas hatch. During this time you should basically forget about the project. Your subconscious mind will use the time to sort through the information you've gathered in the previous steps and may actually construct a solution to the design challenge or at least point you in a valid direction.

Give yourself enough time to let your subconscious mind mull over the data that you have absorbed. It simply isn't possible to do your best work if you wait for a deadline and then rush through an assignment. Quality work happens more easily if you allow time for incubation.

SELECTION

Selection is the step in the design process in which you sift through all of the data you've accumulated and decide on your specific design concept. Because each designer's choices affect the work of all members of the production design team, all the designs need to be discussed in another production meeting.

The lighting designer submits sketches showing the general characteristics of the concept for the lighting design, if such sketches are appropriate. At the least, he or she presents the intended palette and a verbal description of the atmospheric effect of the lighting during the production meeting.

The selection phase of the design process is finished when the director feels satisfied that all design areas support the production design concept.

UNBLOCK YOUR THINKING

How can we get rid of our perceptual blocks? By eliminating the cause, we can usually eliminate the block. Proper identification of the real challenge is extremely important. Many times challenges are not what they first seem to be. If a play has three scenes, the first during late afternoon, the second at sunset, and the third in early evening, one of your design challenges would be to devise ways of making the audience accept and believe the three different time periods. To most of us that would mean gelling the basic acting-area lights with daytime colors and gelling some additional instruments with night colors and adjusting the levels between the two to make the night scene look more "shadowy." Maybe we'd throw in a sunset effect

for fun. That's fairly normal. This type of scene is lit that way all the time. But couldn't the challenge be solved just as well by designing three separate plots for each scene? Wouldn't it be possible to produce the play outdoors and start it just before sunset so that it could be lit realistically as the big instrument in the sky slips below the horizon? How about having each scene in a different theatre and moving the audience between them? These additional solutions to the challenge are the result of nothing more than a very careful examination of the specific question being posed in the challenge.

Define Your Challenge More Broadly

If you thought about the traditional way of cross-fading

between daytime and nighttime colors in the previous problem, you were actually defining the challenge too closely. By unconsciously limiting your quest for possible solutions to the traditionally accepted methods, you were shutting off a whole realm of new, effective (if somewhat quirky) solutions to the challenge. Think creatively about the elements of the challenge, and don't accept only the commonplace answers to the questions posed in the challenge.

Overcome Tunnel Vision

When you are working on a design, it is very easy (and egocentrically convenient) to fail to see your assignment from the viewpoint of others involved in the challenge. It's very easy to forget, when selecting a predominately

IMPLEMENTATION

Quite simply, the implementation phase begins when you stop planning and start doing. At this time you produce the light plot, lighting sectional, and instrument schedule, as well as the other paperwork associated with the lighting design. The lighting designer than supervises the hanging and focusing of the lights and determines the intensity levels and timing for all lighting cues.

amber/yellow palette for the lights, that the costumer has the heroine in a lavender gown. The result will be a gown that's gray instead of lavender. The thoughtless selection of pink as your predominate hue for the lights will similarly kill the light-green walls that the scene designer labored so hard to achieve.

Tunnel vision can be avoided if members of the production design team discuss their ideas in production meetings. By conferring on a regular basis, the director and designers can remain aware of everyone else's work as it progresses from conception to completion.

Avoid Visual Stereotyping
Visual stereotyping refers to seeing what you expect to see rather than what is actually in front of you. It limits your ability to conceive of existing elements in new combinations. If you think of the nighttime sky as simply being blue, then you probably won't experiment with various tones of green and dark lavender, which can provide you with luminescent and realistic nighttime hues. Don't cut yourself off before you start. Critically look at that night sky and you'll see it contains a whole host of colors, tints, and shades.

Remember Details Selectively
People remember things selectively. If we decide that something doesn't have great personal significance, we tend to forget it. To demonstrate this principle, try to recall the lighting patterns in your dorm room, apartment, or home. Where are the sources? What is their distribution pattern? Where are the highlights and shadows? You pass through this place every day, but you don't look at it very closely.

All of us remember details that we have determined are important for us to recall. Albert Einstein was reputed not to have known his own telephone number. When asked why, he reportedly said that he didn't want to clutter up his mind with information that he could look up.

Although it is very important for a lighting designer to have a thorough knowledge of the various areas directly and indirectly related to the field, it is equally important to follow Einstein's dictum and not clutter up your mind with details that can be found in a reference work.

EVALUATION

Evaluation takes place within each step of the design process, and it also occurs when the project is completed. This final evaluation, or review, is not so much a back-patting session as an examination of the methods and materials used to reach the final design goal. You need to evaluate your selections to see if they were really appropriate and to determine if they could be used in the future in another context.

You need to look objectively at the communication process that took place inside and outside the various production conferences. Examine the various interchanges between yourself and the director, producer, and other designers to see if communication can be improved the next time around. Also evaluate the judgments you made to see if anything that might have helped was left out, ignored, or rejected.

As you become more familiar with the design process, you will discover that your own work is more creative and that you can produce it faster and more easily. The design process is a valuable, efficient, time-saving, and frustration-reducing tool. Use it and enjoy.

THE GOBO TRICK

A lot of art is the result of happy accident. When designing the lights for some forgotten production I noticed that one area of the stage seemed to have a rough texture. I went up on stage and looked more closely. The floor didn't have any texture; it was painted a smooth, flat color. Then I looked up at the lights. One of the instruments had a gobo (a thin metal template that creates a shadow pattern) left in it from a previous production. That instrument was creating the texture. Although I took the gobo out of the instrument, I remembered the effect. Now whenever I want to create a textured atmosphere I put gobos in the instruments.

The moral? Always evaluate what you've done, even if you think it's a "mistake." Just because something isn't right for one situation doesn't mean it won't be right for another.

DESIGN PROCESS CHECKLIST

The following checklist provides a short review that will help you use each step of the design process.

Commitment
a. Make a commitment to yourself to do your best work on the project.
b. Overcome any negative feelings toward the project.

Analysis
a. Gather information to clarify and refine the definition of the challenge.
b. Identify areas needing further research.
c. Read the play.
d. Talk to other members of the production design team.

Research
a. Background research
   1. Study the social and artistic history of the period of the play.
   2. Study all the trends and styles of the architecture, lighting fixtures, and the like for the period.
b. Conceptual research
   1. Be a mental pack rat. Think up as many potential solutions to the challenge as possible.
   2. Don't judge or discard any idea. Save them all.

Incubation
a. Just forget about the project. Do something else.
b. Allow enough time for your subconscious mind to work on the challenge.

Selection
a. Develop your solution to the challenge.
b. Don't be afraid to take a piece of one idea and a piece of another to create the most effective solution.

Implementation
a. Stop thinking and start doing.
b. Produce all necessary drawings, sketches, and plans to facilitate the realization of the design.

Evaluation
a. Reflect on the challenge. Did you do everything you could to make it succeed?
b. Review your use of the design process. Did you fully analyze the question? Did you do sufficient background and conceptual research?
c. Did you effectively communicate your ideas and thoughts to the other members of the design team?

C H A P T E R 10

COLOR

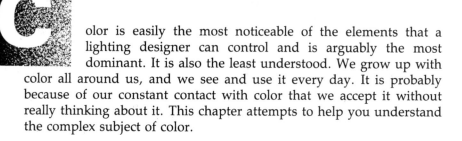

olor is easily the most noticeable of the elements that a
lighting designer can control and is arguably the most
dominant. It is also the least understood. We grow up with
color all around us, and we see and use it every day. It is probably
because of our constant contact with color that we accept it without
really thinking about it. This chapter attempts to help you understand
the complex subject of color.

DEFINING COLOR

Color has a variety of definitions. It can be defined as a perception
created in the brain as a result of stimulation of the retina by light waves
of a certain length. It can also be thought of as the intrinsic physical
properties of specific objects that allow those objects to reflect and
absorb light waves of a certain length. The common denominator for
any definition of color is light, because all color is derived from light.
The phenomenon that we call light is actually the very narrow portion of
the spectrum of electromagnetic radiation that is visible to the human
eye. Color Plate 1 shows the position of visible light on this spectrum, as
well as the positions of some of the other types of radiation. The visible

spectrum stretches in frequency from approximately 750 nanometers to 400. (A nanometer is one billionth of a meter.) Color Plate 2 shows the approximate wavelengths for the various colors of the visible spectrum.

Color Terminology

Without a specific set of terms to describe the various properties of color, almost any discussion of it would quickly degenerate into meaningless comparisons. An example will help explain this phenomenon. If you provided each member of a group of 20 people with 100 **paint chips,** all yellow, but each slightly different, and asked them to identify canary yellow, they would probably select 20 different chips. This is because the connection between the description of any specific color, such as canary yellow, and the brain's understanding of the physical appearance of that color differs, sometimes significantly, from person to person.

The terms that we will be using in our discussion of color are as follows:

- *Hue*—Hue is the quality that differentiates one color from another, such as blue from green or red from yellow.
- *Saturation*—Saturation, also known as chroma, refers to the amount, or percentage, of a particular hue in a color mixture. Fire-engine red has a high, or strong, saturation, because there is a lot of fully saturated color in the mixture. Dusty rose, in contrast, has a low, or weak, saturation, because there isn't a lot of fully saturated color in the mixture; instead, the majority is white or gray.
- *Value*—The relative lightness or darkness of a color is referred to as value. Pale blue has a high value, and dark brown has a low value.
- *Tint*—A color with a high value is referred to as a tint. It is usually achieved by mixing a hue with either white pigment or white light.
- *Shade*—A color with a low value is known as a shade. It is usually created by a mixture of one or more hues and black.
- *Tone*—A color of middle value is frequently referred to as a tone. It is a mixture of a hue with black *and* white.

The color triangle in Color Plate 3 shows the relationships among hue, white, black, gray (the product of mixing black and white), tint, shade, and tone.

Rods: Nerve cells in the retina that are sensitive to faint light.

Cones: Nerve cells in the retina that are sensitive to bright light; they respond either to red, blue, or green light.

SEEING COLOR

Before we learn how color works, we need to understand how we see color. Human sight comprises a complex series of events. When you look at an object, elements within your eye are stimulated by the light being emitted by, or reflected from, the viewed object. An electrochemical reaction occurs in specialized nerve cells in the retina. Two distinct types of light-receptor nerves, **rods** and **cones,** emit minute charges of electricity that are relayed to your brain, where the received data are interpreted as a "picture" that you have seen. The cones are divided into three primary groups: those that respond to the wavelengths of light that correspond to red, blue, and green, respectively.

If a red light enters the eye, the red-responsive cones are stimulated but the others are not. If a light that contains both red and blue wavelengths enters the eye, both the red- and blue-responsive cones are stimulated. In this case the message that is sent to the brain corresponds to the ratio of red and blue light contained in the light mixture that the eye receives. If the light contains more red than blue light, that information is transmitted.

Notice that the eye only sends information to the brain that corresponds to the input it has received. The brain is the organ that does the interpretative mixing of the colors. In the example of the red and blue light, the amount of red and blue in the mixture will be interpreted by the brain to be a particular color such as violet, magenta, or purple.

All perceived color is transmitted to the eye by light. If the light is dim, the cones (color sensors) do not function. The best way to demonstrate this effect is by standing outside on a moonlit night and looking at your surroundings. Everything you see will be a monochromatic gray, with perhaps a slight tint of blue or green if the moonlight is sufficiently bright. You will see no vibrant reds, blues, or greens, because the cones require more light than is being transmitted to your eye. If you look at the same scene during the daytime, the bright sunlight will activate the cones in your eye. Unless your eye has some physical dysfunction or the color-interpretative segment of your brain is impaired, you will see colors.

To further illustrate how the eye sees and the brain interprets color, let's assume that you are standing outside in the sunlight looking at a turquoise (blue-green) color chip, as shown in Color Plate 4. The sunlight, which contains all of the electromagnetic wavelengths of the visible spectrum, strikes the blue-green surface of the color chip. Some of that light is reflected, and some of it is absorbed by the pigment on the paint chip. The majority of those wavelengths of light that correspond to the color of the chip (blue and green) are reflected. The majority of all other wavelengths of light are absorbed by the paint chip.

The reflected blue and green light is received by the eye. The blue and green cones are stimulated by the light, causing them to send electrical impulses to the brain. The relative strength of these signals from the blue and green cones is proportionate to the specific amount of blue and green in the color mix. When the color-sensitive area of the brain is stimulated by these impulses, it interprets that information as a specific color known to that particular brain as turquoise.

COLOR MIXING

Before examining color mixing we must understand some additional terms.

Primary Colors

Primary colors are those hues that cannot be derived or blended from any other hues. In light, the primary colors (Color Plate 5A) are closely related to the color sensitivity of the red, blue, and green cones in the eye.

Secondary Colors

Secondary hues are the result of mixing two primary colors. In the color wheel for light (Color Plate 5A), the mixing of adjacent primaries creates the secondary hues yellow (amber), magenta, and cyan (blue-green). The primary colors in pigment (Color Plate 5B) are red, blue, and yellow. The secondary colors in pigment are purple, green, and orange.

Complementary Colors

Complementary colors can be described as any two hues that, when combined, yield white in light or black in pigment. They can also be described as colors opposite each other on a color wheel. The color wheel for light (Color Plate 5A) shows that the complementary hue for red is cyan. When the two are combined they form white light. In the color wheel for pigment (Color Plate 5B) the complementary of red is green. When the two are mixed, they form black.

Filtered Light

When white light passes through any type of filtering material, such as glass, plastic, or air, a certain portion of the spectrum is absorbed. To fully understand this type of absorption you need to know something about the nature of light and energy.

Light, as we have seen, is a form of radiant energy (part of the electromagnetic spectrum). According to the laws of physics, energy can be neither created nor destroyed, but its form can be changed or converted. This principle can be demonstrated by touching a window through which the sun is shining. The glass will be warmer than a similar window that isn't in the direct sunlight. This is because the energy being absorbed by the glass is being converted from light into heat.

Subtractive Color Mixing in Light   If the glass in the window mentioned above is colored, another type of filtering takes place. Colored filters allow only their own hue to pass through the filtering medium; they absorb all other wavelengths of light.

Color Plate 6A shows a red filter placed in front of a full-spectrum light source. The white light emitted by the lamp is composed of wavelengths from all portions of the visible spectrum. The red filter allows only the wavelengths of light that correspond to its own color to pass. All other light is stopped by the filter and converted into heat.

When two or more filters, such as the secondary hues magenta and cyan, are placed in front of a single source (Color Plate 6B), each filter removes all but its own segment of the spectrum. The resulting blue light is caused by successive filtration. The magenta filter allows only red and blue light to pass through it. The cyan filter absorbs the red portion of the magenta light but allows the blue portion to pass. In practical application, it is usually preferable to use a single filter, rather than multiple filters. By selectively removing portions of the visible spectrum, subtractive color mixing actually reduces the intensity of the output of the source. A yellow or amber color medium of minimal saturation may reduce intensity by about 5 percent, for example, and a heavily saturated dark blue may reduce it by as much as 85 percent. If more than one filter is used, the output of the source can be significantly reduced.

Additive Color Mixing in Light   When several individual hues are transmitted to the eye, added together, and interpreted by the brain, the process is called additive color mixing. Color Plate 7 illustrates color mixing in light. The beams of the three lights are being projected onto a neutral or white surface. When a primary hue, such as red, is mixed with an adjacent primary, such as green, a secondary hue, yellow, is created. (It is interesting to realize that this hue is *not* created on the projection surface but is the result of the red and green cones in our eye being stimulated by the red and green light and our brain interpreting this neurological information as the hue yellow.) This same phenomenon occurs when any two or more hues are additively mixed.

All color is perceived in the same way. The subtle tones, tints, and shades of the various hues that you see are all determined by the level of stimulation that the red, blue, and green cones receive from the light reflected to your eye and by your brain's interpretation of that information.

Integrated Color Wheel

Sir Isaac Newton demonstrated that six principal hues (violet, blue, green, yellow, orange, and red) can be generated when sunlight is passed through a prism. These hues can be placed on a color wheel, as shown in Color Plate 8. Additional hues, which are full chroma equivalents to a mixture of adjacent original hues, can be created and placed between the six principal colors to create a color wheel with twelve specific, fully saturated, hues.

This integrated color wheel can help clarify the interrelationships between pigment and light. For years a semantic problem has hindered easy understanding of these relationships. The use of the same words to describe some of the primary and secondary hues for pigment and light has tended to create some confusion. Although the words red, blue, green, and yellow are used to describe colors in both pigment and light, the specific hues are not identical. The integrated color wheel resolves this problem by renaming the primary colors in light to more accurately reflect the true color relationship that exists between the various hues in pigment and light.

THE PRACTICAL APPLICATION
OF COLORED LIGHT IN THE THEATRE

In any discussion of color there is bound to be a disparity between theoretical principles and practical results. Although the principles of color theory are certainly applicable in the practical use of color, the end results will be somewhat different from the results projected by the theory. This is because of the impurities and contaminants found in all stage paints, dyes, lamps, and color media.

Meaning of Color

People react to color. Sometimes that response is subtle and subconscious, and at other times it is overtly physical. Doctors and drug rehabilitation counselors have discovered that an extremely violent patient will often become calm and manageable in about 15 or 20 minutes if placed in an all-pink environment. Many hospitals now have "pink rooms" in which everything—the floor, ceiling, walls, doors—is painted the same hue of pink.

The meanings of color are constantly changing. Color meanings are influenced by many factors: cultural background, personality, adjoining colors, and individual mood. The variability of these factors is the primary reason that the following list of affective meanings is necessarily ambiguous. Moreover, these definitions are simply common interpretations of the meaning of specific colors and should not be thought of as being the "correct" ones.

- yellow: stimulating, cheerful, exciting, joyful, serene, unpleasant, aggressive, hostile
- orange: warm, happy, merry, exciting, stimulating, hot, disturbed, distressed, unpleasant
- red: happy, affectionate, loving, exciting, striking, active, intense, defiant, powerful, masterful, strong, aggressive, hostile
- green: youthful, fresh, leisurely, secure, calm, peaceful, emotionally controlled, ill
- blue: pleasant, cool, secure, comfortable, tender, soothing, social, dignified, sad, strong, full, great
- violet: dignified, stately, vigorous, disagreeable, sad, despondent, melancholy, unhappy, depressing
- black: sad, melancholy, vague, unhappy, dignified, stately, strong, powerful, hostile, distressed, fearful, old
- white: pure, tender, soothing, solemn, empty
- brown: secure, comfortable, full, sad, disagreeable

Practical Color Use

Lighting designers normally follow some general color guidelines when selecting their palettes. The following discussion provides a survey of examples and general practices. However, any competent designer will advise you that there are many occasions when it is appropriate, logical, and right to ignore the normal and the conventional if doing so will support the visualization of the production concept.

There are some very pragmatic reasons for using colored light onstage. The light from theatre spotlights is relatively bright and harsh. In its uncolored state and at close to full intensity, it will tend to bleach any color out of the scenery, costumes, and makeup. If colors that are compatible with the scenery and costumes are used to filter the stage lights, however, the scenic designer's and costume designer's color palettes and values will be maintained.

As we have seen, the mixing of complementary hues creates white light. In the discussion on color theory this principle was demonstrated with fully saturated hues. In practical application fully saturated hues are rarely used because of their adverse effect on the other designers' palettes and on actors' skin tones. Complementary hues of low chroma are frequently used, however, because pigments lit with additively mixed white light are enhanced rather than bleached. This color enhancement is caused by the brain's interpretation of retinal stimulation, as demonstrated in Color Plate 9. Color Plate 9A shows white light striking a white surface. Since the white light is composed of all

---

HOW TO CREATE HUMIDITY WITH LIGHT

A major portion of the lighting designer's job is to create an atmosphere supportive of the production concept. In the box "How Does It Really Look" in Chapter 9, I discussed the University of Arizona production of *Rain*, where the lighting designer made the set look "desert" hot rather than "tropical" hot. It is actually fairly easy to manipulate the apparent humidity of the onstage picture. To do so, simply increase the saturation of the color mix used in the acting areas. In *Rain* the lighting designer first lit the whole set with a double-hung (two instruments hung immediately adjacent to each other, each gelled with a different color) complementary mix of very low saturation—No-Color Yellow and No-Color Blue.

When we finally stopped tinkering with the colors, that mix had changed to hues of medium saturation—Golden Amber and Steel Blue—and the look of the stage picture had changed to the hot, sticky, moist heat of the tropics. The reason for this change in audience perception has to do with the phenomenon of aerial perspective, which is the visual expression of depth through the gradation of color saturation from more fully saturated in the foreground to less saturated in the background.

According to the principles of aerial perspective, the farther an object is from you, the less saturated it seems to be. As humidity goes up, the effects of aerial perspective are enhanced because there

is more moisture in the air to diffuse the reflection of light from objects to your eye. The color of distant objects becomes even less saturated, and their outlines less distinct. All human beings have learned this principle through observation. As a lighting designer you can play on this unconsciously learned response by increasing the saturation of close objects (in relationship to distant objects—background scenes, ground rows, and so forth) in a scene to create the appearance of high humidity. Conversely, to create the appearance of low humidity, all you need to do is decrease the difference in saturation between the light falling on the background and foreground elements of the set.

Source light: The apparent source of light that is illuminating a scene or object.

wavelengths of light, the white surface simply reflects all the light rather than absorbing or filtering out any specific portion of the spectrum. Color Plate 9B shows two complementary hues of low saturation (light blue and light yellow) striking the same white surface. These low-saturation hues emphasize a relatively narrow portion of the spectrum (blue and yellow), although there is still a large proportion of the full spectrum (white light) in the mix. The white surface reflects the pale blue and pale yellow, as well as the white light, to your eye. Because blue and yellow are complementary, your brain interprets the mixture of those two lights as white. However, the cones are more strongly stimulated by the blue and yellow light than they would be with plain white light. Interestingly, the brain interprets this stronger color stimulation as a richer, more vibrant color. This phenomenon works for all complementary color mixes. Although the specific color reflectivity and absorption of any colored light from any particular costume or set color will depend on the characteristics of that particular hue, the principles of color vibrancy remain constant.

Warm and Cool Colors

"Warm" and "cool" refer to the psychological effect that certain colors seem to possess. Most people feel a sense of warmth with colors in the red-orange-yellow color range and a sense of coolness with colors in the blue-green-lavender range. Lighting designers frequently make use of these psychological color keys to indicate **source light** (warm) and shadow (cool).

Color Direction

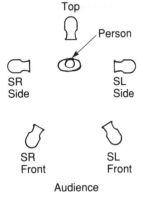

The direction (relative to the audience) from which each color strikes the actor has a great deal to do with how much color blending the audience sees. Basically, light striking an actor from a front light can be seen more readily by the audience than can the light from the side or top. Therefore, the major color impact that the audience sees results from the colors used in the front lights.

Figure 10.1 shows how color blending takes place. Any color that we use on these instruments would additively mix according to the amount of overlap between the instruments and their position relative to the observer. In the proscenium theatre you would see the following: the two side-front lights would blend fairly uniformly; the stage-left side light would blend with the stage-left side-front light and a little bit with the top light; the stage-right side light would similarly blend with its adjacent side-front light and the top light; the top light would additively

Figure 10.1

Direction of the light (relative to the observer) affects color blending. (See text for details.)

mix with all four lights, but only on top of the actor's head and shoulders.

Complementary Tint Theory

The gross oversimplification of the concept of warm and cool colors as directional indicators of source and shadow has unfortunately resulted in some garish stage lighting over the years. When the interaction between hues of a complementary mix is inadequate, as when the angle between the two sources in a two-color mix is so wide that there is almost no overlap of the colors, an uneven additive color mix is the unhappy result. For example, when Roscolux 20, Medium Amber, is used from one side of the stage and Roscolux 68, Sky Blue, is used from the other, the actor will end up looking amber on one side and blue on the other. However, the complementary tint theory works extremely well if approached with care and a little good judgment. If an actor is lit by two instruments that overlap adequately and are colored with relatively complementary tints, such as Roscolux 09, Pale Amber Gold, and Roscolux 60, No-Color Blue (see Figure 10.2), the majority of his face and body will be washed with both colors, which additively mix to yield a slightly warm white light. Only on the extreme sides of his face, where he is lit by only the Pale Amber Gold or the No-Color Blue, will the actor seem to be slightly warmer or cooler.

There is a theory that having one side of the actor appear to be slightly cool in comparison to the other enhances the modeling qualities of the light. Another theory holds that modeling is more related to distribution and intensity than color and that the color should be evenly distributed on both sides of the actor. Neither practice is necessarily better than the other. They both work well in given circumstances. However, to achieve a smooth blend it will be necessary to have all visible areas of the actor's body covered with light of both colors. This can be accomplished by **double hanging** the lights from each direction as shown in Figure 10.3A. Double hanging also enables the designer to shift between colors by increasing or decreasing the intensity of one color or the other.

Another method of overlapping the colored light to achieve a relatively uniform additive mix is shown in Figure 10.3B. With this method, however, it isn't possible to do an effective color shift between the warm and cool lights because, with the staggered position of the instruments, the modeling on the actor would change if you were to make one color brighter than the other.

When you use a complementary color mix, the additive color mix increases the apparent life in a much wider range of colors than if the

Double hang: To place two instruments adjacent to each other to light an area that normally would be lit by one instrument. Normally done to allow a color shift during a scene or to provide an additive color mix.

Person

Figure 10.2

Complementary tints can be used to create a more vibrant white light. (See text for details.)

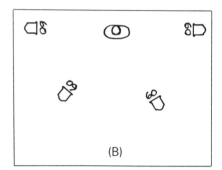

Figure 10.3

Color blending techniques: (A) double hanging; (B) alternating colors.

scene were lit with a single color that closely approximates the hue resulting from the additive mix.

The palettes used by the scenic and costume designers generally dictate the specific complementary hues that are chosen by a lighting designer. The lighting designer usually selects specific hues that will enhance the primary palettes of the other designers, using the guideline that every hue heightens its own color and suppresses its complementary. If the scenic or costume designer is using a full-spectrum palette, the lighting designer may combine three or more colors, such as low-chroma versions of the three secondary colors—yellow, cyan, and magenta—to create white light. When more specific hues are used to create the white-light mix, the range of hues affected by the color-enrichment characteristics of a complementary mix are similarly broadened.

The lighting designer can also produce a white-light mix that is not exactly complementary—either slightly warm or cool—to create a corresponding warming or cooling of the stage environment. This type of not-quite-complementary color mixing is very helpful in establishing an atmospheric feeling of heat or cold on the stage.

Color Media

Three transparent color media are used to color the light output of stage lighting instruments. Each medium has its own particular characteristics and advantages.

Gel   Gel is the least expensive of the color light filters. It is made from animal gelatin and colored with a variety of primarily synthetic dyes. Its principal disadvantages are that it fades rather quickly, particularly when used with T-H lamps, and is subject to being eaten by vermin. It's amazing how a cockroach can put three strategically placed holes in a sheet of gel and make it almost impossible to cut an 8-inch gel from a full 20-by-24-inch sheet. Gel is also fragile when dry and totally destroyed when wet. Primarily because it bleaches and deteriorates much more rapidly than do plastic media, the use of gel is decreasing rapidly.

Plastic   The primary filters used in stage lighting instruments are generally made from either mylar or polyester because of the rugged, long-lasting qualities of these plastics. Mylar and polyester are both considerably stronger and much more heat-resistant than gel. They are

---

COMPLEMENTARY COLOR SHADOWING

Complementary color shadowing is another interesting challenge to the lighting designer. Complementary color shadowing refers to the physiological reaction of seeing shadow colors that are complementary to the specific hue of the source light. An example will help illustrate this phenomenon. Color Plate 10 shows two intersecting light sources, one gelled with a fairly heavily saturated magenta, and the other with a magenta of low saturation. They are projecting onto a white surface. An object has been erected to throw shadows from both beams onto the projection surface. The shadow of one light is magenta, but the other is green!

The brain constantly tries to balance the input that it receives from the eye to create a white base. The eye recognizes that it is receiving input from multiple sources because of the difference in specific color between the two sources. The only way that the brain can logically create the white base that it seeks from these two magenta sources is to interpret one of the hues—the less saturated one—to be the complement of magenta: green.

I've used magenta in this example simply because the magenta/green mix is very visible and provides a startling example. However, the principle holds true for any other related color mix as well: green gels will have magenta shadows, blue gels will have yellow shadows, yellow gels will have blue shadows, and so forth.

While this is an interesting party trick and one that never fails to amaze anyone who sees it, there is a rational, productive reason for lighting designers to understand this phenomenon. When you work with a related tint mix (a color mix in which all of the hues are tints, tones, and shades of one color), you are going to get complementary color shadowing. For example, if you choose to work in a related tint mix of lavender, depending on the specific hues that you select, you will probably have some ugly looking greenish shadows lurking about the stage. However, if you add a top light in a complementary hue to the mix, you create a resultant white light that reduces the effects of the complementary color shadowing to the point where it isn't visible. Additionally, by putting the complementary hue in the top light, you haven't significantly altered the effects of your related tint design on the sets, costumes, and skin tones.

available in a wide and ever-increasing variety of colors. The low-saturation tints bleach out very slowly, and the more heavily saturated shades last for a relatively long time, even under the intense ultraviolet radiation emitted by T-H lamps.

Glass   Glass is used infrequently as a filter although it is certainly the longest lasting and most fade resistant of all the media. Its palette is extremely limited when compared with plastic color media; it is expensive and heavy and will shatter if dropped. The most prominent use of glass is in rondels, the glass filters used with striplights. These are generally available in red, blue, green, and amber.

The difference between the theory and practice of color mixing is only a matter of degree, not principle. Although an understanding of the laws of physics that govern the mixing of color is very helpful in using color in the theatre, the only way that a lighting designer can develop any real understanding of, and facility in, the use of color is through experimentation and experience.

HEAT PROTECTION FOR PLASTIC COLOR MEDIA

Heat is one of the prime enemies of plastic color media. A recently developed material, Thermoguard, manufactured by the Artifex Corporation, when placed between the lens of the instrument and the color media, will reflect a high percentage of the infrared radiation (heat) back toward the lamp, while allowing the visible spectrum to pass unimpeded. The material is a transparent heat-reflective coating bonded to a clear polyester base.

Thermoguard will increase the life of your gels and will actually reduce the heat onstage. When used with heavily saturated gels, a 2-inch air space needs to be maintained between the gel and the Thermoguard material. The reflective coating *must* face the heat source. If the material is put into the instrument backwards, the heat from the lamp will melt the polyester base, destroying the filter.

ANALYZING THE SCRIPT

t some point in the information-gathering stage of the design process you will read and begin to analyze the script. In Chapter 9, ''The Design Process,'' I suggested that you carry a notebook and jot down your ideas so that you don't forget them. But not everyone is comfortable working that way. Some people make copius notes in the margins of the script; others sketch or jot down only a few key ideas on scraps of paper and keep them in a folder. Some work on a strictly intuitive basis; others reason out every detail of the design. One designer can actually see the lighting for each scene in his mind's eye, while another works with ideas stored from previous productions he has worked on. Regardless of personal working style, every designer needs to make a detailed analysis of the script as part of the design process. A designer's analysis is not a literary analysis. Although the analytical processes are similar, the end result of a designer's analysis is a performance-oriented set of stimuli rather than a literary critique.

Script analysis comprises two distinct processes. The first process is the textual analysis—the script is read (usually several times) for the intellectual and emotional stimuli that will create specific visual images in the mind of the designer. These images are the creative seeds of the lighting design. The second process is the analysis of those visual images. The designer analyzes the specific visual images obtained from textual analysis into the four controllable qualities of light—distribution, intensity, movement, and color.

The visual concept of a production frequently starts with ideas gleaned from the script; however, it is always modified and enhanced through discussions with the other members of the production design team during the initial production meetings. In these meetings the director and designers freely exchange ideas on the style and context of the production concept. (See the box entitled "Talk It Over" in Chapter 9 for more information on the evolution of the production concept.) In these production meetings the lighting designer also sees the color palettes being used by both the scenic and costume designers.

It is equally important that the lighting designer conduct background research of the type suggested in Chapter 9. Assuming that the production style is relatively realistic, it is imperative that the designer understand what light actually looks like in the physical location of the play. An understanding of the emotional basis—tragic, happy, sad, and so forth—of the play as a whole, as well as the individual scenes and moments within those scenes, is essential. Probably more than any other element, the emotional tone of these segments determines the duration or timing of the fades used with the cues that light these scenes.

IN THE BEGINNING, THINK CREATIVELY

If the lighting is to be an integral, creative part of the production concept, you need to let the words, images, and music of the production meetings and script stimulate your imagination into creating a visual image, or series of images, that support the production concept. To help that process along, think in terms of the functions of light (visibility, selective focus, modeling, mood) that will help or enhance the production concept.

Probably the last things you should think about during the early stages of the creative process are the tools of the designer (instruments, dimmers, cable, and so forth). This type of tunnel-vision thinking will inevitably limit your creative thought processes. If you count your instruments before you have developed your concept, you're erecting an almost insurmountable roadblock to creativity. An effective concept can always be adapted to equipment limitations, but thinking about the limitations before developing a concept simply blocks creativity.

From the information gathered from the script and production meetings, as well as from background research, the lighting designer should have a clear idea, image, or series of images of the psychological and atmospheric quality of the light for the production. Some designers like to synthesize these thoughts and images into a written statement that helps communicate the intent of the lighting design to other members of the production design team.

SCRIPT ANALYSIS

Although it is not at all unusual for designers to read scripts many times, they undertake the first three readings of the script with specific objectives in mind.

First Reading

The first time you sit down with the script, just read it for fun. Discover the flavor of the play. Learn its general story line, the nature of its characters, their socioeconomic status, and their interrelationships. One of the first things you see when you open the script is the description of the physical environment of the play. Usually written in italics just before the opening lines, it describes the set and, occasionally, the costumes, sound, and lights. Unless you are working from an original script, these descriptions are usually taken from the stage manager's prompt book for the first major professional production of the play and explain the specific designs for that particular production. These descriptions shouldn't be thought of as the correct design solutions for the play; they are just one way that the show can be designed. Your production is entitled to a fresh design treatment that will be appropriate to its personnel, time, place, and budget. To believe that you have to, or should, copy the original design is an insult to your creative ability. Use the descriptive information in the script along with the other information you gather to synthesize an original design concept.

Second Reading

During the second reading of the script you should be looking for specific moments and incidents within the play that stimulate your imagination and provide you with strong visual and textural images and feelings. These inspirations are random, often disconnected, thoughts and impressions about the appearance of the various design elements. Jot them in your notebook. If they are more visual than verbal, sketch them.

Motivated light cue: Indicated or caused by some specific action within the script, like the beginnings and endings of scenes and acts or a character's turning a light switch on or off.

Unmotivated light cue: Change in the lights not specifically called for in the script.

As you continue to reread the play you will get more ideas. Ideas will also appear when you are not reading the script. They can materialize when you are talking to the director, discussing the play with another designer, eating breakfast, or walking to class. Don't judge the ideas at this point. Gather information now, and weed later.

Third Reading

In the third reading you are looking for specific mechanical information rather than broad-based concepts. Specifically, you are looking for any special lighting requirements, such as the appearance of the ghost in Shakespeare's *Hamlet* or the electric cross in Preston Jones's *The Last Meeting of the Knights of the White Magnolia*. At this time you also begin marking the location of both motivated and unmotivated light cues. A **motivated light cue** is caused by some specific action contained within the script, like the beginnings and endings of scenes or acts or a character's turning a light switch on or off. **Unmotivated light cues** are changes in the lights that are not specifically called for in the script. They are harder to detect; and, in fact, you may not see the need for any until you watch a rehearsal or two. For example, you're watching a rehearsal of *The Petrified Forest*, which is set in a lonely roadside diner in northern Arizona. The set is fairly large, and two of the main characters have some important dialogue while they sit at a small table on one side of the set. Other characters are onstage but are unimportant to the scene. You decide to help focus the audience's attention on the couple by boosting

---

SNEAKY TRICK NUMBER 102

There will be times when you will want to shift the audience's attention from place to place on the set. Sometimes you'll want to make that obvious, as when you're changing from location to location on a unit set. For these types of cues, you'll usually use a timed cross-fade of between 3 and 5 seconds duration. At other times, however, you won't want the audience to be aware of what you're doing, as when you're trying to shift the audience's point of focus from one area of the set to another in a realistic interior. On these occasions, if you boost or drop the intensity of the lights only a little (10 or 15 points on a 100-point scale) and prolong the fade over 60 or 90 seconds, the audience will not consciously *see* the fade but will feel it, and their attention will be drawn to the area of highest intensity.

the intensity of the lights on the table just a little bit. This specific use of selective focus is an unmotivated light cue. Mark your script with the location of both motivated and unmotivated cues.

Information regarding any special effects—fires, battery-powered torches, wall sconces, or other practicals, special projections, and so forth—that influences the budgets (both time and fiscal) should also be noted at this time.

Information from the third reading is gathered not only from reading the script but also from production meetings and additional conferences with other members of the production design team. As with the first and second readings, put all the information you collect in your notebook.

Image of light: A picture or concept of what the light should look like for a production.

Plan angle: The ground-plan view of an object.

Hanging positions: The various locations around the stage and auditorium where lighting instruments are placed.

Key light: The brightest light in a scene.

Fill light: Light used to fill the shadows created by the key light.

ANALYSIS OF THE IMAGE OF LIGHT

So far, this chapter has shown you how to evolve an image of the way the light should look for a production. To transfer that image from your mind's eye onto paper, you must be able to analyze the **image of light** for its component elements of distribution, intensity, movement, and color.

Lighting Key

A brief digression is necessary before we plunge into the analysis of the image of light. As I've already indicated, you have to be able to transfer your image of light onto paper if you want to be able to re-create it on the stage. The lighting key (Figure 11.1) is a drawing that indicates the **plan angle** and color of the various sources that illuminate your image of light. The lighting key is used by the designer as the primary guide for determining the **hanging positions** of the lights and can be an effective tool when discussing the design with other members of the production design team.

Analysis for Distribution and Intensity

The analysis of the image of light for distribution and intensity is one of the prime factors in determining the location of the lighting instruments for a production. Modeling of actors and settings is principally a function of the direction and intensity of the light that strikes them. For these reasons it is essential that you be able to determine the direction and relative intensities of the **key** and **fill lights** that are illuminating your image of light if you hope to re-create that image onstage.

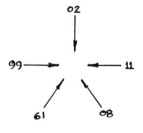

Figure 11.1

A lighting key.

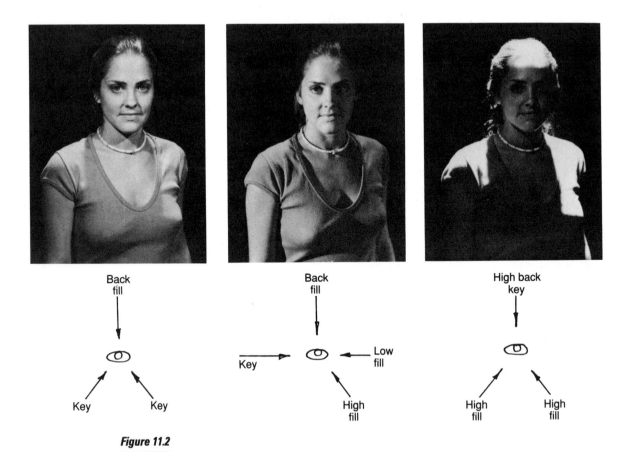

Figure 11.2

Analysis of photographs for distribution and intensity. The length of the arrows indicates the relative intensity of the individual lights.

Figure 11.2 demonstrates how an image can be analyzed for distribution and intensity and the results codified through the use of the lighting key. Each picture has a different emotional impact on the viewer; but the perceived differences are caused only by lighting, for the model's pose is the same in all three. The model in Figure 11.2A is lit with a relatively smooth light evenly keyed from each front-side as shown in the accompanying lighting key. A back fill light provides some extra depth to the figure. In Figure 11.2B the model is strongly key lit from the left side. The fill lights from high front-side and low side smoothly fill the shadows. Again, a high back light helps to separate the model from the background and provides depth to her face. In Figure 11.2C the model is lit with a high back key light. The smooth front fill makes her face visible.

Analysis for Movement

During the analysis phase the lighting designer usually considers movement of light only in terms of his or her feelings about the rhythm and flow of the production. After seeing a finished blocking rehearsal, the designer will have a much better feeling for the specific rhythm, flow, and movement of the production. As movement is probably the most easily adjusted of all the qualities of light, the setting of the times for the various cues is customarily done during the lighting rehearsal and adjusted during the technical and dress rehearsals (see Chapter 16, "Rehearsal and Performance Procedures").

Analysis for Color

The designer needs to pay close attention to the indications of color in his or her image of light, because those color clues provide the basis for creating the color portion of the lighting key. Color is probably the

---

KEY AND FILL LIGHTS

The terms *key* and *fill* are used to describe the relationship between the direction and relative intensity of light striking an object. The key light is the most intense, primary source of light for a scene; and the fill light is the slightly dimmer or more diffused light used to fill the shadows created by the key.

The concept of key and fill lights is simply an organizational tool. It can help codify your thinking as you struggle to determine the direction, intensity, color, and movement of the various sources that are illuminating your image of light.

The application of the concept of key and fill lights can best be explained by example. When you are analyzing the image of light, you should either see or rationalize a source light—a source or sources of illumination for the image. If your image consists of a picture of the set as it is lit for a particular (or hypothetical) moment in the play, you should be able to look around that picture and pick out the sources—table lamps, windows, fireplaces, and so forth. If your image of light is more abstract—the face of a tired old woman staring off into the distance—you should be able to analyze that face and see where the dominant light is coming from (her left, right, center, or front). In either case, the dominant light in the scene will be the key light; the less intense lights will be the fill lights.

primary means that the lighting designer has for indicating the climate and temperature of a scene. It is also a key element in creating psychological atmosphere. Chapter 10 provided a number of practical tips for the use and application of color in lighting.

This chapter has introduced you to the specific steps that a designer goes through when analyzing the script. The end product of this analytical process is the creation of the image of light. The image of light is the beginning point for the creation of the lighting key, which is the reference point to which the designer will continually return during the implementation phase of plot production. The next chapter, "The Lighting Key," contains specific information about converting the image of light into a lighting key.

THE LIGHTING KEY

The lighting key is the codification of the image of light. But to be able to translate that image of light into a meaningful symbol, you have to understand how light works. Quite specifically, you have to be able to *see* light.

Light is a molding medium; it sculpts and shapes our perception and understanding of people, objects, and things. In the first section of this chapter we'll explore (with visual aids) the effects that can be achieved by manipulating two of the controllable qualities of light—distribution and intensity—to affect the functions of light: visibility, selective focus, modeling, and mood.

MODELING WITH LIGHT

As I said before, light affects the appearance of objects. Before you can hope to be a lighting designer, you have to understand the modeling effects of light. The series of photographs in Figure 12.1 illustrates how varying the direction of a single source of light affects the pattern of highlight and shadows on a model's face. To help you begin to understand how changing the direction and angle of a light affects the modeling characteristics of that light, each photograph is accompanied by a drawing that shows the relative plan and **sectional angles** of the light.

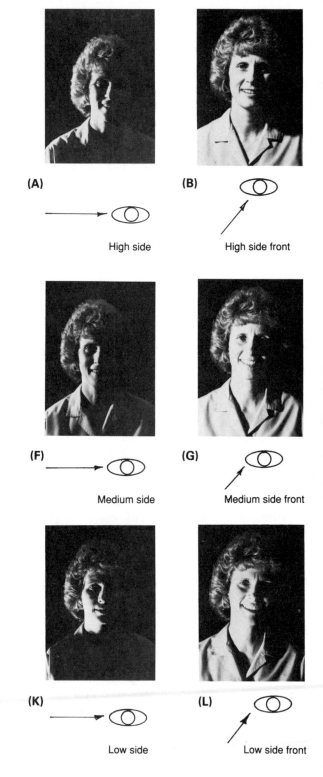

(A)

High side

(B)

High side front

(F)

Medium side

(G)

Medium side front

(K)

Low side

(L)

Low side front

Figure 12.1

Effects of varying the
direction of the light.

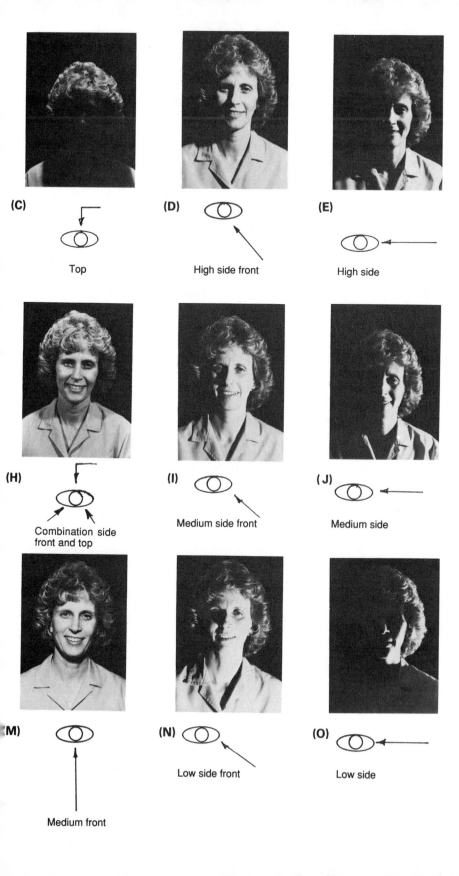

(C)

Top

(D)

High side front

(E)

High side

(H)

Combination side
front and top

(I)

Medium side front

(J)

Medium side

(M)

Medium front

(N)

Low side front

(O)

Low side

Sectional angle: The angle of intersection between the axis of the cone of light emitted by an instrument and the working height—usually the height of an actor's face (about 5 feet 6 inches)—of the lighting area.

Stage picture: The visual appearance of the stage during a specific moment in a play.

When analyzing a photo, or a **stage picture,** it is almost impossible to discuss one quality or function of light without touching on another. Changing the direction (distribution) of the light affects both selective focus and mood. As you compare the photos in Figure 12.1, notice how you almost invariably look at the area of highlight first. Glance away from the photos; then try to look at a shadow area first. It is almost impossible. Even when you concentrate and tell yourself, "I'm going to look at a shadow area first," you *will,* in all probability, see the highlight first. This graphic demonstration of selective focus shows the power of the instinctive human reaction that designers understand and use to manipulate the focus of the audience's attention.

Notice how your emotional response to the photos changes with the visibility of the model's face. Most people will feel relatively at ease looking at those photos where her face is fully visible. They will feel a little uncomfortable or uneasy looking at those photos where her face is fully or partially shadowed because they cannot read her facial nonverbal communication—the thoughts and intentions mirrored in her eyes and facial expressions. Again, by learning or intuition, lighting designers know, understand, and use the very powerful effects of visibility on the creation of mood in the stage picture.

Surrounding an actor with a number of light sources provides the potential for modeling with light. In Figure 12.2 the direction of the light varies, but the intensity of those individual lights is held constant. A front light (Figure 12.2A) by itself is unflattering; it tends to flatten and compress facial and bodily features. Side lights (Figure 12.2B) and top light (Figure 12.2C) create highlights along the edges of the head and body but cause deep shadows across the face and front of the body. A combination of side and top lights (Figure 12.2D), together with a front light that fills the shadows created by the side and top lights, reveals the form of the model by surrounding her with light.

When lit from the side-front at about 45 degrees in plan and section (Figure 12.2E), the model is smoothly illuminated, but her facial and bodily features are slightly compressed. If a top light or back light is added to the side-front light (Figure 12.2F), the resultant rim or edge light creates a highlight that adds depth to the face and body. As you can see, the greatest potential for modeling is achieved when the model is surrounded with light.

CREATING THE LIGHTING KEY

After you have analyzed your image of light, you must address yourself to the challenge of codifying your thoughts on the direction and placement of the key and fill lights as dictated by that image. This

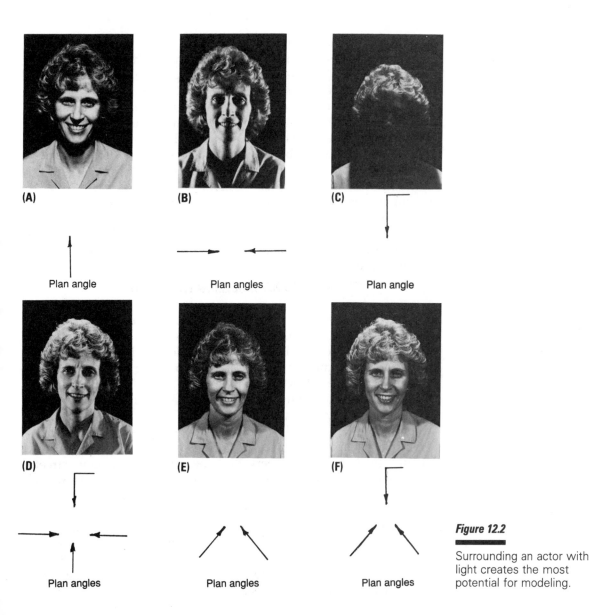

Figure 12.2

Surrounding an actor with light creates the most potential for modeling.

process can best be described through example. Suppose that we want to light somebody standing in the middle of an otherwise bare stage. To light her effectively, we have to create a mental image of how we want her to look. My mental picture of the scene is as follows: It's a bitterly cold, January day in Minnesota. A young girl is standing in the middle of a snow-crusted field. The sun is frozen close to the horizon; its pale, washed-out color etches jagged shadows across the field. (Specific descriptive information about the scene is vitally important, for the quality of light varies for different locales, times of the day, and times of the year.) So far, this description should provide you with enough information to "see" the scene in your mind's eye.

A cautionary note is appropriate before we launch into an analysis of this scene. Each analysis is a product of an individual's imagination. Every analysis is a unique creation of an individual designer, and as long as those analyses subscribe to the stylistic parameters stipulated in the production concept, each person's analysis is equally valid. With this proviso firmly in mind, my analysis of this scene follows: The key light is the sunlight coming from a fairly low angle in back of, and slightly to the side of, the young girl. This light should have a harsher, more strident quality than the light reflected from the snow (front), which is both soft and directionless and seems to insinuate itself into the strong shadows created by the key light.

MORE ABOUT MODELING WITH LIGHT

An excellent way to learn more about the modeling capabilities of light is to develop a lighting morgue—a collection of photographs of people, objects, and paintings that you analyze for the direction, intensity, and color of their key and fill lights.

Another simple way to learn about light is to look at everyday objects—buildings, statues, trees, parked cars, and so forth—and critically examine the way they are illuminated. See how the appearance of a ball field changes from early morning to noon, noon to afternoon, late afternoon to dusk and early morning. Notice how the range of intensity between highlights and shadows on a statue in the park is compressed on cloudy days (as compared with clear days). Notice how the sharp-edged shadow that you see under a car on a clear day has no clearly definable edge, is softer, and not so black on a cloudy day. Look at the same building on a clear day and on a cloudy day and notice how the vibrancy has gone out of the colors on the cloudy day—how the building looks more dreary. Notice how the appearance of a city street changes radically between daytime and night—how the patterns of highlight and shadow radically alter when the streetlights and shop windows are the primary sources of light.

Only when you begin to develop your critical eye, when you begin to see how things *really* look—how light shapes our perception of what we see—can you begin to use light to manipulate the audience's understanding of the actors, sets, and costumes of the play that they are watching.

Figure 12.3

Key light for the "girl in the snowfield" exercise.

Figure 12.4

Fill lights for the "girl in the snowfield" exercise.

The quality of the light chosen for a scene generally dictates the type of lighting instruments used. The back-side key light (sunlight) calls for an ERS, because the beam of light emitted by that instrument is generally hard-edged and cohesive. The soft, directionless quality of the front fill light suggests that a Fresnel spotlight, with its soft, diffused light, would be the correct instrument to use. The sunlight (key light) in our image strikes the girl over her left shoulder and from slightly above her horizontal axis, or stage floor, as illustrated in Figure 12.3. To re-create this effect, you have to place the instrument at the same angle relative to the actress as the sunlight seen in the image of light.

The fill light in our image of light is directionless and smoothly fills the shadows. To re-create this effect, two Fresnel spotlights should be placed in positions where they will provide a smooth, apparently directionless light on the front of the girl. Instruments placed at a sectional angle of about 45 degrees provide a fairly normal angle of light. This sectional angle provides a feeling of directionless light, particularly when the two instruments are placed between 60 and 90 degrees apart so that they smoothly cover the front of the girl with light but don't override the intensity of the key light (see Figure 12.4).

If the key light ERS and the two fill light Fresnels are each circuited into separate dimmers, then the relative intensities of the three instruments can be varied independently until the proper relationship (as determined by your mental picture of the image of light) is established.

While the selection and placement of the instruments and the setting of intensities for the individual lights are of primary importance in the re-creation of the image of light, the selection of color will greatly enhance the overall mood and feeling of the scene. Again, remember that there isn't a "correct" solution to this challenge. Each designer may select a different color palette, but all palettes should be based on an interpretation of the image of light. A realistic interpretation of this scene might find us selecting Roscolux 06, No-Color Straw, for the sunlight or key light. Since the shadow of a color is usually perceived as the complement of that color, Roscolux 53, Pale Lavender, might be selected for the front fill light. The use of these colors will produce a realistic, thin tint of yellow for the sunlight and a cool, relatively complementary lavender tint for the shadow fill.

The selection of other colors will create different, although still relatively realistic, psychological impacts on the audience. If, for some strange reason, you decide that you want the scene to have a warm or soft feeling, then you might want to go to warmer colors, say Roscolux 09, Pale Amber Gold, for the sunlight and use a not-quite-complementary hue such as Roscolux 55, Lilac, for the fill lights. (When additively mixed, Roscolux 09 and 55 produce a warm-white hue rather than the pure white that a truly complementary blend would yield.) On the other hand, you might want to enhance the bitterly cold feeling of the scene. In this case you might want to select Roscolux 61, Mist Blue, for the sunlight, and use a related, but more saturated hue such as a Roscolux 64, Light Steel Blue, or Roscolux 57, Lavender, for the fill. Working with a palette composed of closely related tints can have a significant psychological impact on your audience, but you need to remember that using a very narrow range of related (rather than complementary) colors on your lights will suppress any complementary colors in both the sets and costumes. This is fine as long as the set and costume designers are aware of the effects that your narrow color selection will have on their palettes and approve of this restriction.

In the theatre a lighting designer rarely has an opportunity to create an isolated design such as the one just described. Plays exist in time as well as space, and the lighting designer must adapt the lighting key to accommodate the full production, not just an isolated moment in the play. We will use *The Playboy of the Western World*, by John Millington Synge, to illustrate the development of a lighting key for a complete production.

Let's assume that the image for this production could be stated as "a bright, twinkling Irish morning." Our analysis of this statement leads us to conclude that achieving the concept of a bright, twinkling Irish morning on the stage will require creation of (1) a light and cheery atmosphere, (2) no shadows, and (3) thin tints of springlike colors.

If an actor in our play were surrounded with light, as shown in Figure 12.5, we would have achieved one of our stated objectives—no shadows. If we adjusted the dimmers that control those lights to a fairly bright setting, we would achieve another of our objectives—a bright

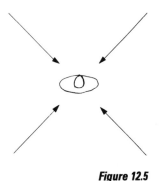

Figure 12.5

Four-source lighting key for *Playboy of the Western World.*

atmosphere. By selecting happy, springtime, pastel colors we would also meet the third objective—a "cheery" springlike atmosphere.

This brief analysis of the image of light has already given us much of the information needed for completing the basic lighting key for our production. Specifically, we have determined the distribution for the basic lighting of each lighting area (four diagonal cross lights) and the basic range of the color palette (pastel tints). Let me hasten to add that this particular solution is not the "correct" analysis of the image of light. There are myriad other possibilities, all of them equally "correct." You could have light from more or fewer directions (Figure 12.6A and B). You could also interpret the concept of "springtime pastel colors" to mean thin tints of cool colors as opposed to warm—it just depends on your personal understanding of the idea of a springtime atmosphere.

With the foregoing proviso firmly in mind, we make the conscious decision that our lighting key is going to be based on a five-sided distribution pattern (Figure 12.7). This pattern will provide a smooth, shadowless light that will support our interpretation of the image of light. Additionally, the top or back light (the arrow at the top of the pentagon) will provide a nice rim or halo light around the head and shoulders of the actors to prevent them from blending into the set.

Before selecting specific colors for the lighting instruments, the color palettes of the scenic and costume designers must be studied. This "color study" normally occurs during the various production conferences as each designer (scenic, costume, lighting) presents his or her design and color concepts. The reason that the lighting designer must know what colors the other designers are using is relatively simple. Colored light can drastically alter the apparent color of the sets and

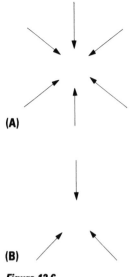

(A)

(B)

Figure 12.6

Six- and three-source lighting keys for *Playboy of the Western World.*

"NORMAL" LIGHTING ANGLES

I've mentioned "normal" lighting angles several times in this text. Normal is a relative term, but for most people a "normal" sectional angle for light striking the face is between 30 and 60 degrees. The reason for this is simple. If you live in the temperate regions of the world (where some 80 to 90 percent of the world's population lives), the sun angle relative to your body position varies between these two extremes during most daylight hours. Forty-five degrees is an average of these two extremes, and so when you recreate onstage that "average" sectional sun angle, you are in effect creating a situation that duplicates what we've learned to identify as ordinary or "normal."

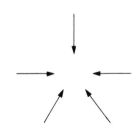

Figure 12.7

Five-source lighting key for *Playboy of the Western World.*

Figure 12.8

The set design for *Playboy of the Western World.*

costumes, and it isn't in the interests of a unified production concept to change the other designers' work without their knowledge and consent.

During the initial conferences of our hypothetical *Playboy* production, the design team decided that the play would be produced in a realistic style. Based on this concept the lighting designer will want the set to appear as though it were being lit by the source lights that are located on the set. To determine the nature of these sources, and their locations, it will be necessary to look at a scenic rendering or model of the set. The scenic sketch (Figure 12.8) shows that there are oil lamps on the counter and each table, there is a peat fire glowing in the fireplace, and the window and door are open. Each of these sources would provide light of differing hues. The sunlight, according to our analysis of the image of light, is cool-white, bright, and cheerful. The fireplace is warmer and redder than the sunlight, and the oil lamps give off a soft, amber glow.

Using this analysis and information as a guide, Roscolux 61, Mist Blue, is selected to represent the bright, clean sunlight. Roscolux 02, Bastard Amber, is chosen for the firelight, and Roscolux 09, Pale Amber Gold, is selected to represent the color emitted by the oil lamps.

Now that the colors have been selected to represent the various sources, they need to be applied to the lighting key. The application of color to the basic distribution pattern of the lighting key should support the thesis that the source lights are providing the light for the environment of the play. To achieve this goal, the light from stage left should be colored to represent the fireplace color, Bastard Amber, because the fireplace is on the stage-left side of the set. The oil lamp color (Pale Amber Gold) is used from a direction (stage right) that supports the visual impression that the oil lamps are primarily on the downstage-right part of the set. The light approaching the stage from an upstage direction should represent the sunlight (Mist Blue), because the window and doorway are on the upstage wall of the set.

Figure 12.9 shows the colors assigned to the specific distribution pattern that we had previously determined from our analysis of the image of light. The stage-left side light is assigned Bastard Amber, to support the concept that the fireplace is lighting the room from this direction. The top-back light is colored with Roscolux 61, Mist Blue, because this supports the idea that any light approaching the stage from this direction would be sunlight coming through the window or door. The stage-right side light and the stage-right front light are colored with Pale Amber Gold, to support the notion that the primary source light for this side of the stage comes from the oil lamps.

This leaves the stage-left front light as the only uncolored instrument. Since there is no specific source light coming from this direction, it will be necessary to refer back to the image of light to determine the appropriate color for this instrument. The image of light specifies that the atmosphere should resemble a "twinkling spring morning." Roscolux 51, Surprise Pink, is selected for use from this direction, because this bright, cheerful color will blend with the Pale Amber Gold (used in the other front light) to produce a warm white light that supports the concept of a cheery morning that is dictated by the image of light.

In this chapter you've learned how to translate your image of light into a lighting key. In the next chapter you'll learn how to use the lighting key as the basis for creating the light plot.

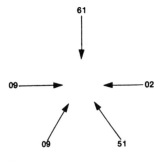

Figure 12.9

Five-source lighting key, with color, for *Playboy of the Western World*.

USING THE LIGHTING KEY TO DRAW THE LIGHT PLOT

efore we get into the practical matters of using the lighting key to draw the light plot, you need to know something about acting areas and lighting areas.

ACTING AND LIGHTING AREAS

Acting areas are those spaces on the stage where specific scenes, or parts of scenes, are played. In some plays the entire setting is the acting area (usually the case with a realistic interior setting). In other plays the setting may be divided into several smaller acting areas. A unit set for Anouilh's *Becket*, where one part of the set is used for scenes in Canterbury Cathedral, another for the French seacoast, and another for a hovel in an English forest, illustrates the use of many separate acting areas in one setting. The shape and size of an acting area (Figure 13.1), although roughly determined by the shape of the setting, are specifically determined by the blocking patterns used by the actors.

A lighting area is a cylindrical space (Figure 13.2) approximately 8 to 12 feet in diameter and about 7 feet tall. As you'll see later, the actual size of a lighting area is roughly determined by the diameter of the beam of light of the instruments that are being used to light the area.

In order to provide a uniform base of lighting for the acting area (so that actors will look the same regardless of where they move within the

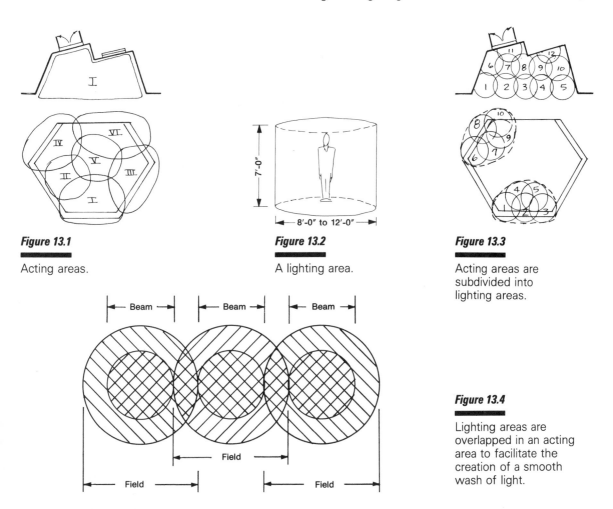

Figure 13.1

Acting areas.

Figure 13.2

A lighting area.

7'-0"

8'-0" to 12'-0"

Figure 13.3

Acting areas are subdivided into lighting areas.

Beam   Beam   Beam

Field

Field   Field

Figure 13.4

Lighting areas are overlapped in an acting area to facilitate the creation of a smooth wash of light.

acting area), we will need to subdivide the acting areas into lighting areas as shown in Figure 13.3.

At this point, we'll digress further to explain *how* the process of subdividing acting areas into lighting areas facilitates smooth lighting. To achieve a smooth wash of light throughout the acting area, light from instruments in adjacent lighting areas is overlapped by about one-third, as shown in Figure 13.4. If the light from the field of these two instruments is overlapped, it will nearly equal the intensity of the light from the beam of a single instrument. If the light from all of the instruments lighting the individual lighting areas within an acting area is overlapped according to this plan, a smooth wash of light will be achieved for the entire acting area. (Further explanation of this process is offered in the box titled "Beam and Field Angles Explained.")

USING THE LIGHTING KEY
TO DRAW THE LIGHT PLOT

Now you know that the acting areas are subdivided into lighting areas to facilitate the production of a smooth wash of light throughout the acting area. But where do you go from here? You simply use the lighting key as a guide for placing and coloring the instruments that will be used to illuminate each lighting area. Again, this process is best explained by example. We've learned that the shape of the acting areas determines the number and arrangement of the lighting areas. In our hypothetical

---

BEAM AND FIELD ANGLES EXPLAINED

There is a rational reason why lighting designers need to know the beam and field angles for the various instruments they will be using. You may remember from Chapter 4 that the beam angle is the central cone of light whose outer limit is defined as that point where the light diminishes to 50 percent of its intensity when compared with the center of the beam. The field angle is the portion of the cone of light outside the beam angle whose outer limit is defined as that point where the light diminishes to 10 percent of the output of the center of the beam.

As shown in Chapter 4 (Table 4.2), the field angle for any ellipsoidal reflector spotlight (the most commonly used stage lighting instrument) is approximately twice its beam angle. In practical terms this relationship means that when adjacent lighting areas are overlapped by one-third, the beam angle of the instruments lighting those areas will illuminate the central, or "un-overlapped," portion of the lighting area, and the field angle will illuminate the overlapped area. The result of the overlap of the adjacent fields is an additive effect that brings the intensity level of the overlapped areas up to approximately the same as the central "un-overlapped" areas. This results in a relatively smooth, consistent level of illumination throughout the acting area.

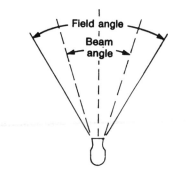

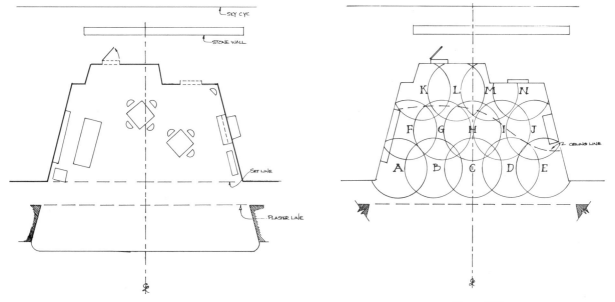

Figure 13.5

Acting (left) and lighting areas for *Playboy of the Western World.*

production of *The Playboy of the Western World,* discussed in Chapter 12, the whole set is a single acting area. In order to draw the light plot it will be necessary to subdivide that acting area into lighting areas, as shown in Figure 13.5.

To create a smooth wash of light over the entire acting area the lighting designer needs to replicate the lighting key (Figure 12.9, page 155) in each of the lighting areas. This process of duplication is demonstrated for a single lighting area in Figure 13.6.

Unfortunately, it isn't always possible to achieve an exact duplication of the lighting key in every lighting area, because the walls of the set prevent the use of sidelight in the lighting areas that are adjacent to the walls, and the ceiling interferes with a great deal of the top and back light. More challenges are imposed by the physical limitations of the auditorium, which generally inhibit some of the front-of-house hanging positions.

When a situation occurs that makes it difficult to place an instrument exactly where it is needed, the lighting designer must make a design decision. If the light can't be placed in a position where it will replicate the angle specified in the lighting key, the compromise solution should be guided by the principles outlined in the lighting key and the designer's interpretation of the image of light. For example, it isn't possible to use direct stage-left sidelight for area J (see Figure 13.7),

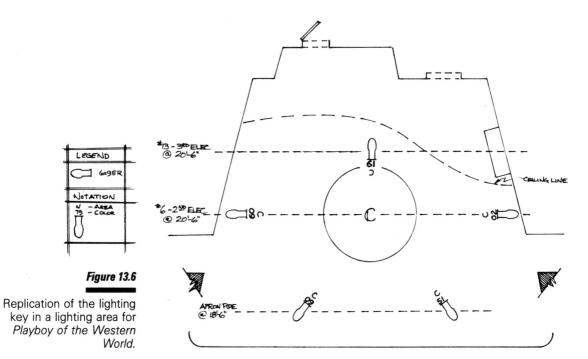

Figure 13.6

Replication of the lighting key in a lighting area for *Playboy of the Western World.*

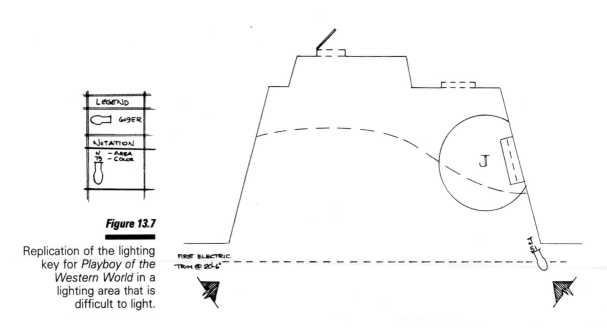

Figure 13.7

Replication of the lighting key for *Playboy of the Western World* in a lighting area that is difficult to light.

because the wall gets in the way. Two possible compromise solutions to this challenge might be (1) put an instrument on the stage-left end of the **first electric,** as shown in Figure 13.7; (2) eliminate the instrument. The choice of which solution to use should be guided by your interpretation of the image of light and the lighting key.

To complete the basic, or first, layer of the lighting design it will be necessary to duplicate, as closely as possible, the lighting key in every lighting area. This process of replication results in a basic light plot that creates the atmosphere and look dictated by the image of light.

First electric: The onstage pipe for lighting instruments that is closest, from the onstage side, to the proscenium arch.

LAYERING

A lighting design exists in time as well as space. It ebbs and flows as the mood of the play changes. To create a temporal development in the lighting design, mechanisms must be designed into the light plot.

Layering is primarily an organizational tool of the lighting designer. It refers specifically to the process of designing layers of light.

EFFECTS AND SUPPORT LIGHTS

Apparent onstage sources of light—windows, table lamps, fireplaces, and so forth—can be thought of as psychological key lights. They are, apparently, the source of illumination for the set. According to the definition of key and fill lights, any lights used to fill the shadows caused by these key lights would be fill lights. That's the principle, and it works. However, at this point an interesting paradox raises its ugly head. In practice, apparent onstage sources—lamps, fires in fireplaces, and so forth—are deliberately kept dim so that they won't be the center of the audience's attention. (As you learned in Chapters 1 and 11, the audience is compelled to look at the brightest spot in a stage picture.) While the apparent sources, called effects or effects lights, are relatively dim, lighting designers normally place stage lights (ERSs, Fresnels, PARs, and so forth) in positions where they can create light that looks as if it is emanating from, and the color of, the effects light. These support lights (lights used to support or reinforce an effect) can be thought of as keys, and the acting area lights can be thought of as fills. These support lights are usually gelled in a hue that is more saturated than but in the same color range as the color of the lights approaching the acting areas from the same general direction as the effect. The color of these acting-area lights will be specified in the lighting key. The reason for the disparity in saturation is so that the effect of the support light will be more noticeable as the actors get closer to the effect—table lamp, fireplace—that the support light is reinforcing.

The first layer of light for our hypothetical production of *Playboy* was created when we implemented our interpretation of the image of light—"a bright, twinkling Irish morning." This image works well for Acts II and III, which take place in the morning and afternoon, respectively. However, Act I takes place in the early evening. The "twinkling morning" look simply doesn't translate as night. In order to create an appropriate look of early evening for Act I it will be necessary to do one of two things: (1) create a completely separate lighting key and design for Act I or (2) create some supplemental "early evening" lighting that can be used in conjunction with the basic "twinkling Irish morning" lights.

From an aesthetic standpoint a completely separate plot for Act I would be the preferred solution, but a separate design would necessitate a very large instrument inventory.

The supplemental lighting solution would achieve relatively similar results with a considerably smaller number of instruments. The instruments used to create this second layer of light need to be positioned and colored to create the look of "indoor evening" in the pub, where the principal sources of light are oil lamps and the peat fire. Any light coming in the window and door should have the appearance of "night light" rather than daylight.

Since this second layer of light needs to be integrated with the "twinkling Irish morning" lights to achieve the look of "early evening," it will be necessary to select angles and colors that work to support the premise that the pub is actually lit by the oil lamps and the peat fire.

A wash of "night" colors (Roscolux 79, Bright Blue) could be used to flood the stage from the front-of-house positions, as shown in Figure 13.8A. By balancing the intensities of these night colors with those of the basic lighting key we can ensure that the blue lights won't override the basic hues that were selected for the lighting key. They will, however, provide a blue wash over the whole acting area that will fill any shadow or underlit areas with a blue light to help create the illusion of nighttime.

Additional instruments could be hung to augment the color selected to reinforce the source lights—the oil lamps and peat fire—in the first layer of the plot. These instruments, as shown in Figure 13.8B, should be colored in more fully saturated hues than their "first layer" counterparts, and they should be hung in positions that will support the effects of the source lights.

Additional layers of light can be used for a variety of purposes. Figure 13.8C shows the location of those instruments that are used to create the "daylight" and "night light" that come through the window and door.

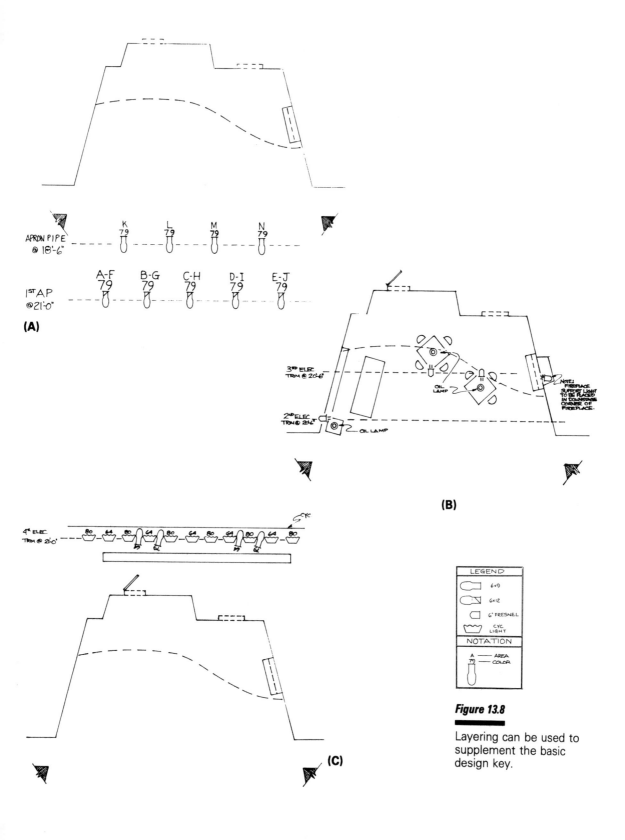

(A)

APRON PIPE
@ 18'-6"

K	L	M	N
79	79	79	79

1ST A.P.
@ 21'-0"

A-F	B-G	C-H	D-I	E-J
79	79	79	79	79

(B)

3RD ELEC
TRIM @ 20'-8"

2ND ELEC
TRIM @ 20'-6"

OIL LAMP

OIL LAMP

NOTE:
FIREPLACE
SUPPORT LIGHT
TO BE PLACED
IN DOWNSTAGE
CORNER OF
FIREPLACE.

(C)

4TH ELEC
TRIM @ 21'-0"

CYC

80 64 80 64 80 64 80 64 80 64 80

LEGEND

6×9
6×12
6" FRESNEL
CYC LIGHT

NOTATION

A — AREA
79 — COLOR

Figure 13.8

Layering can be used to supplement the basic design key.

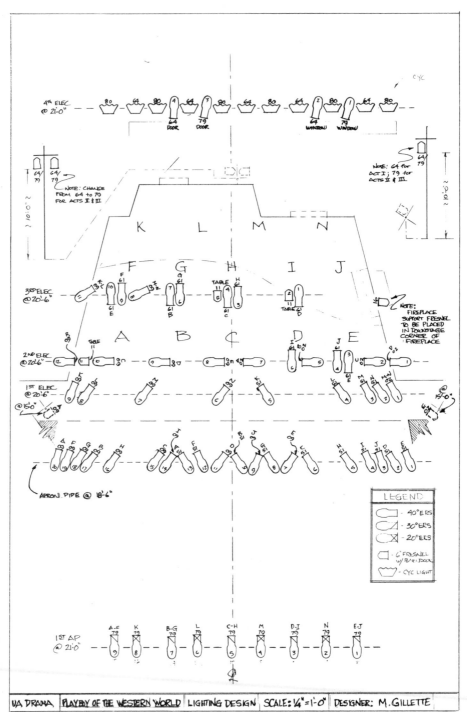

Figure 13.9

Light plot for a proscenium production of *Playboy of the Western World.*

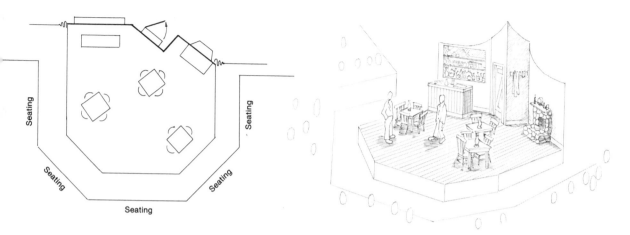

Figure 13.10

Scenic design for a thrust production of *Playboy of the Western World.*

As indicated at the beginning of this discussion, layering is primarily an organizational tool of the lighting designer. It isn't really necessary to divide your thinking about the design into segments, but many designers find that this compartmentalization of the design into specific segments, or layers, makes it easier to concentrate on solving the challenges imposed by the individual elements of the design. Figure 13.9 shows the finished light plot for *Playboy of the Western World.*

DESIGNING LIGHTING KEYS FOR THRUST AND ARENA STAGES

Designing lights for an arena or thrust stage is not significantly different from designing for a proscenium theatre. The only substantive difference is the location of the audience. In the thrust configuration, as you will recall, the audience sits on three sides of the stage, and in an arena theatre it surrounds the stage. It is the lighting designer's responsibility to light the stage so that all spectators, regardless of where they are sitting, are able to see the production equally well.

We can use our hypothetical production of *The Playboy of the Western World* to demonstrate the relative lack of difference between designing lighting for the three modes of stages. Figure 13.10 shows a sketch of the modified scenic design that would work for a thrust production of our play. Note that the side walls have been removed so the spectators sitting on the sides of the thrust stage can see all of the action. Also notice that because the walls are gone, the ceiling has been eliminated.

The image of light remains the same as before, simply because the concept of how we are going to produce the play hasn't changed. The

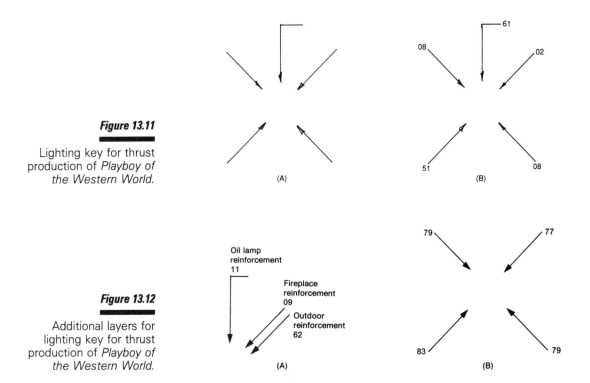

Figure 13.11

Lighting key for thrust production of *Playboy of the Western World.*

(A)   (B)

Figure 13.12

Additional layers for lighting key for thrust production of *Playboy of the Western World.*

Oil lamp reinforcement
11

Fireplace reinforcement
09

Outdoor reinforcement
62

(A)   (B)

distribution of the design key has been slightly modified because of the position of the audience relative to the stage. We are still surrounding the actors with light to re-create our "bright, twinkling Irish morning" as shown in Figure 13.11A. The color of the design key also remains relatively unchanged, although we will lower the saturation of the "warm" color because of the proximity of the audience, as shown in Figure 13.11A.

The second layer for our thrust production could concentrate on enhancing the source lights—oil lamps, fireplace, window, and door (Figure 13.12A). The third layer (Figure 13.12B) would concentrate on creating the "night" wash.

The lighting design for an arena production of our play would be very similar to the thrust design. The set for the arena production is shown in Figure 13.13. Notice how all of the walls that might in any way interfere with the spectators' sight lines have been removed. The scenic design has been essentially reduced to a furniture arrangement, with just enough set left to provide a hint of what the cottage or pub actually looks like. The set has been shifted to a diagonal angle so that the entrances are lined up with the auditorium entryways.

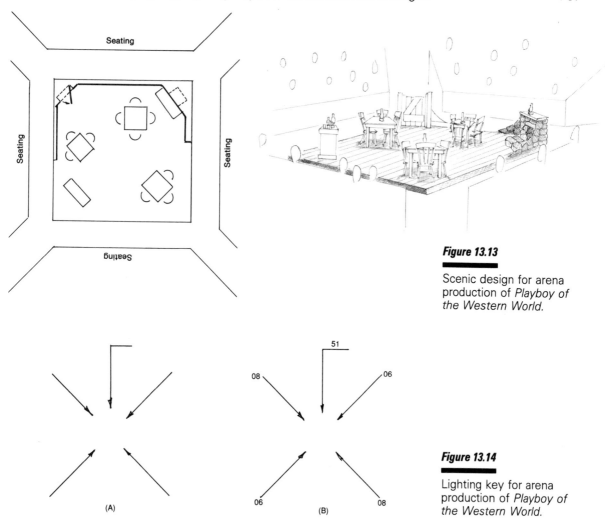

Figure 13.13

Scenic design for arena production of *Playboy of the Western World.*

Figure 13.14

Lighting key for arena production of *Playboy of the Western World.*

The distribution of the lighting key for the arena production is no different from the thrust stage configurations (Figure 13.14A). The color portion of the design key is also different, but only because we want everyone looking at the play to get the same feeling. For the proscenium and thrust productions we were able to have the light coming from the direction of the door and window gelled with colors that would support the "outdoors" look of the light coming through the window and door. Because we now have the audience surrounding the stage however, we need to create the same feeling of "interior" lighting from all angles. These changes are shown in the color selection for the design key illustrated in Figure 13.14B.

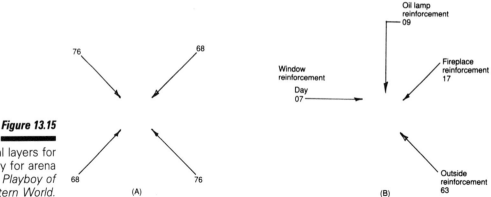

Figure 13.15

Additional layers for lighting key for arena production of *Playboy of the Western World.*

Similarly, the "night" layers must place lights in positions that will enhance the idea of "night" for all of the viewing audience, as shown in Figure 13.15A. In this particular design the third layer of light is used to support both the internal and external source lights. These lights need to be reasonably directional, as shown in Figure 13.15B, because the apparent source lights that they are reinforcing (sunlight, moonlight, peat fire) are also directional. The instruments that are reinforcing the oil lamps are placed over the general area of the lamps, simply because the light from the oil lamps illuminates everything around it.

The only other type of design modification that needs to be made when working in an arena theatre is caused by the fact that the instruments are probably hung closer to the actors than in either a thrust or proscenium configuration. Because of this you will want to use less-saturated color media, since the closer the instrument is to the actor, the stronger the effect of any color that is used with that instrument.

Other than these relatively minor adjustments required by the positioning and proximity of the audience, there really aren't any significant changes in philosophy, practice, or techniques when designing for thrust or arena threatres.

DRAFTING
FOR LIGHTING DESIGN

ecause the product of lighting design—light—is probably the most intangible and abstract of all the theatrical design elements, some specialized paperwork is needed to help carry out the designer's intentions.

GRAPHIC STANDARDS FOR LIGHTING DESIGN

The purpose of the paperwork associated with the drafting of a lighting design—light plot, lighting section, instrument schedule—is to provide sufficient information to the master electrician and crew to enable them to hang and circuit the lighting equipment for the entire production. There are some definitions, conventions, and standards that you need to know before you begin to draw the light plot.

The Light Plot

The light plot is a scale mechanical drawing—a "road map"—that indicates where the lighting instruments should be placed (Figure 14.1). More specifically, the light plot is a "horizontal offset section with the cutting plane passing at whatever levels are required to produce the most descriptive view of the instrumentation in relation to the set(s)"

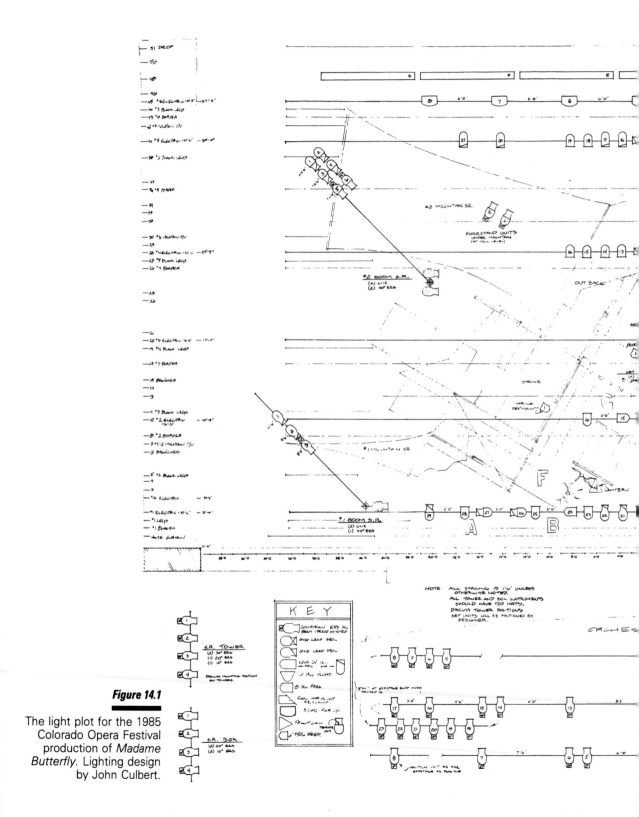

Figure 14.1

The light plot for the 1985
Colorado Opera Festival
production of *Madame
Butterfly*. Lighting design
by John Culbert.

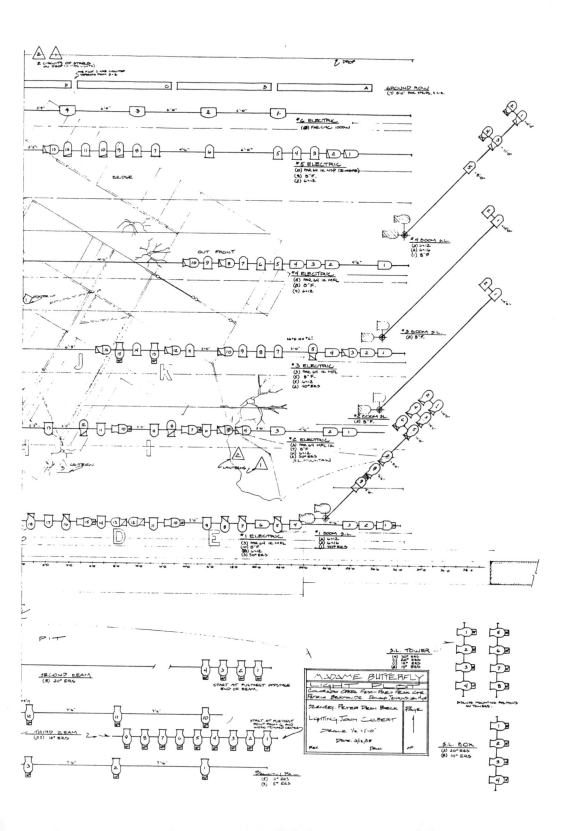

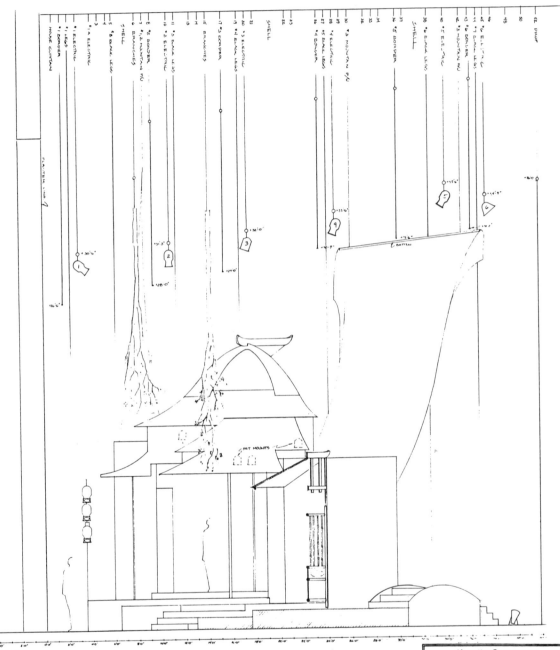

Figure 14.2

The lighting section for
the 1985 Colorado Opera
Festival production of
Madame Butterfly.
Lighting design by John
Culbert.

MADAME BUTTERFLY

SECTION

Design by PETER DEAN BECK

according to the United States Institute of Theatre Technology's (USITT's) graphic standards for stage lighting.

Although there is no universally accepted style of drafting light plots, all good plots will have certain things in common. The primary purpose of a light plot is to depict, in scale (usually ½ or ¼ inch to 1 foot), the exact location of all lighting instruments being used in the production. The plot shows the location of the set(s) in relationship to the physical structure of the theatre. The plot also includes a legend describing each of the symbols used on the plot, as well as a title block that details pertinent information about the production. (More information about the legend and title block is provided later in this chapter.)

Center line: A leader line that runs perpendicular to the set line from the midpoint or center of the opening of the proscenium arch.

The Lighting Section

The lighting section (Figure 14.2) is usually a composite side-view drawing (if the set is basically symmetrical) that shows the position of the lighting equipment in relationship to the set and the physical structure of the theatre. If the set is significantly asymmetrical, then two sections will normally be drawn, one looking stage right from the **center line,** the other looking stage left. This drawing, used primarily by the designer, has several purposes: to check sightlines of the lighting instruments, to assist in determining the appropriate trim height for horizontal masking, and to ensure that the lighting equipment won't interfere with any scenic elements and vice versa.

The Instrument Schedule

The instrument schedule (Figure 14.3), also known as the hookup sheet, is a specification sheet that contains everything that you might want or need to know about every instrument used on the production. It identifies each instrument by its instrument number and specifies its type, hanging location, focus area, circuit, dimmer, lamp wattage, and color. A section for special remarks is used to note anything else that might be appropriate, such as focusing notes, auxiliary or nonstandard equipment that needs to be attached to the instrument, and so forth.

Standards for Drafting in Lighting Design

Because so much data must be included on a light plot or lighting section, the USITT has developed a set of standards and conventions for drafting in lighting design. This section details the pertinent elements of those recommendations.

Lettering   All lettering should be legible and the style should allow easy and rapid execution. Characters that generally conform to the

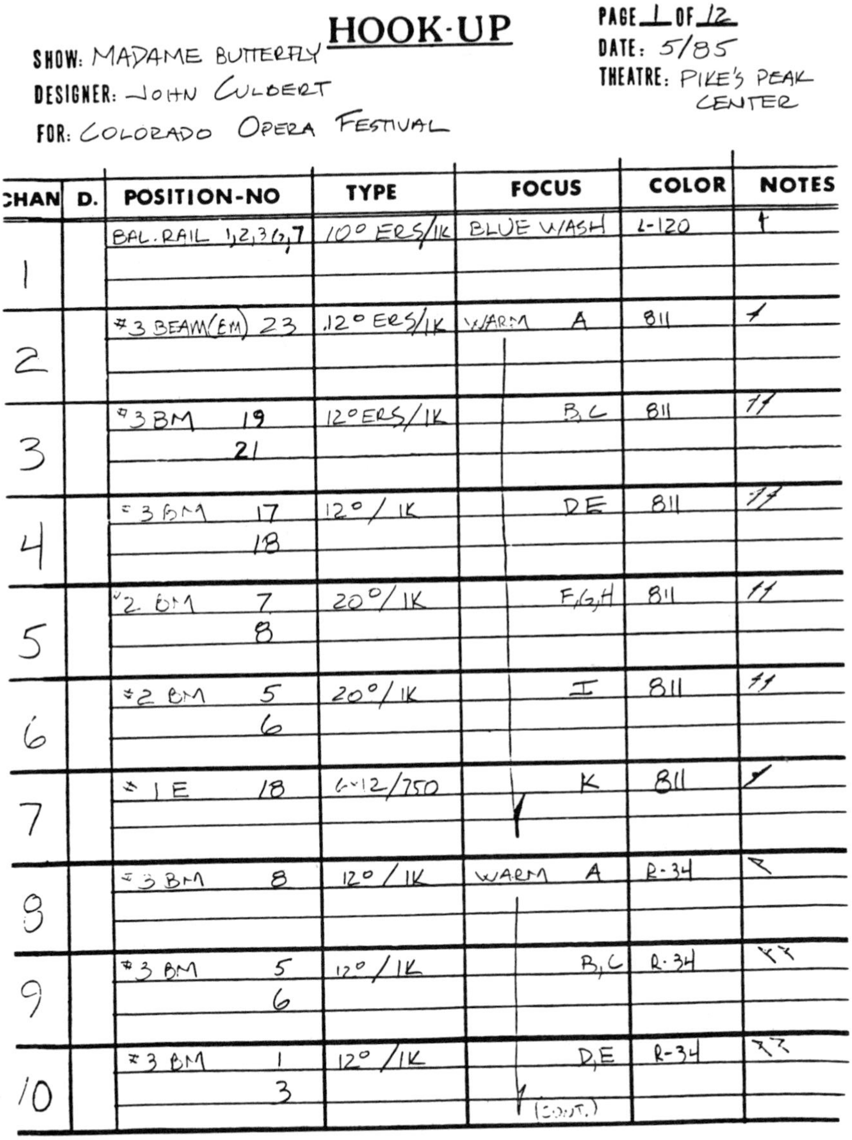

HOOK-UP

SHOW: MADAME BUTTERFLY

DESIGNER: JOHN CULBERT

FOR: COLORADO OPERA FESTIVAL

PAGE 1 OF 12

DATE: 5/85

THEATRE: PIKE'S PEAK CENTER

CHAN	D.	POSITION-NO	TYPE	FOCUS	COLOR	NOTES
1		BAL. RAIL 1,2,3,6,7	10° ERS/1K	BLUE WASH	L-120	†
2		#3 BEAM (EM) 23	12° ERS/1K	WARM A	811	/
3		#3 BM 19 21	12° ERS/1K	B,C	811	//
4		#3 BM 17 18	12° / 1K	D,E	811	//
5		#2 BM 7 8	20° / 1K	F,G,H	811	//
6		#2 BM 5 6	20° / 1K	I	811	//
7		#1 E 18	6×12/750	K	811	/
8		#3 BM 8	12° / 1K	WARM A	R-34	⟋
9		#3 BM 5 6	12° / 1K	B,C	R-34	//
10		#3 BM 1 3	12° / 1K	D,E (CONT.)	R-34	//

Figure 14.3

A sample page from the instrument schedule (hook-up sheet) for the 1985 Colorado Opera Festival production of *Madame Butterfly*. Lighting design by John Culbert.

single-stroke gothic style (Figure 14.4) meet these requirements. In general, only uppercase letters should be used, although lowercase letters can be used for special purposes.

Title Block   The title block (Figure 14.5) should be in the same location on all drawings of a single project. The title block should be located in

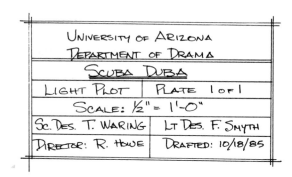

ABCDEFGHIJKLM
NOPQRSTUVWXYZ
1234567890

Figure 14.4

Single-stroke gothic lettering.

University of Arizona
Department of Drama
Scuba Duba

Light Plot	Plate 1 of 1
Scale: ½" = 1'-0"	
Sc. Des. T. Waring	Lt Des. F. Smyth
Director: R. Howe	Drafted: 10/18/85

Figure 14.5

A title block.

either the lower-right-hand corner or in a strip along the bottom of the drawing. In either case, the block should include the following information:

1. Name of producing organization and/or theatre
2. Name of production
3. Drawing title
4. Drawing number
5. Predominant scale of the drawing
6. Date the sheet was drafted
7. Designer(s) of the production
8. Drafter, if different from designer
9. Approval of drawing, if applicable
10. Dates of revisions

Symbols   The normal procedure in drawing a light plot is to use symbols to represent the various types of lighting instrument being used. The USITT-recommended symbols are illustrated in Figure 14.6.

Legend   Each light plot must have a legend, or instrument key (Figure 14.7), which indicates the meaning of each symbol used on the plot.

3" Fresnel	Par 38
6" Fresnel	Par 56
8" Fresnel	Par 64
12" Fresnel	10" Scoop
2-panel barndoor	14" Scoop
4-panel barndoor	14" Scoop
Floor-mounted strip light	Followspot
Pipe-mounted strip light	
10" Beam projector	35mm slide projector
16" Beam projector	Practical
Effects projector	

	3½" × 6" ERS	8" × 9" ERS
	3½" × 8" ERS	8" × 10" ERS
	3½" × 10" ERS	8" × 11" ERS
	6" × 9" ERS	30 ERS designated by degree
	6" × 12" ERS	Z Variable focal length
	6" × 16" ERS	Gobo
	6" × 22" ERS	Iris
	4½" × 6½" ERS	Top hat

Figure 14.6

USITT-recommended lighting symbols.

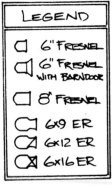

Figure 14.7

A sample legend.

Instrument Notation   The symbol for each instrument drawn on a light plot normally has a great deal of information associated with it: the area of focus, color, instrument number, lamp wattage, circuit, and dimmer. Figure 14.8 shows the specific location, relative to the instrument symbol, where this information should be placed. The meaning of each follows:

- *Focus area*—The focus area for each instrument, identified by a letter placed in front of the lens housing, corresponds to the same letter that identifies a specific lighting area on the plot.
- *Color*—This reference is to the number of the specific color medium that will be used on that instrument.
- *Instrument number*—Each instrument is assigned a number so that it can be cross-referenced with the instrument schedule. (See the

box titled "Instrument Numbers" for specific information on instrument numbering.)

- *Lamp wattage*—Since most instruments will accommodate lamps with a variety of wattages, it is important that the specific wattage of the lamp used for each instrument in the production be noted.
- *Circuit number*—This identifies the stage circuit into which the instrument should be plugged. The circuit number can be assigned by the lighting designer but is frequently left to the discretion of the master electrician.
- *Dimmer number*—This identifies the specific dimmer that will control the instrument.

Only relevant information need be included. For example, if the theatre for which you're designing has a dimmer-per-circuit system, then it would be unnecessarily redundant to include both the circuit and

Figure 14.8

Peripheral information notation standard.

INSTRUMENT NUMBERS

The specific number assigned to each lighting instrument is determined by two factors: (1) its hanging location and (2) its position relative to the other instruments on that pipe. On the portion of the instrument schedule shown in Figure A you'll notice that the instrument numbers are specified as 1E1, 1E2, and so on. The first portion of the number, 1E, refers to its hanging location—in this case, the first electric. The second portion of the number (1, 2, and so forth), refers to the instrument's sequential position on the pipe. In the proscenium theatre, the numbering of any electric starts at the left end of the pipe when viewed as if you were standing with your back against the upstage portion of the stage house (Figure B).

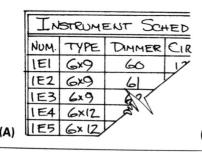

(A)

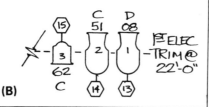

(B)

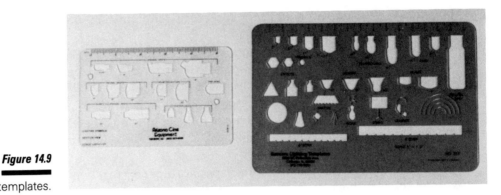

Figure 14.9

Lighting templates.

dimmer number. Similarly, if you've made a note in the legend that all 6 × 9 ERSs are to be equipped with 500-watt lamps, then you won't have to include the lamp wattage in each 6 × 9 symbol.

Under normal circumstances, instrument notations such as I've described are made only on the light plot, not on the lighting section. The lighting section is used mainly as a guide for checking the physical compatibility of the various elements of the design—lighting equipment, set, theatre structure, masking—and the inclusion of any of these technical data would be unnecessary.

Lighting Templates   Lighting templates (Figure 14.9) are used to facilitate the drawing of the various stage lighting symbols. Templates are readily available in scales of ¼ inch = 1 foot and ½ inch = 1 foot.

Line Weights   The USITT recommends the following line weights be used for drafting light plots and sections.
Pencil: Thin: .3 mm
         Thick: .5 mm
Pen: Thin: .010 inch–.0125 inch
         Thick: .020 inch–.025 inch
In either pen or pencil, an extra-thick line, .035 inch to .040 inch (.9 mm) may be used, as necessary, for emphasis (plate border, suitable section cutting-plane line, and so forth).

Drafting Conventions   The drafting conventions for lighting design generally subscribe to the USITT-recommended graphic standards for scenic design and production shown in Figure 14.10.

While it is normal and convenient to have the outline of the set on the light plot, the most important visual elements on the light plot are

Type	Style	Notes and Line Weights

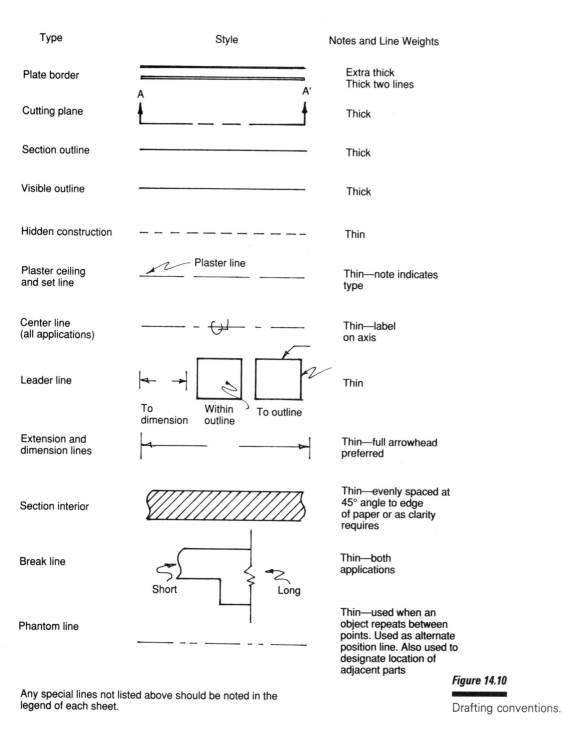

Plate border — Extra thick / Thick two lines

Cutting plane — Thick

Section outline — Thick

Visible outline — Thick

Hidden construction — Thin

Plaster ceiling and set line — Thin—note indicates type

Center line (all applications) — Thin—label on axis

Leader line — Thin

Extension and dimension lines — Thin—full arrowhead preferred

Section interior — Thin—evenly spaced at 45° angle to edge of paper or as clarity requires

Break line — Thin—both applications

Phantom line — Thin—used when an object repeats between points. Used as alternate position line. Also used to designate location of adjacent parts

Figure 14.10

Drafting conventions.

Any special lines not listed above should be noted in the legend of each sheet.

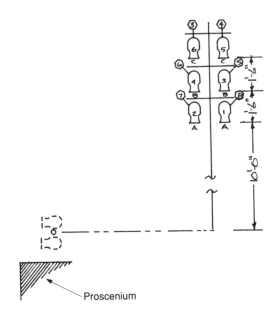

Figure 14.11

Alternate position drafting
technique for depicting
booms.

Proscenium

the lighting symbols; therefore, those symbols should be drawn with a solid "thick" line. So that it recedes in visual importance, the set should be drawn with a solid "thin" line. Any portion of the set that would interfere with the lighting symbols or notes should be eliminated. Lighting pipes should be drawn with a hidden-construction-line style.

Lighting booms offer an interesting challenge to the general rule that a light plot is a **ground plan** view. Typically, booms are drawn in front elevation (using a "thick" line) to show the height of the boom and the placement of the instruments. If there is enough space on the plot, the elevation is drawn with its base marking the place onstage where the boom will stand. However, booms are often located in cramped areas between the set and masking where there is no room on the plot to draw an "in situ" elevation. In these cases the elevation is frequently drawn toward the side of the plot, and an alternate position line is drawn from the base of the elevation to the actual place where the boom will stand, as shown in Figure 14.11. A plan view of the boom, including the instruments (use the hidden-construction-line style) is drawn in position on the plot.

DRAFTING THE PLOT

The lighting designer needs to acquire several specific drawings from other members of the production design team before he or she can start to draw the light plot:

1. the ground plan(s) of the scenic design
2. the **sectional(s)** of the scenic design
3. a scale ground plan of the stage and auditorium
4. a scale sectional drawing of the stage and auditorium
5. a layout of, and specifications for, the stage lighting system(s) of the theatre

The ground plans of the theatre and set are traced, using a thin line, onto the tracing paper to be used for the light plot. The layout of the stage lighting system provides information about the location of the

Ground plan: A scale mechanical drawing in the form of a horizontal offset section with the cutting plane passing at whatever level, normally a height of 4 feet above the stage floor, required to produce the most descriptive view of the set.

Sectional: A drawing, usually in scale, of an object that shows what it would look like if cut straight through at a given plane.

DRAFTING FOR LIGHTING DESIGN

As we have seen, the lighting designer uses two principal mechanical drawings to record the information that is needed to hang, circuit, and focus the lighting design, the light plot, and the lighting section. The purpose of these drawings is to guide the master electrician and crew. The amount and kind of information shown on the paperwork associated with a lighting design varies greatly from production to production and designer to designer. But a set of basic criteria pertains to the drawings associated with any lighting design.

1. The light plot and lighting section should be drawn to scale.
2. The light plot should show the location of the lighting instruments in relationship to the set and the physical structure of the theatre.
3. All drawings should adhere to the tenets of good mechanical drafting techniques.
4. Lighting instrument symbols and associated lettering should be represented by a thick line; all other elements should be drawn using a thin line, unless a thick or extra-thick line is needed for emphasis.
5. A legend should be used to explain all symbols used on the plot.
6. Each lighting instrument or fixture should be numbered to allow for its easy identification on the hookup sheet, or instrument schedule.
7. All pertinent data regarding each instrument should be included on the instrument schedule.
8. The title block should adhere to the criteria noted in the text.

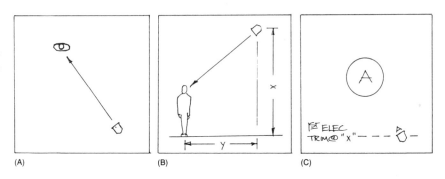

Figure 14.12

A sectional view of the
hanging position of a
lighting instrument
provides an accurate
picture of the angle from
which the light will strike
the actor.

various stage circuits (connecting strips, floor and wall pockets, and so
on). The sectionals of the set and the stage/auditorium are traced to
create the basic visual information necessary for the lighting section.

Information regarding the lighting key, beam and field angles, and
lighting areas was presented in Chapters 12 and 13. However, additional technical information on determining the sectional angle of the
light for each instrument may prove helpful.

Determining the Sectional Angle

The lighting key codifies the plan angle and color for each instrument,
but it doesn't provide any information about the sectional angle for each
instrument. Although the sectional angle should be determined from an
analysis of the desired appearance of the light, in fact the sectional
angles of almost all lighting instruments (except top lights) will usually
be between 30 and 60 degrees, with 45 degrees being fairly normal and
typical. (See the box in Chapter 12 titled " 'Normal' Lighting Angles" for
the reason for this apparently arbitrarily selected angle.)

Dance and other applications in which the revelation of form is
more important than the visibility of the face are notable exceptions to
this generalization about the sectional angle. Dance lighting frequently
makes very effective use of side lighting in which the angle of approach
is parallel with the stage floor.

The trim height for an instrument with a given sectional angle can
be determined very easily if you construct a **working sectional.** Figure
14.12A shows the plan view of a single lighting instrument. Figure
14.12B shows a sectional view taken at right angles to the axis of that
same instrument. The **trim height** (x) will be specified by the lighting
designer. (See the box titled "What Determines a Pipe's Trim Height?"
for an explanation of how the trim height is determined.) Since any
point along the axial line (the central axis of the beam of light emitted by

the instrument) would provide the "correct" sectional angle, the axial line can be extended until it reaches the predetermined trim height. At that point a vertical line can be dropped to the stage floor, and the distance from that point to the center of the lighting area can be measured (y). This information is recorded on the light plot by placing the symbol for the instrument at the measured floor distance (y) from the center of the lighting area, as shown in Figure 14.12C. The trim height for the pipe (x) is noted at the end of the pipe on the plot.

Selecting Instrument Size

At the same time that the sectional angle is being determined, the lighting designer can also determine the appropriate size of instrument to use. From the beam and field angle information (see box titled "Beam and Field Angles Explained" in Chapter 13) or from the manufacturer's specification sheets for specific lighting instruments, beam and field angle templates can be constructed. These thin, triangular pieces of cardboard (Figure 14.13A) are actually sectional representations of the

Working sectional: A drawing showing the sectional angle for a lighting instrument; used to determine its trim height or hanging position; not to be confused with the lighting section.
Trim height: Height above the stage floor at which an instrument will be hung.

WHAT DETERMINES A PIPE'S TRIM HEIGHT?

The trim height of any instrument or pipe will be determined by a number of factors. In many arena and thrust theatres a permanent lighting grid hangs over the stage. Since the height of these grids is rarely adjustable, the trim height for any instruments attached to them is also fixed. Most proscenium arch theatres also have some fixed positions such as the ante-proscenium cuts, balcony rails, and other "in-house" positions. However, the counterweight system that is part of most proscenium arch theatres' permanent equipment provides the

means for the lighting designer to specify the trim height for onstage lighting instruments.

Any number of factors will contribute to a designer's decision to trim a particular pipe at a specific height. Among the more practical considerations are the size of the stage, the height of the scenery, the height of any fixed hanging positions, the throw distance of the instruments being used, the maximum safe working height of equipment used to focus the instruments, and so forth. Aesthetic considerations such as whether the production

concept calls for the instruments to be masked or seen by the audience would also be considered. After factoring all of the available information, the lighting designer will specify the trim height for any movable pipes.

Given all of the elements that need to be considered when making this important decision, onstage electrics for productions in medium-sized theatres with counterweight systems are normally trimmed at a height between 18 and 26 feet.

Maximum throw distance: The point at which the output of a stage lighting instrument drops to 50 footcandles.

Throw distance: How far light from an instrument travels from its hanging position to the center of its area of focus.

cone of light emitted by a specific instrument. The angle is cut to match the field angle of the instrument; and the length matches, in scale, the **maximum throw distance** of that particular instrument. A composite template (Figure 14.13B), made from acetate, consolidates all of the information onto one template. The center line, which coincides with the instrument axial line, is a scale rule marked with 5-foot increments. Fanning out on either side of the center line are lines noting degrees of arc.

Figure 14.14 shows how to use the composite beam and field angle template. After the working sectional for an instrument has been drawn, the apex of the template is placed at the hanging point specified for that instrument. An appropriately sized instrument will have a field angle that slightly overlaps the lighting area and a maximum throw distance longer than the **throw distance** measured to the center of the lighting area.

This method of instrument selection is suggested only as a general guide. In the final analysis, the designer needs to make instrument selections based on what is aesthetically appropriate for the particular situation.

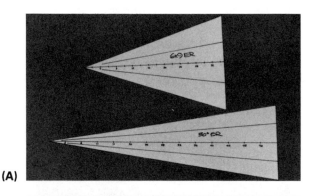

(A)

Figure 14.13

Beam and field angle templates. (A) Cardboard templates for 6 × 9 and 6 × 16 ERSs. (B) A composite plastic template.

(B)

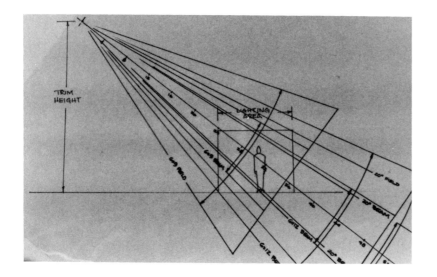

Figure 14.14

How to use a beam and field angle template.

LIGHTING INSTRUMENT SPECIFICATION SHEETS

It is extremely useful for a lighting designer to assemble a collection of data sheets that specify the photometric data (beam, field angle, light output at specific throw distances, and the like) for the instruments of the various manufacturers (see example). The maximum throw distance is the farthest distance at which the instrument can effectively be used. At this distance the light emitted by the instrument measures 50 footcandles, which is used as the industry standard and is considered to be the lowest effective illumination level for stage use.

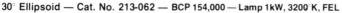

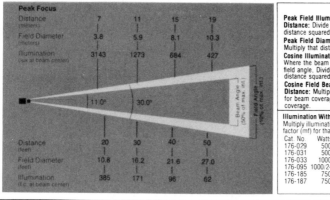

A portion of an instrument specification sheet for the Colortran 30-degree ellipsoidal reflector spotlight.

Plotter: A computer-controlled machine that draws graphic representations on large-sized paper.

Cut list: A list that details the number of gels of specific size and color that will be used on a production; for example, 12 pieces of Roscolux 09 for 6-inch ERSs, 6 pieces of Lee 154 for 8-inch Fresnels, and so forth.

Computer Graphics

In the past few years a number of computer software programs have been created to assist the lighting designer. Some of the programs are complete packages that, with the aid of a **plotter,** will draw light plots and sectionals as well as create and maintain the instrument schedule or hookup sheets. Frequently when the program is designed to create an instrument schedule, the information in the database can be rearranged to provide a **cut list** as well as a variety of other helpful types of paperwork.

Programs that have a graphic component (those that can draw plots and sectionals) generally need a computer that has a large storage capacity (such as that offered by a hard disk) while those that work only on the instrument schedules and other non-graphic paperwork can generally be operated on most basic office-model personal computers.

DRAWING THE PLOT: A SUGGESTED SEQUENCE

It is easy to be apprehensive when confronted with the challenge of drawing a light plot. The following sequence may help ease some of that frustration. However, remember that this is only a suggested procedure. It isn't the "only" way to do it, nor does it provide for every contingency. Nevertheless, it does provide a reasonably accurate list of "what to do first" and should help you through the necessarily complex job of producing the lighting designer's preliminary paperwork—the light plot, lighting section, and instrument schedule.

1. Draw a "rough" plot first. You can make all sorts of smudges, erasures, and corrections on this copy and then, when you have it the way you want it, lay another piece of Clearprint over it and trace your final clean copy.
2. Draw the theatre structure and set using a "thin" line.
3. Draw in your lighting areas using a "thin" line. On your rough plot you can draw circles for the lighting areas if doing so will help you visualize. Most designers assign each area a letter to differ-

entiate between them. When you draw the final plot, don't draw the circles; just place the appropriate letters in the center of the areas. If placing the letters in the center of the area interferes with the location of any lighting equipment, move the letter, not the equipment.
4. Replicate the lighting key in each area. Use a "thick" line for the symbols for all lighting equipment. (If you, as lighting designer, are going to be assigning circuits to each instrument, do so when you draw each instrument.)

Specific information about these software systems and the hardware needed to run them can be found in advertisements and articles in trade magazines such as *Lighting Dimensions* and *Theatre Crafts* as well as in many well-stocked computer shops.

In the past 10 years lighting design has seen the computer board become the dominant system for intensity control in the theatre simply because the computer can reproduce the designer's intentions (during production) faster, more accurately, and for less money than any other system. I suspect that computer graphics will similarly become the dominant mode in lighting graphics in the future. However, just like the computer in the light booth, this computer and its software will be a tool to *help* the designer save time and be more accurate in his or her work. It will not replace the designer's need to know the basics—how to draw a plot or sectional and how to keep accurate and up-to-date associated paperwork.

When you plot the location of the instruments, it is usually easiest to start with an area that will be the least encumbered by set pieces and masking. For proscenium and thrust productions, this is usually one of the areas down center. For arena productions, the least encumbered areas are usually center stage. If you're a little hazy on how to replicate the key in the lighting areas, you might want to review Chapter 13.

5. Proceed to replicate the keys for any additional layers of lights, such as the support lights for any sources (practical lamps, windows, fireplaces, and so forth); washes; cyc and ground-row lighting; off-stage atmospheric lights such as hallways, adjoining rooms, and so forth. Don't forget to circuit each instrument, practical, and effect.

6. When you've laid in all your lights and made any necessary adjustments, number all of your instruments according to the guide-lines laid down earlier in this chapter.

7. Using your light plot and the ground plans of the set(s) and theatre as your guides, draw a rough lighting section. If you find that some lighting equipment interferes with the set or masking, make any necessary adjustments to the section *and the plot*.

8. Trace the final copies of the light plot and section.

9. Fill in all necessary data on the instrument schedule or hookup sheet.

DESIGN EXAMPLES

he design process (see Chapter 9) provides a useful analytical approach to the process of design. That methodology will remain the same regardless of the **form** (proscenium, thrust arena) or type (drama, musical theatre, dance) of production situation in which you find yourself. However, there are some pragmatic differences between these forms and types of theatre that will affect your work as a designer. Chapter 13 showed how the lighting key varies with the form of stage; this chapter will expand on that beginning and show how the form of theatre and type of production affect the lighting design.

DESIGNING FOR THEATRE TYPE

Theatre in the twentieth century inherited the proscenium stage that had developed, in various ways and through various detours, from the days of Greek drama. Nevertheless, as a ripple effect of the Little Theatre movement of the 1920s and 1930s, fledgling companies, with little money, began to produce theatre in "found" spaces. Existing barns, churches, feed stores, grocery stores, libraries, old movie houses, and other large, relatively open buildings were all candidates for takeover. Many of these groups relished the enforced intimacy between the actors and audience that shoehorning theatres into these cramped spaces provided. Whether by accident or design, many of these converted theatre spaces didn't have the room to erect a proscenium stage and auditorium. For whatever reasons, thrust and arena stages sprung up all over the country, and all three forms prevail today.

Proscenium Stage

The proscenium arch is essentially a picture frame through which the audience views the play (Figure 15.1). Proscenium staging forces a separation between the audience and the action of the production, creating the least intimate observer-action relationship of the three basic forms of stage.

The traditional proscenium production preserves the "magic" of the theatre. In many of the more elaborate productions, the scenery and set props are moved mechanically. The audience doesn't see the stagehands or stage machinery that moves the scenery; they just see the settings "magically" transformed before their eyes. To help create the magical mood essential to this style of production, the lighting

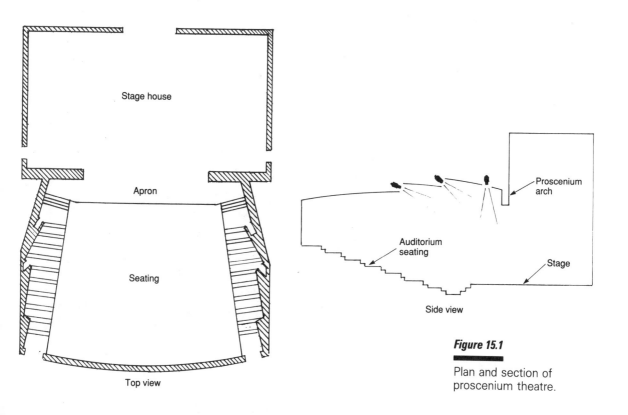

Figure 15.1

Plan and section of proscenium theatre.

Style: In this context, style refers to the specific compositional characteristics that distinguish the appearance of one type of design from another. Using this definition, the various design styles—realism, expressionism, surrealism, and so forth—are delineated by the differences in their compositional principles.

Form: In this context, elements that have similar physical characteristics. For example, arena, thrust, and proscenium theatres have different *forms* of stage configuration.

Drop-and-wing set: A setting primarily composed of two-dimensional scenery, normally one or more drops upstage and a series of portals placed between the drops and the proscenium.

instruments are frequently masked so that the audience won't be aware of the source of the lighting. While it can be aesthetically pleasing to have the instruments hidden from view, this practice frequently compromises the lighting by reducing the number of hanging locations available to the designer. It is reasonably easy to adequately mask onstage instruments behind borders or in the wings without adversely affecting the lighting to any serious degree. Attempting to hide the front-of-house positions is another matter. Almost any attempt to conceal the instruments will have a negative effect on the flexibility of the designer's choices. Most Broadway and regional professional houses have many, if not all, of the front-of-house instruments exposed to view by some members of the audience (Figure 15.2). Although the instruments aren't particularly attractive, the audience usually doesn't notice them once the production is under way.

The **style** and **form** of the setting in a proscenium production will, to a great extent, determine the availability of hanging positions. The traditional box setting with a ceiling severely limits side-, top-, and back-lighting approaches. Box settings without ceilings still restrict the use of sidelight but open the set to both top- and some back-light angles. **Drop-and-wing sets** (frequently used in traditional musicals and ballet) enable the designer to make effective use of side, top, and some back lighting. An open setting, one that is essentially a series of platforms with few vertical elements, provides the designer with the most flexibility because it opens the playing area to approaches from all directions—front, side, top, and back.

Figure 15.2

A proscenium theatre and auditorium. University of Arizona, Department of Drama.

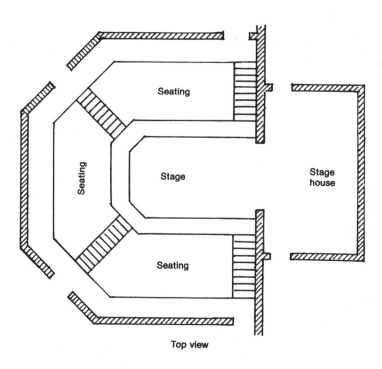

Top view

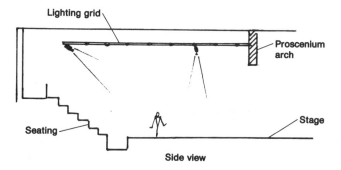

Side view

Figure 15.3

A typical thrust stage arrangement.

Thrust Stage

A thrust stage can be loosely defined as any form of playing area that is surrounded on three sides by the audience. Because the audience views the action of the play from three sides, as shown in Figure 15.3, the designer generally needs to surround the actors with light more completely than would be necessary on a proscenium stage. On a thrust stage the downstage areas (the space toward the front of the thrust) usually contain only furniture pieces as shown in Figure 15.4. Since there are usually no large walls or other vertical elements to interrupt

Figure 15.4

Thrust theatre. Tyrone
Guthrie Theater,
Minneapolis, Minnesota.
Seating an audience of
1,441, no seat is farther
than 52 feet from the
stage. Photo by Robert
Ashley Wilson.

WHEN POSSIBLE, COMPROMISE

Many times you will be able to create better designs if you sit down and chat. If the scene designer has created an elegant living room design, but the set has a ceiling, your overhead hanging positions are obviously gone. Right? Not necessarily. Sit down and chat with the designer. See if he or she would be able to put beams or some other visual elements on the ceiling that would enable a hole or slot to be cut through which you could focus your instruments. If holes or slots can't be cut, perhaps you could hide small instruments, such as 6-inch Fresnels or PAR 38's, behind the beams.

Remember that theatre is a collaborative art, but collaboration can't happen without communication.

the lighting approach angles on the three open sides of the stage, it would seem that the designer would have more flexibility to select the appropriate angle of approach for each instrument. This flexibility can be limited if the theatre doesn't have a well-designed **grid** system above and beyond the stage area. All is not lost, however, because the judicious and creative use of booms and lighting ladders to provide temporary lighting positions in unusual places can solve a multitude of problems.

The challenge of masking lighting instruments for a thrust-stage production is considerable. In fact, it is almost impossible to mask the instruments from every seat in the house; and if all instruments *are* effectively masked, it is often at the expense of the lighting design. In such cases, it is preferable to sacrifice the masking. Although members of the audience may see the instruments, if they aren't lit directly (see the box titled "Try to Avoid Blinding Your Audience") and can't clearly see the audience on the opposite side of the stage, they will generally accept the exposed instruments as a convention and concentrate on the action of the play.

Grid: A network of steel I beams supporting elements of the counterweight system.

Arena Stage

An arena stage can be defined as any stage space surrounded on all sides by the audience, as shown in Figure 15.5. It is unusual to find an arena theatre where the last row of seats is more than 20 to 25 feet from the stage. The Arena Stage in Washington, D.C., is a large example of this type of theatre, because the last row of the auditorium is

---

TRY TO AVOID BLINDING YOUR AUDIENCE

When working on a thrust or arena stage, you always confront the challenge of light shining from the opposite side of the stage into the eyes of the audience. Although, ideally, you'd like to keep the light off the audience entirely, the audience's proximity to the stage normally makes it impossible to prevent some spill. If the light falls on the feet, shins, or maybe the knees of audience members closest to the stage, they will probably not be bothered by the light; if it gets much higher, they will tend to become distracted by it.

To reduce ambient spill, and to keep the audience from seeing the hot spots of the lenses, use snoots or top hats on all ERSs and on those Fresnels that don't have barn doors.

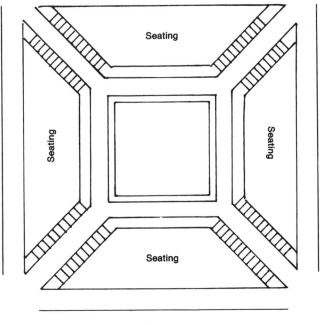

Top view

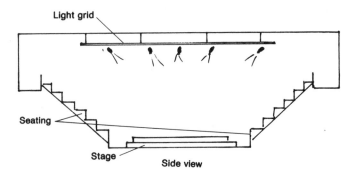

Figure 15.5

A typical arena theatre configuration.

approximately 35 feet from the stage (Figure 15.6). This intimate observer-action relationship dictates that most of the acting-area instruments, which are hung relatively close to the actors, will serve double duty. Wide field-angle instruments, such as 6 × 9 and 40- or 50-degree ERSs and 6-inch Fresnels, provide front lights for one section of the audience while they backlight the action for the audience on the opposite side of the stage.

The use of color in lighting for the arena stage probably requires more subtlety, both in design and execution, than does the lighting for

Figure 15.6

Arena theatre. The interior of the 827-seat Arena Stage in Washington, D.C.

either proscenium or thrust stages. Pale tints and colors of lower than normal saturation are generally used in arena productions because hues of even medium saturation have a tendency to overwhelm skin tones and the palettes of the scenic and costume designers if used at the close ranges generally dictated by the proximity of instruments to the stage.

The settings used in arena productions are generally limited to furniture and low-profile pieces that offer little interference with the approach angles for the light. The challenge of inadequate hanging locations can be solved with the same type of creative ingenuity recommended during the discussion of booms and ladders in the section on thrust stages.

While fairly steep sectional angles are normally used to prevent light from shining on the audience, there is rarely a problem with heavy facial shadows on arena stages because each lighting area is usually lit from at least three (and more normally four) sides, and the bounce light from the floor (even when it's painted black) tends to fill any remaining shadows.

DESIGNING FOR THEATRICAL FORM

The previous section was devoted to a general discussion of how the different forms of theatre affect the execution of the lighting design. Since craft principles are best demonstrated through example, in this section we will study lighting designs for proscenium, thrust, and arena productions of Tennessee Williams' *The Glass Menagerie*. We will discuss the musical *Cabaret* and use *The Nutcracker* to illustrate lighting principles for dance production.

An advisory digression before we begin. Each lighting design is a product of a unique set of circumstances: the theatre in which the play is produced, the personalities and creativity of the production design team, the production budgets (both time and fiscal), the dedication and talent of the lighting crew, and so forth. No design should ever be thought of as "correct," as the only solution to the design challenge. In that vein, these designs are only examples. They show one designer's reaction to the production circumstances. They work; but they aren't "right," and they aren't wrong. They are simply what they are: examples.

Drama: The Glass Menagerie

Notes about *The Glass Menagerie* in my designer's notebook (see Chapter 9) might look like the following:

> *The Glass Menagerie* is primarily a memory play. Memories are usually soft and faded, like tattered, forgotten baby blankets. The mind plays gentle tricks with harsh reality of what has been. It smooths off the painful edge of injury and mutes the high points of happiness. Pleasant moments from the past well up in gentle colors and soft focus. Even the unwatchable can be seen through the soft diffusion and blending of time and distance. Memories, both good and bad, change and fade with the passage of time. Reality is nonexistent. Only special moments remain.

Laura is soft and gentle. She possesses the depth and transparent delicacy of her menagerie of tiny animals. If one personality could combine the brilliant clarity of delicate crystal wind chimes with the velvet kiss of a soft summer night, that person would be Laura. Like glass, she appears hard but can, with only a little pressure, shatter into a thousand shimmering pieces.

Amanda is also soft. She has the softness of a chiffon gown lazily twirling to the music of a waltz at the cotillion on a warm, long ago, Mississippi summer night. While Laura is clear and bell-like, Amanda is delicate pale tints of blue and lavender. A faded memory of herself, she lives in the past because the present is too hard, too harsh. We wonder if her memories of Blue Mountain are based on her past, or if she created the reality of her past to get through her present. Even the stridency and harshness of Amanda is softened through the dimness of memory.

This play belongs to Laura and Amanda. It's Tom's memory of them. As it is his memory, he only wanders through the play to act as a foil to them; he is the narrator of his own memory. He is more real than any of the others. At the beginning of the play and during those moments when he steps out of the play to narrate, he is real. He is contemporary. There must be a separation between Tom and the portrayal of his remembered self.

The Gentleman Caller is also a memory. He is more vibrant than Laura and Amanda because he was a swirl of activity in Tom's memory. He was the All-American ideal, the go-getter, the positive I'm-going-to-succeed young man that Amanda wanted her children to be.

The world of Tom's memory and Tom's world as the narrator must be visually separated by the quality of the light. The world of memory should be soft and faded. The Wingfield's apartment should be lit with out-of-focus ERSs and soft Fresnels. No hard edges should be evident anywhere. Colors in the memory scenes should be mostly tints of pale lavenders, blues, pinks, and a little **neutralizing** amber. The candlelight scene will need soft but deep shadows and some "candle color" support for Laura and the Gentleman Caller's faces. The street of Tom's memories must also be soft, but Tom must always be hard, clear, and real.

Tom's world as narrator should have the harsh glare of reality about it. The light should be hard-edged; and, to help create Tom's sense of isolation, it should have the look of night about it.

Neutralization: The result of mixing complementary hues. In light, the creation of white. In pigment, the creation of dark gray.

General Design Notes

A different lighting key is used for each design to show how the same stimuli can result in a number of equally effective solutions to the design challenge. Notice how the saturation of the

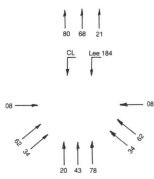

Figure 15.7

Light key for proscenium production of *The Glass Menagerie.*

colors decreases as we move from the proscenium to the thrust and finally the arena design.

Notes on the Proscenium Production   The lighting key for the proscenium production of *The Glass Menagerie* is shown in Figure 15.7. The scenic sketch, light plot, section, and instrument schedule are shown in Figures 15.8–15.11.

The production concept specifies soft pastels and color shifts to enhance the moods of the individual scenes. Since front lights provide the most reflectivity to the audience, the medium-saturation color washes—Roscolux 20, Medium Amber; 43, Dark Pink; and 78, Trudy Blue—are hung in the second AP to provide the dominant color-change mechanism. The side-front lights provide good facial modeling and visibility. They are double hung into each lighting area with Roscolux 34, Flesh Pink, and 62, Booster Blue, to enhance the color-shift capabilities. (When used together, these two colors result in a warm-white mix. When used separately, they enhance either the warm or cool color-shift capabilities of the design.) The side lights provide good body definition and help to separate the actors from the background. They are gelled with 08, Pale Amber Gold, which is a warm, low-saturation tint that will combine with the R62 to produce a white edge or rim light. The R08 is neutral enough that it won't create any strange shadow colors (see box titled "Complementary Color Shadowing" in Chapter 10) when combined with any of the front or side-front lights. The top lights

Figure 15.8

Scenic design for proscenium production of *The Glass Menagerie.*

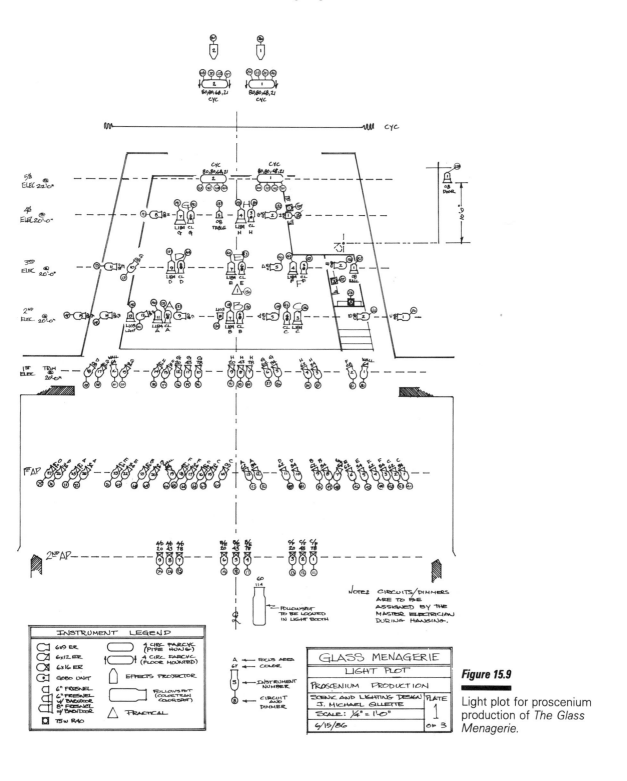

Figure 15.9

Light plot for proscenium production of *The Glass Menagerie*.

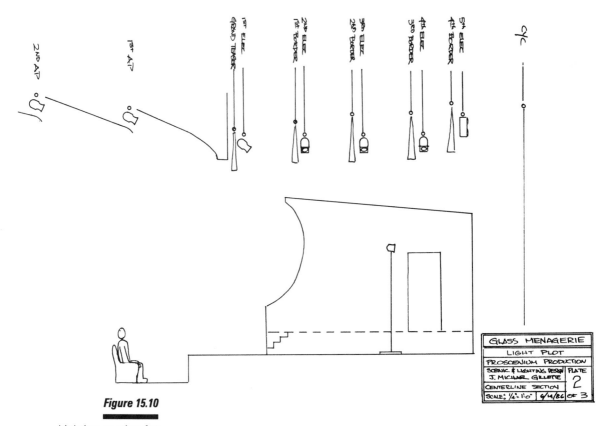

Figure 15.10

Lighting section for proscenium production of *The Glass Menagerie*.

highlight the head and shoulders and help separate the actors from their background. They are gelled with Lee 184, Cosmetic Peach, because its very pale cool-brown hue is an excellent neutral blending color and its soft diffused quality will help fill shadows. The clear top light with the medium breakup gobo is used to provide texture—primarily in combination with the saturated washes during Tom's narrative sequences.

The R-40 (flood) lamps hung over the door arches simply light the doorways. The light from these lamps, which are normally run at low intensity, is very diffused and puts a little fill light into the archways to soften the harsh shadow lines frequently encountered here.

The support light for the floor lamp is a 6-inch Fresnel hung directly above the practical and gelled with Lee 103 to provide a warm pool of light around it when the floor lamp is on. Support lights for the candles used in the scene between Laura and the Gentleman Caller are hung in the first AP and focused on area C.

The followspot focuses tightly on Tom's head during his narration sequences. The specified Colortran Colorspot doesn't have a fan, and

INSTRUMENT SCHEDULE

PRODUCTION: GLASS MENAGERIE - PROSCENIUM   PAGE 1 OF 4

INST #	TYPE	LOCATION	AREA	COLOR	CIR	DIM	LAMP	REMARKS
2AP1	6x16	2ND AP	C/F		11	11	"	
2AP2	6x16	"	C/F		12	12	"	
2AP3	6x16	"	C/F		13	13	"	
2AP4	6x16	"	B/E		17	17	"	
2AP5	6x16	"	B/E		18	18	"	
2AP6	6x16	"	B/E		19	19	"	
2AP7	6x16	"	A/D		23	23	"	
2AP8	6x16	"	A/D		24	24	"	
2AP9	6x16	"	A/D		25	25	"	
1AP1	6x12	1ST AP	C	34	41	41	1000w	
1AP2	6x12	"	F	62	42	42	"	
1AP3	6x12	"	F	34	43	43	"	
1AP4	6x12	"	F	62	44	44	"	
1AP5	6x12	"	E	34	45	45	"	
1AP6	6x12	"	E	62	46	46	"	
1AP7	6x12	"	SL WALL	64	48	48	"	
1AP8	6x12	"	B	34	49	49	"	
1AP9	6x12	"	B	62	51	51	"	
1AP10	6x12	"	D	34	52	52	"	
1AP11	6x12	"	D	62	53	53	"	
1AP12	6x12	"	A	34	56	56	"	
1AP13	6x12	"	A	62	57	57	"	
1AP14	6x12	"	C	09	60	60	"	
1AP15	6x12	"	C	34	62	62	"	
1AP16	6x12	"	C	62	63	63	"	
1AP17	6x12	"	F	34	64	64	"	
1AP18	6x12	"	F	62	65	65	"	
1AP19	6x12	"	SR WALL	64	66	66	"	
1AP20	6x12	"	B	34	67	67	"	
1AP21	6x12	"	B	62	68	68	"	
1AP22	6x12	"	E	34	69	69	"	
1AP23	6x12	"	E	62	70	70	"	
1AP24	6x12	"	A	34	72	72	"	

INSTRUMENT SCHEDULE

PRODUCTION: GLASS MENAGERIE - PROSCENIUM   PAGE 2 OF 4

INST #	TYPE	LOCATION	AREA	COLOR	CIR	DIM	LAMP	REMARKS
1AP25	6x12	1ST AP	A	62	73	73	1000w	
1AP26	6x12	"	D	34	74	74	"	
1AP27	6x12	"	D	62	75	75	"	
1E1	6x9	1ST ELEC	SL WALL	64	80	80	1000w	KEEP FOCUS OFF "
1E2	6x9	"	F	08	81	81	"	
1E3	6x12	"	H	34	83	83	"	
1E4	6x12	"	H	62	84	84	"	
1E5	6x12	"	G	34	86	86	"	
1E6	6x12	"	G	62	87	87	"	
1E7	6x12	"	H	78	89	89	"	
1E8	6x12	"	H	43	90	90	"	
1E9	6x12	"	H	20	91	91	"	
1E10	6x12	"	G	78	94	94	"	
1E11	6x12	"	G	43	95	95	"	
1E12	6x12	"	G	20	96	96	"	
1E13	6x12	"	H	34	97	97	"	
1E14	6x12	"	H	62	98	98	"	
1E15	6x12	"	G	34	100	100	"	
1E16	6x9	"	SR WALL	64	101	101	"	KEEP FOCUS OFF "APT."
1E17	6x12	"	G	62	103	103	"	
1E18	6x9	"	D	08	105	105	"	
2E1	6"F	2ND ELEC	C	08	120	120	750w	
2E2	6x9	"	B	08	122	122	750w	
2E3	6x9	"	C	LIB4	126	126	750w	
2E4	8"F	"	C	NONE	128	128	1000w	
2E5	6x9	"	A	08	129	129	750w	
2E6	6x9	"	B	NONE	132	132	750w	
2E7	8"F	"	B	LIB4	133	133	750w	
2E8	6"F	"	E	L103	134	134	500w	CHANDELIER " SUPPORT"
2E9	6x9	"	C	08	137	137	750w	
2E10	6x9	"	A	NONE	139	139	750w	
2E11	8"F	"	A	LIB4	140	140	1000w	

INSTRUMENT SCHEDULE

PRODUCTION: GLASS MENAGERIE - PROSCENIUM   PAGE 3 OF 4

INST #	TYPE	LOCATION	AREA	COLOR	CIR	DIM	LAMP	REMARKS
2E12	6x9	2ND ELEC	F	08			750w	
2E13	6"F	"	LAMP SUPPORT	L103			500w	
2E14	6x9	"	B	08			750w	
2E15	6x9	"	A	08			750w	
3E1	6"F	3RD ELEC	HALL	08			500w	
3E2	6x9	"	E	08			750w	
3E3	6x9	"	F	NONE				GOBO - MEDIUM BREAKUP
3E4	8"F	"	F	LIB4			1000w	BARNDOOR
3E5	6x9	"	D	08			750w	
3E6	6x9	"	E	NONE			750w	GOBO - MED. BREAKUP
3E7	8"F	"	E	LIB4			1000w	
3E8	6x9	"	D	NONE			750w	GOBO - MED. BREAKUP
3E9	8"F	"	D	LIB4			1000w	
3E10	6x9	"	G	08			750w	
3E11	6x9	"	E	08			750w	
4E1	6"F	4TH ELEC	H	08			500w	
4E2	6x9	"	G	08			750w	
4E3	6x9	"	H	NONE			750w	GOBO - MED. BREAKUP
4E4	8"F	"	H	LIB4			1000w	
4E5	6"F	"	TABLE SPEC	08			500w	FULL FLOOD
4E6	6x9	"	G	NONE			750w	GOBO - MED. BREAKUP
4E7	8"F	"	G	LIB4			1000w	
4E8	6x9	"	H	08			750w	
5E1	FOR CYC	5TH ELEC	CYC	80,80,82			4-1K	
5E2	FOR CYC	"	CYC	80,80,82			4-1K	
SL1	6"F	STAGE DOOR	DINING DOOR	08			500w	BARNDOOR TO DOOR EDGE
SPEC	SLIDE PROJ	LINE 8	—	—			8-25w	CHANDELIER
US1	FOR CYC	US of CYC	CYC	80,80,82			4-1K	
US2	FOR CYC	"	"	80,80,82			4-1K	
US3	STREET PROJ	"	"	—				DISCUSS SLIDES w/ DESIGNER
US4	STREET PROJ	"	"	—				" "

INSTRUMENT SCHEDULE

PRODUCTION: GLASS MENAGERIE - PROSCENIUM   PAGE 4 OF 4

INST #	TYPE	LOCATION	AREA	COLOR	CIR	DIM	LAMP	REMARKS
US DOOR	R40	US DOOR	—	—			75w	ANGLE DOWN @ 60°
DOOR	R40	MIDDLE DOOR	—	—			75w	"
DOOR (B)	R40	DS DOOR	—	—			75w	"

Figure 15.11

Instrument schedule for proscenium production of *The Glass Menagerie*.

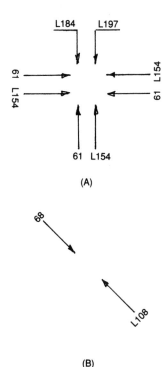

(A)

(B)

the lamp is incandescent so that it can be put on a dimmer to unobtrusively dim it out when Tom segues from narrator to participant in the scene. It is gelled with Roscolux 114, Hamburg Frost, to soften the edge of the beam and Roscolux 60, No-Color Blue, to help it cut through the warm pinks and lavenders of the other lights.

The cyc lights are used to wash the building flats on either side of the set and the cyc in back of it. Each four-lamp cyc light is gelled with two dark blues (Roscolux 80, Primary Blue, and Roscolux 84, Zephyr Blue), one medium blue (Roscolux 68, Sky Blue), and a neutralizing complementary (Roscolux 21, Golden Amber).

The seamless plastic projection screen cyc is painted with dyes and paint. It is lit from front and back to give greater depth to the scene during the evening and storm scenes. The effects projectors contain slides showing the building of storm clouds during the dinner scene.

Because of the number of instruments and the complexity of the color shifts, this production should be equipped with a dimmer-per-circuit lighting system equipped with a computer board.

Notes on the Thrust Production   The lighting key for the thrust production is shown in Figure 15.12. The scenic sketch, light plot, section, and instrument schedule are shown in Figures 15.13–15.16.

Figure 15.12

Lighting key for thrust production of *The Glass Menagerie.*

Figure 15.13

Scenic design for thrust production of *The Glass Menagerie.*

The thrust production lighting design uses a two-color shift. The two colors—Lee 154, Pale Rose, and Roscolux 61, Mist Blue—are double hung, as shown in Figure 15.12A, to give a color range from soft pink through lavender to pale blue. The top lights (Lee 184, Cosmetic Peach, with a medium breakup pattern) are a compromise solution. They provide the color neutralization of the Lee 184 with the textural effects

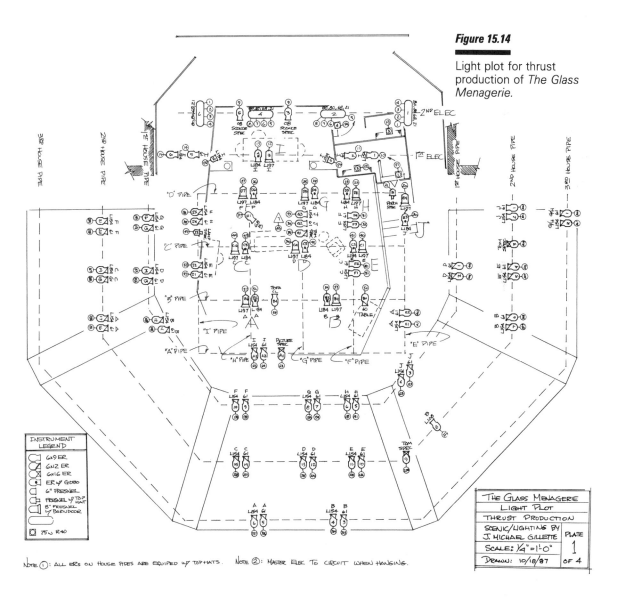

Figure 15.14

Light plot for thrust production of *The Glass Menagerie.*

NOTE ①: ALL ERs ON HOUSE PIPES ARE EQUIPED W/ TOP HATS.   NOTE ②: MASTER ELEC TO CIRCUIT WHEN HANGING.

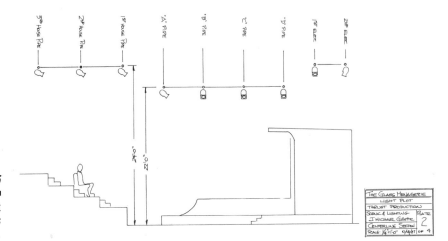

Figure 15.15

Lighting section for thrust production of *The Glass Menagerie.*

of the medium breakup pattern. The Lee 197, Alice Blue, top wash is used in conjunction with the goboed top light during Tom's narrative sequences.

For the candlelit scene between Laura and the Gentleman Caller, area C is crosslit according to the lighting key shown in Figure 15.12B. The Lee 108, Straw, is a candlelight support and the Roscolux 68, Sky Blue, provides visibility while still maintaining the idea of "shadow."

Father's picture, the sofa, and the table holding Laura's menagerie are lit with specials to highlight those areas when necessary. Rather than using followspots for Tom's narrative sequences, a location just in front of the stoop is designated as the "narrative spot." Three ungelled specials are triangulated on that spot. Additional specials provide support lights for the floor lamp, porch light, and wall sconces.

The method of circuiting the dimmers is based on the area color-shift concept. Each lighting area has all three instruments of the same color patched into the same dimmer. The top lights are ganged by areas—AB, CDE, FGH, I, and J. This method uses a moderate number of dimmers while still allowing for color shifting.

Notes on the Arena Production   Figure 15.17 is the lighting key for the arena production. Figures 15.18–15.21 are the scenic sketch, light plot, lighting section, and instrument schedule for this production.

The color-shift technique used in this production relies on a close interplay between the saturated overhead color wash (Roscolux 59, Indigo) and the diagonally crossing acting-area lights (Roscolux 02,

INSTRUMENT SCHEDULE

PRODUCTION: GLASS MENAGERIE - THRUST   PAGE 1 OF 4

INST#	TYPE	LOCATION	AREA	COLOR	CIR	DIM	LAMP	REMARKS
3P1	6x12	3RD HOUSE PIPE	G/4	G1	300	7	1KW	
3P2	6x12	"	G/4	L154	301	17	1KW	
3P3	6x12	"	B	G1	333	2	1KW	
3P4	6x12	"	B	L154	334	12	1KW	
3P5	6x12	"	A	G1	336	1	1KW	
3P6	6x12	"	A	L154	337	11	1KW	
2P1	6x9	2ND HOUSE PIPE	J	G1	200	10	750W	
2P2	6x9	"	J	L154	201	20	750W	
2P3	6x16	"	TOM SPEC	NONE	204	41	1KW	PATCH W/ 2P9 & G1
2P4	6x12	"	E	G1	205	5	1KW	
2P5	6x12	"	E	L154	207	15	1KW	
2P6	6x12	"	B	G1	208	2	1KW	
2P7	6x12	"	B	G1	209	12	1KW	
2P8	6x9	"	B	L108	227	31	750W	PATCH W/ H1
2P9	6x16	"	TOM SPEC	NONE	230	41	1KW	PATCH W/ 2P3 & G1
2P10	6x12	"	E	G1	232	5	1KW	
2P11	6x12	"	E	L154	233	15	1KW	
2P12	6x12	"	D	G1	234	4	1KW	
2P13	6x12	"	D	L154	235	14	1KW	
2P14	6x12	"	C	G1	237	3	1KW	
2P15	6x12	"	C	L154	238	13	1KW	
2P16	6x12	"	A	G1	251	1	1KW	
2P17	6x12	"	A	L154	253	11	1KW	
2P18	6x12	"	C	G1	256	3	1KW	
2P19	6x12	"	C	L154	257	13	1KW	
2P20	6x12	"	F	G1	258	6	1KW	
2P21	6x12	"	F	L154	259	16	1KW	
1P1	6x12	1ST HOUSE PIPE	D	G1	102	4	1KW	
1P2	6x12	"	D	L154	104	14	1KW	
1P3	6x12	"	J	G1	123	10	1KW	
1P4	6x12	"	J	L154	125	20	1KW	
1P5	6x12	"	H	G1	131	8	1KW	

INSTRUMENT SCHEDULE

PRODUCTION: GLASS MENAGERIE - THRUST   PAGE 2 OF 4

INST#	TYPE	LOCATION	AREA	COLOR	CIR	DIM	LAMP	REMARKS
1P6	6x12	1ST HOUSE PIPE	H	L154	133	18	1KW	
1P7	6x12	"	G	G1	134	7	1KW	
1P8	6x12	"	G	L154	135	17	1KW	
1P9	6x12	"	F	G1	138	6	1KW	
1P10	6x12	"	F	L154	139	16	1KW	
1P11	6x12	"	B	G1	148	2	1KW	
1P12	6x12	"	B	L154	149	12	1KW	
1P13	6x12	"	D	G1	152	4	1KW	
1P14	6x12	"	D	L154	153	14	1KW	
1P15	6x12	"	G	G1	158	7	1KW	
1P16	6x12	"	G	L154	159	17	1KW	
A1	6x16	GRID PIPE A	PICTURE SPEC	NONE	63	34	1KW	
A2	6x12	"	I	G1	64	9	1KW	
A3	6x12	"	I	L154	65	19	1KW	
B1	6x12	GRID PIPE B	TABLE	NONE	52	32	500W	
B2	8"F	"	B	L197	53	25	1KW	W/ BARNDOOR
B3	6x9	"	B	L184	54	21	750W	W/ MED. BREAKUP GOBO
B4	6x9	"	SOFA	NONE	55	33	500W	
B5	6x9	"	A	L184	56	21	750W	W/ MED. BREAKUP GOBO
B6	8"F	"	A	L197	57	25	1KW	W/ BARNDOOR
C1	8"F	GRID PIPE C	E	L197	40	26	1KW	W/ BARNDOOR
C2	6x9	"	E	L184	41	22	750W	W/ MED. BREAKUP GOBO
C3	6x9	"	D	L184	42	22	750W	"
C4	8"F	"	D	L197	36	26	1KW	W/ BARNDOOR
C5	6x9	"	C	L184	43	22	750W	W/ MED. BREAKUP GOBO
C6	8"F	"	C	L197	44	26	1KW	W/ BARNDOOR
D1	6"F	GRID PIPE D	PATCH SPEC	NONE	21	35	750W	W/ 2" TOP HAT
D2	8"F	"	H	L197	22	27	1KW	W/ BARNDOOR
D3	6x9	"	H	L184	23	23	750W	W/ MED. BREAKUP GOBO
D4	6x9	"	G	L184	24	23	750W	" "

INSTRUMENT SCHEDULE

PRODUCTION: GLASS MENAGERIE - THRUST   PAGE 3 OF 4

INST#	TYPE	LOCATION	AREA	COLOR	CIR	DIM	LAMP	REMARKS
D5	6x9	GRID PIPE D	G	L197	25	27	1KW	W/ BARNDOOR
D6	6x9	"	F	L184	26	23	750W	W/ MED. BREAKUP GOBO
D7	8"F	"	F	L197	27	27	1KW	W/ BARNDOOR
E1	6x9	GRID PIPE E	A	L154	61	11	750W	
E2	6x9	"	A	G1	60	1	750W	
E3	6x9	"	J	L184	30	29	750W	W/ MED. BREAKUP GOBO
E4	8"F	"	J	L197	20	30	1KW	W/ BARNDOOR
F1	6x9	GRID PIPE F	C	L154	51	13	750W	
F2	6x9	"	C	G1	50	3	750W	
F3	6x9	"	F	L154	32	16	750W	
F4	6x9	"	F	G1	31	6	750W	
G1	6x12	GRID PIPE G	TOM SPEC	NONE	35	41	1KW	PATCH W/ 2P9 & 2P3
G2	6x9	"	J	G1	34	10	750W	
G3	6x9	"	J	L154	33	20	750W	
H1	6x9	GRID PIPE H	B	68	37	31	1KW	PATCH W/ 2P8
I1	6x12	GRID PIPE I	E	G1	59	5	1KW	
I2	6x12	"	E	L154	58	15	1KW	
I3	6"F	"	LAMP SPEC		49	36	500W	W/ 2" TOP HAT
I4	6x12	"	H	G1	39	8	1KW	
I5	6x12	"	H	L154	38	18	1KW	
1E1	6x9	1ST ELEC	I	L154	10	19	750W	
1E2	6x9	"	I	G1	11	9	750W	
1E3	8"F	"	I	L197	12	28	1KW	W/ BARNDOOR
1E4	6x9	"	I	L184	13	24	750W	W/ MED. BREAKUP GOBO
1E5	6x9	"	I	G1	14	9	750W	
1E6	6x9	"	I	L154	15	19	750W	

INSTRUMENT SCHEDULE

PRODUCTION: GLASS MENAGERIE - THRUST   PAGE 4 OF 4

INST#	TYPE	LOCATION	AREA	COLOR	CIR	DIM	LAMP	REMARKS
2E1	FRESNEL	2ND ELEC	SL WALL	B0,B0,R2,U	1-4	42,43,44,45	4-1KW	PATCH W/ 2E6 (BY COLOR)
2E2	FRESNEL	"	US WALL	B0,B0,R2,U	5-8	42,43,44,45	4-1KW	PATCH W/ 2E4 (BY COLOR)
2E3	6x9	"	SCONCE SPEC	CB	9	37	500W	PATCH W/ 2E5
2E4	FRESNEL	"	US WALL	B0,B0,R2,U	5-8	42,43,44,45	4-1KW	PATCH W/ 2E2 (BY COLOR)
2E5	6x9	"	SCONCE SPEC	CB	9	37	500W	PATCH W/ 2E3
2E6	FRESNEL	"	SR WALL	B0,B0,R2,U	1-4	42,43,44,45	4-1KW	PATCH W/ 2E1 (BY COLOR)
1	R40	FRONT DOOR	-	-	F1	38	75W	ANGLE DOWN @ 45°
2	R40	LR ARCH	-	-	F2	38	75W	" " "
3	R40	UL ARCH	-	-	F3	38	75W	" " "
4	R40	DINING RM DOOR	-	-	F4	38	75W	" " "
5	6"F	DINING RM	I	L154	F6	39	500W	TWOFER W/ 6
6	6"F	" "	I	L154	F10	39	500W	TWOFER W/ 5
7	-	REMEMBERED TIMES C/D	-	-	45	40	8-15W	CHANDELIER

Figure 15.16

Instrument schedule for thrust production of *The Glass Menagerie.*

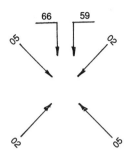

Figure 15.17

Lighting key for arena
production of *The Glass
Menagerie.*

Bastard Amber, and 05, Rose Tint). By varying the intensity differential between these two sets of lights, colors that range between a very delicate rose-pink and deep purple can be achieved. The goboed top light gelled with Roscolux 66, Cool Blue, provides a complementary hue to enliven the mix and provide some needed texture for Tom's narrative sequences.

The diagonal orientation of the lighting in the apartment area results in a slightly different look when compared with the "on-axis" orientation of the lights outside of the apartment.

Candlelight support lights are not used for the scene between Laura and the Gentleman Caller because the lights from the candles should provide the needed light. The dark blue "Alley specials" will be used to help create the concept of night outside the apartment. Various other support lights and specials are used as necessary.

Again, as in the thrust production, a "narrative spot" will be established, and that location will be lit with specials rather than followspots.

The circuiting of the dimmers will be similar to that for the thrust production. Each lighting area has all four of the instruments gelled with R02 and R05 patched into the same dimmer. The top lights are ganged by areas—ABC, DEF, G, HI, and J.

Figure 15.18

Scenic design for arena
production of *The Glass
Menagerie.*

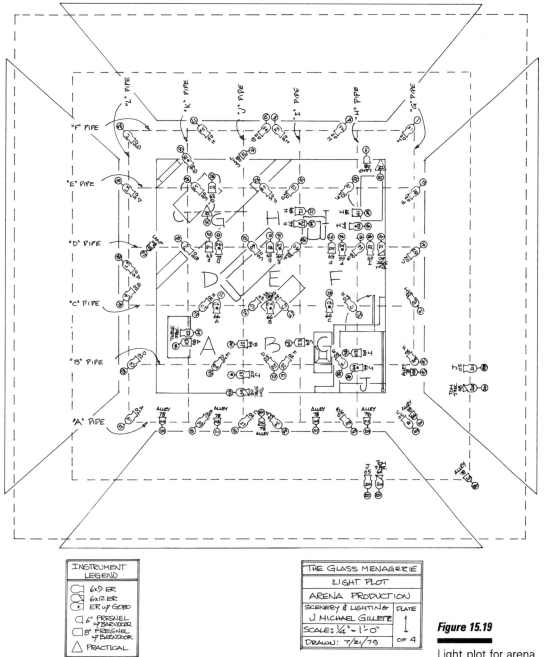

INSTRUMENT
LEGEND

6x9 ER
6x12 ER
ER w/ GOBO
6" FRESNEL
w/ BARNDOOR
8" FRESNEL
w/ BARNDOOR
PRACTICAL

THE GLASS MENAGERIE
LIGHT PLOT
ARENA PRODUCTION

SCENERY & LIGHTING J. MICHAEL GILLETTE	PLATE
SCALE: ¼" = 1'-0"	1
DRAWN: 7/21/79	OF 4

Figure 15.19

Light plot for arena
production of *The Glass
Menagerie*.

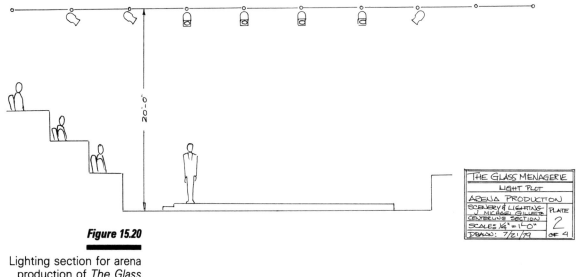

Figure 15.20

Lighting section for arena
production of *The Glass
Menagerie.*

Musicals: Cabaret

The lighting key for *Cabaret* is shown in Figure 15.22. Figures 15.23–
15.26 show the scenic sketch, light plot, lighting section, and instrument
schedule.

There are two significant differences between most musical and
non-musical forms of theater: the use of (1) songs and (2) dance within
the context of the story to further the plot, provide character development, and so forth. As a consequence, the style of most musicals is
generally less realistic than is that of non-musical theatre. This "less
realistic" style frequently results in a color palette that is more saturated
than its more realistic counterparts; the addition of dance requires that
principles of dance lighting, which focuses on illuminating the whole
body, be integrated with those of dramatic lighting, which (to a great
extent) focuses on lighting the face.

The colors selected for lighting design in this particular production
of *Cabaret* were dictated by three primary considerations: (1) the full-
spectrum colors of the costume and set; (2) the heavy, smoke-filled,
sensuous atmosphere needed for the cabaret; and (3) the need for a
lighter, more realistic atmosphere for those scenes outside the cabaret.

Complementary colors of light saturation (Roscolux 62, Booster
Blue, and 02, Bastard Amber) were selected for the front lights because
they would be appropriately neutral for both the cabaret scenes and

INSTRUMENT SCHEDULE

PRODUCTION: GLASS MENAGERIE - ARENA   PAGE 1 OF 3

INST #	TYPE	LOCATION	AREA	COLOR	CIR	DIM	LAMP	REMARKS
A1	6x9	"A" PIPE	C	05	102	3	500w	
A2	6"F	"	ALLEY	78	104	22	500w	
A3	6x9	"	B	05	105	2	500w	
A4	6"F	"	ALLEY	78	107	23	500w	
A5	6x9	"	A	05	108	1	500w	
A6	6"F	"	ALLEY	78	109	23	500w	
A7	6x9	"	C	02	110	3	500w	
A8	6"F	"	ALLEY	78	111	23	500w	
A9	6x9	"	B	02	113	2	500w	
A10	6"F	"	ALLEY	78	114	23	500w	
A11	6x9	"	A	02	117	1	500w	
B1	6x9	"B" PIPE	E	05	85	5	500w	
B2	6x9	"	F	02	87	6	500w	
B3	6x9	"	D	05	88	4	500w	
B4	6x9	"	E	02	93	5	500w	
B5	6x9	"	D	02	98	4	500w	
C1	6x9	"C" PIPE	H	05	64	8	500w	
C2	6x9	"	C	66	65	11	500w	w/ MED. BREAKUP GOBO
C3	6x9	"	G	05	67	7	500w	
C4	6x9	"	B	66	68	11	500w	w/ MED. BREAKUP GOBO
C5	6x9	"	I	02	70	9	500w	
C6	6x9	"	A	66	71	11	500w	w/ MED. BREAKUP GOBO
C7	6x9	"	H	02	73	8	500w	
D1	6x12	"D" PIPE	LAMP SPEC	60	42	21	500w	
D2	6x9	"	J	05	43	10	500w	
D3	6x9	"	B	02	45	2	500w	
D4	6x9	"	F	66	46	12	500w	w/ MED BREAKUP GOBO
D5	8"F	"	F	59	47	17	1KW	
D6	6x9	"	A	02	48	1	500w	
D7	6x9	"	E	66	50	12	500w	w/ MED. BREAKUP GOBO
D8	8"F	"	E	59	51	17	1KW	

INSTRUMENT SCHEDULE

PRODUCTION: GLASS MENAGERIE - ARENA   PAGE 2 OF 3

INST #	TYPE	LOCATION	AREA	COLOR	CIR	DIM	LAMP	REMARKS
D9	6x9	"D" PIPE	C	05	52	3	500w	
D10	6x9	"	D	66	53	12	500w	w/ MED. BREAKUP GOBO
D11	8"F	"	D	59	54	17	1KW	
D12	6x9	"	B	05	56	2	500w	
D13	6"F	"	LAMP SPEC	08	57	24	500w	CHANDELIER SUPPORT
E1	6x9	"E" PIPE	E	02	25	5	500w	
E2	6x9	"	D	02	29	4	500w	
E3	6x9	"	F	05	32	6	500w	
E4	8"F	"	G	59	35	18	1KW	
E5	6x9	"	E	05	36	5	500w	
F1	6x9	"F" PIPE	I	02	1	9	500w	
F2	6x9	"	H	02	4	8	500w	
F3	6x9	"	I	05	8	9	500w	
F4	6x9	"	G	02	9	7	500w	
F5	6x9	"	H	05	17	8	500w	
G1	6x9	"G" PIPE	F	02	21	6	500w	
G2	6x9	"	C	02	41	3	500w	
G3	6x9	"	I	05	61	9	500w	
G4	6x9	"	F	05	81	6	500w	
G5	6"F	"	ALLEY	78	82	22	500w	
G6	6"F	"	ALLEY	78	101	22	500w	
H1	8"F	"H" PIPE	I	59	24	19	1KW	
H2	6x9	"	I	66	44	14	500w	w/ MED. BREAKUP GOBO
H3	8"F	"	J	59	86	20	1KW	
H4	6x9	"	J	66	84	15	500w	w/ MED. BREAKUP GOBO
I1	8"F	"I" PIPE	H	59	27	19	1KW	
I2	6x9	"	H	66	49	14	500w	w/ MED. BREAKUP GOBO
I3	8"F	"	C	59	89	16	1KW	

INSTRUMENT SCHEDULE

PRODUCTION: GLASS MENAGERIE - ARENA   PAGE 3 OF 3

INST #	TYPE	LOCATION	AREA	COLOR	CIR	DIM	LAMP	REMARKS
J1	6"F	"J" PIPE	LAMP SPEC	08	10	24	500w	CHANDELIER SUPPORT
J2	8"F	"	B	59	90	16	1KW	
J3	6x9	"	J	02	91	10	500w	
J4	6x9	"	TBM SPEC	08	92	21	500w	
K1	6x9	"K" PIPE	G	66	18	13	500w	w/ MED BREAKUP GOBO
K2	6x9	"	TABLE SPEC	—	64	25	500w	
K3	8"F	"	A	59	94	16	1KW	
L1	6x9	"L" PIPE	G	05	20	7	500w	
L2	6x9	"	D	05	40	4	500w	
L3	6x9	"	A	05	58	1	500w	
L4	6x9	"	G	02	78	7	500w	
Z1	CHAN.	NEW PIPE	—	—		26	75W	HANG NEW PIPE BETWEEN "J" & "K"
Z2	FLOOD LAMP	BY DESK	—	—		27	60W	
201	6x9	1ST HOUSE PIPE	J		209	10	500w	
202	6x12	"	TBM SPEC		210	21	500w	
203	6"F	"	ALLEY		220	22	500w	
204	6x12	"	TBM SPEC		224	21	500w	
205	6x9	"	J		225	10	500w	

INSTRUMENT SCHEDULE

PRODUCTION: ___   PAGE ___ OF ___

INST #	TYPE	LOCATION	AREA	COLOR	CIR	DIM	LAMP	REMARKS

Figure 15.21

Instrument schedule for arena production of *The Glass Menagerie.*

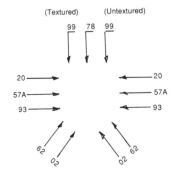

Figure 15.22
_____

The lighting key for
Cabaret.

Figure 15.23
_____

Scenic design for *Cabaret*,
by Tom Benson. Produced
at the University of
Arizona.

those more intimate scenes outside the cabaret. However, those colors had enough saturation to enhance the costume and set colors in both locations. By balancing the color mix between the 02 and 62, the stage could be made neutral, cool, or warm as appropriate. The full saturation necessary for the scenes inside the cabaret was supplied by the Roscolux 20 (Medium Amber), 57A (Lavender), and 93 (Blue Green) used on the vertical striplights and Fresnels on either side of the stage. These saturated color washes, used in conjunction with the acting-area lights, enhanced the costumes and scenery and provided the sidelight necessary to outline the bodies of the dancers during the production numbers.

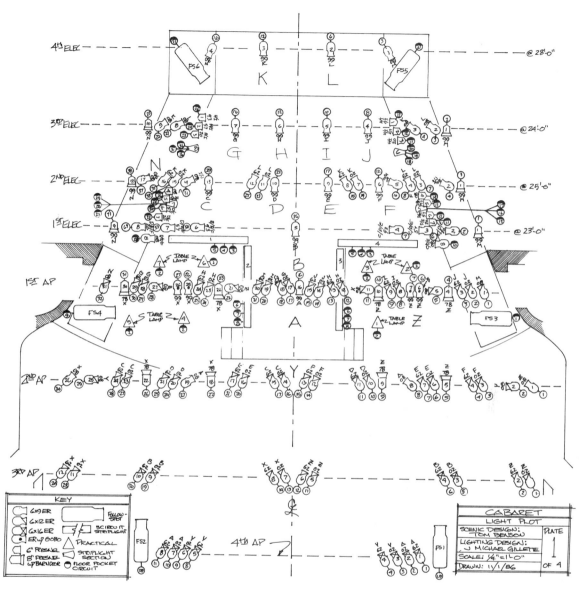

Figure 15.24

The light plot for *Cabaret*.

During the musical numbers, the set was generally lit with psychologically appropriate color washes; and the six followspots, using white or lightly tinted light, were used to highlight the various leads.

The downstage area of the cabaret audience was lit with a textured top wash (Roscolux 99, Chocolate) to support the concept that the area

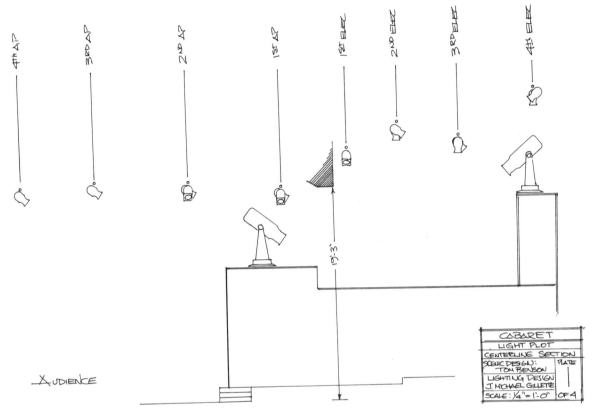

Figure 15.25

Lighting section for
Cabaret.

was lit by the practical lamps on each table. Since the director wanted the "onstage" audience to be visible at all times, during the out-of-the-cabaret scenes, the textured top light was combined with a deep blue (Roscolux 78, Trudy Blue) to reduce the area's apparent visibility. (The deep blue looks like a shadow color but allows the "real" audience to see the shadow detail.)

Dance: The Nutcracker

If there is a difference in lighting for dance, as opposed to lighting for legitimate theatre, it is a matter of degree, not principle.

As indicated during the discussion of *Cabaret*, in legitimate theatre you are concerned with lighting the face so that the audience can see the thoughts and emotions of the actors, whereas in dance you are more concerned in revealing the form of the body. To achieve this goal, the

INSTRUMENT SCHEDULE

PRODUCTION: CABARET PAGE 1 OF 6

INST #	TYPE	LOCATION	AREA	COLOR	CIR	DIM	LAMP	REMARKS
1E1	6"F	1ST ELEC	M	99	1E1	56	500w	w/ BARNDOOR
1E2	6x9	"	C/D/E	20	1E2	63	500w	
1E3	6x9	"	C/D/E	57	1E6	65	500w	
1E4	6x9	"	C/D/E	93	1E7	67	500w	
1E5	6x9	"	B	99	1E36	38	500w	
1E6	6x9	"	D/E/F	93	1E50	66	500w	
1E7	6x9	"	D/E/F	57	1E53	64	500w	
1E8	6x9	"	D/E/F	20	1E69	60	500w	
1E9	6"F	"	N	99	1E71	51	500w	w/ BARNDOOR
2E1	6"F	2ND ELEC	M	99	2E3	57	500w	
2E2	6x9	"	I/J	08	2E4	32	500w	
2E3	6x9	"	L	02	2E7	12	500w	
2E4	6x9	"	L	62	2E8	24	500w	
2E5	6x9	"	G/H	08	2E10	31	500w	
2E6	6x9	"	F	99	2E12	42	500w	
2E7	6x9	"	K	02	2E14	11	500w	
2E8	6x9	"	K	62	2E15	23	500w	
2E9	6x9	"	E	99	2E17	41	500w	
2E10	6x9	"	D	99	2E22	40	500w	
2E11	6x9	"	L	02	2E23	12	500w	
2E12	6x9	"	L	62	2E25	24	500w	
2E13	6x9	"	C	99	2E29	39	500w	
2E14	6x9	"	I/J	08	2E31	32	500w	
2E15	6x9	"	K	02	2E33	11	500w	
2E16	6x9	"	K	62	2E35	23	500w	
2E17	6x9	"	G/H	08	2E37	31	500w	
2E18	6"F	"	N	99	2E38	52	500w	
3E1	6"F	3RD ELEC	M	99	3E2	58	500w	
3E2	6x9	"	L	08	3E3	36	500w	
3E3	6x9	"	K	08	3E4	35	500w	
3E4	6x9	"	J	99	3E8	46	500w	
3E5	6x9	"	I	99	3E10	45	500w	
3E6	6x9	"	H	99	3E12	44	500w	
3E7	6x9	"	G	99	3E16	43	500w	

INSTRUMENT SCHEDULE

PRODUCTION: CABARET PAGE 2 OF 6

INST #	TYPE	LOCATION	AREA	COLOR	CIR	DIM	LAMP	REMARKS
3E8	6x9	3RD ELEC	L	08	3E21	34	500w	
3E9	6x9	"	K	08	3E22	33	500w	
3E10	6"F	"	N	99	3E23	53	500w	
4E1	6x9	4TH ELEC	M	08	4E3	55	500w	
4E2	6x9	"	L	99	4E6	48	500w	
4E3	6x9	"	K	99	4E12	47	500w	
4E4	6x9	"	N	08	4E16	50	500w	
1AP1	6x12		M	08	1AP1	54	750w	
1AP2	6x12		J	02	1AP2	10	750w	
1AP3	6x12		J	62	1AP3	22	750w	
1AP4	8"F		Z	78	1AP4	85	1K	
1AP5	6x12		B	08	1AP5	26	750w	
1AP6	6x9		Z	99	1AP6	82	500w	w/ MED. BREAKUP GOBO
1AP7	6x9		Z	99	1AP7	82	500w	w/ MED. BREAKUP GOBO
1AP8	6x12		I	02	1AP8	9	750w	
1AP9	6x12		I	62	1AP9	21	750w	
1AP10	8"F		Z	78	1AP10	85	1K	
1AP11	6x12		X	08	1AP11	78	750w	
1AP12	6x12		H	02	1AP12	8	750w	
1AP13	6x12		H	62	1AP13	20	750w	
1AP14	6x12		J	02	1AP14	10	750w	
1AP15	6x12		J	62	1AP15	22	750w	
1AP16	6x9		A	99	1AP16	37	500w	
1AP17	6x12		G	02	1AP17	7	750w	
1AP18	6x12		G	62	1AP18	19	750w	
1AP19	6x12		I	02	1AP20	9	750w	
1AP20	6x12		I	62	1AP21	21	750w	
1AP21	6x12		Z	08	1AP22	79	750w	
1AP22	8"F		X	78	1AP23	83	1K	
1AP23	6x12		H	02	1AP24	8	750w	
1AP24	6x12		H	62	1AP25	20	750w	
1AP25	6x9		99	99	1AP26	81	500w	w/ MED. BREAKUP GOBO

INSTRUMENT SCHEDULE

PRODUCTION: CABARET PAGE 3 OF 6

INST #	TYPE	LOCATION	AREA	COLOR	CIR	DIM	LAMP	REMARKS
1AP26	6x9	1ST AP	X	99	1AP27	81	500w	w/ MED. BREAKUP GOBO
1AP27	6x12	"	B	08	1AP28	26	750w	
1AP28	6x12	"	G	02	1AP29	7	750w	
1AP29	6x12	"	G	62	1AP30	19	750w	
1AP30	8"F	"	X	78	1AP31	83	1K	
1AP31	6x12	"	N	08	1AP32	49	750w	
2AP1	6x9	2ND AP	Z	08	2AP1	80	500w	
2AP2	6x12	"	Y	08	2AP2	88	750w	
2AP3	6x12	"	F	02	2AP3	6	750w	
2AP4	6x12	"	F	62	2AP4	18	750w	
2AP5	8"F	"	Z	78	2AP5	84	1K	w/ BARNDOOR
2AP6	6x12	"	E	02	2AP6	5	750w	
2AP7	6x12	"	E	62	2AP7	17	750w	
2AP8	6x9	"	A	08	2AP8	25	500w	
2AP9	8"F	"	Z	78	2AP9	84	1K	w/ BARNDOOR
2AP10	6x12	"	D	02	2AP10	4	750w	
2AP11	6x12	"	D	62	2AP11	16	750w	
2AP12	6x12	"	F	02	2AP14	6	750w	
2AP13	6x12	"	F	62	2AP15	18	750w	
2AP14	6x12	"	C	02	2AP16	3	750w	
2AP15	6x12	"	C	62	2AP17	15	750w	
2AP16	6x12	"	E	02	2AP20	5	750w	
2AP17	6x12	"	E	62	2AP21	17	750w	
2AP18	8"F	"	X	78	2AP22	82	1K	w/ BARNDOOR
2AP19	6x9	"	A	08	2AP23	25	500w	
2AP20	6x12	"	D	02	2AP24	4	750w	
2AP21	6x12	"	D	62	2AP25	16	750w	
2AP22	8"F	"	X	78	2AP26	82	1K	w/ BARNDOOR
2AP23	6x12	"	C	02	2AP27	3	750w	
2AP24	6x12	"	C	62	2AP28	15	750w	
2AP25	6x12	"	Y	08	2AP29	88	750w	
2AP26	6x9	"	X	08	2AP30	77	500w	

INSTRUMENT SCHEDULE

PRODUCTION: CABARET PAGE 4 OF 6

INST #	TYPE	LOCATION	AREA	COLOR	CIR	DIM	LAMP	REMARKS
3AP1	6x12	3RD AP	Z	02	3AP1	75	750w	
3AP2	6x12	"	Z	62	3AP2	76	750w	
3AP3	6x16	"	B	02	3AP5	2	750w	
3AP4	6x12	"	B	62	3AP6	14	750w	
3AP5	6x12	"	Z	02	3AP11	75	750w	
3AP6	6x12	"	Z	62	3AP12	76	750w	
3AP7	6x12	"	X	02	3AP13	75	750w	
3AP8	6x12	"	X	62	3AP14	76	750w	
3AP9	6x16	"	B	02	3AP19	2	750w	
3AP10	6x16	"	B	62	3AP20	14	750w	
3AP11	6x12	"	X	02	3AP23	75	750w	
3AP12	6x12	"	X	62	3AP24	76	750w	
4AP1	6x16	4TH AP	A	62	4AP1	13	750w	
4AP2	6x16	"	A	02	4AP2	1	750w	
4AP3	6x16	"	Y	02	4AP3	86	750w	
4AP4	6x16	"	Y	62	4AP4	87	750w	
4AP5	6x16	"	Y	62	4AP8	87	750w	
4AP6	6x16	"	Y	02	4AP9	86	750w	
4AP7	6x16	"	A	02	4AP10	1	750w	
4AP8	6x16	"	A	62	4AP11	13	750w	
STAGE RIGHT WALKWAY RAIL								
1	6"F	SR WALK TOP RAIL	H/I	93	FP25	66	500w	2FER w/ 5
2	6"F	"	H/I	57	FP24	64	500w	2FER w/ 6
3	6"F	"	H/I	20	FP23	61	500w	2FER w/ 7
4	6"F	"	C	08	FP26	27	500w	
5	6"F	"	D/E	93	FP25	66	500w	2FER w/ 1
6	6"F	"	D/E	57	FP24	64	500w	2FER w/ 2
7	6"F	"	D/E	20	FP23	61	500w	2FER w/ 3
8	6x9	"	D/E/F	08	FP22	29	500w	

INSTRUMENT SCHEDULE

PRODUCTION: CABARET PAGE 5 OF 6

INST #	TYPE	LOCATION	AREA	COLOR	CIR	DIM	LAMP	REMARKS
—STAGE LEFT WALKWAY RAIL—								
1	6"F	SL WALKWAY TOP RAIL	H/I	93	FP13	67	500w	2FER w/ 5
2	6"F	"	H/I	57	FP12	65	500w	2FER w/ 6
3	6"F	"	H/I	20	FP11	63	500w	2FER w/ 7
4	6"F	"	F	08	FP14	28	500w	
5	6"F	"	D/E	93	FP13	67	500w	2FER w/ 1
6	6"F	"	D/E	57	FP12	65	500w	2FER w/ 2
7	6"F	"	D/E	20	FP11	63	500w	2FER w/ 3
8	6x9	"	C/D/E	08	FP10	30	500w	
—STRIPLIGHTS—								
1	6x8	FLOOR	C/D	20,57,93	FP 3,4,5	68,69,70	300w	PATCH BY COLOR w/ 4
2	6x8	RUNWAY	A/B	20,57,93	FP 6,7,8	71,72,73	300w	PATCH BY COLOR w/ 3
3	6x8	RUNWAY	A/B	20,57,93	FP 6,7,8	71,72,73	300w	PATCH BY COLOR w/ 2
4	6x8	FLOOR	E/F	20,57,93	FP 3,4,5	68,69,70	300w	PATCH BY COLOR w/ 1
5	6x8	DL VERTICAL	E/F	20,57,93	FP 15,16,17	63,65,67	300w	PATCH BY COLOR w/ 7
6	6x8	UL VERTICAL	J/I	20,57,93	FP 18,19,20	62,65,67	300w	PATCH BY COLOR w/ 8
7	6x8	DR VERTICAL	C/D	20,57,93	FP 27,28,29	62,64,66	300w	PATCH BY COLOR w/ 5
8	6x8	UR VERTICAL	G/H	20,57,93	FP 30,31,32	62,64,66	300w	PATCH BY COLOR w/ 6
—FOLLOWSPOTS—								
1	–	LIGHT BOOTH	–	114, 28, 62, 34, 09	LB1	90	1K	ALL FOLLOWSPOTS TO
2	–	DIRECTOR BOOTH	–	114, 28, 62, 34, 09	DB1	91	1K	BE COLORTRAN
3	–	DL TOWER	–	114, 28, 62, 34, 09	FP1	92	1K	COLORSPOTS
4	–	DR TOWER	–	114, 28, 62, 34, 09	FP9	93	1K	
5	–	UL TOWER	–	114, 28, 62, 34, 09	FP21	94	1K	
6	–	UR TOWER	–	114, 28, 62, 34, 09	FP33	95	1K	
—"AUDIENCE" TABLE LIGHTS								
1	PRAC.	"AUDIENCE" TABLE	–	–	FP2	89	25w	
2	"	"	–	–	FP2	89	25w	
3	"	"	–	–	FP2	89	25w	
4	"	"	–	–	FP2	89	25w	
5	"	"	–	–	FP2	89	25w	

INSTRUMENT SCHEDULE

PRODUCTION: CABARET PAGE 6 OF 6

INST #	TYPE	LOCATION	AREA	COLOR	CIR	DIM	LAMP	REMARKS
6	"	"	–	–	FP2	89	25w	
7	"	"	–	–	FP2	89	25w	

Figure 15.26

Instrument schedule for *Cabaret*.

axis of the light should be parallel with the axis of the dancer's movement, and it should light the dancer's whole body.

While, ideally, you would place lights parallel with the axis of every movement in a dance, that ideal is also impractical. However, much of dance movement happens in any number of combinations based on the three patterns illustrated in Figure 15.27. These areas can be effectively covered with the use of side lights, top lights, and side-front lights, with a few front lights for visibility, as shown in the

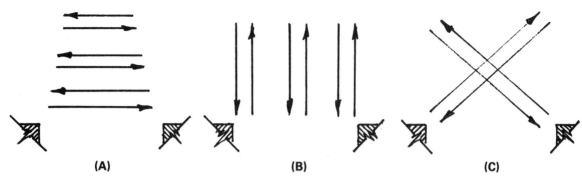

(A)   **(B)**   **(C)**

Figure 15.27

Typical dance movement patterns: (A) side to side or cross-stage; (B) up and down stage; (C) diagonal.

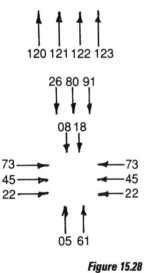

Figure 15.28

Lighting key for *The Nutcracker*.

lighting key and plot for *The Nutcracker* (Figures 15.28 and 15.29). The lighting section and instrument schedule for *The Nutcracker* are shown in Figures 15.30 and 15.31.

The Nutcracker could be described as a collection of individual dances, each possessing its own particular emotional quality and style. A flexible design based on color shifts over a wide range of hues provides a good solution to this challenge. Four color washes (Roscolux

---

DANCE BOOMS

Almost every lighting design for dance will have six to eight booms located in the slots (the spaces between the wings [legs] in a drop-and-wing setting). The figure illustrates a typical dance boom. The lowest lights on the boom, frequently referred to as shinkickers or shinbusters (for obvious reasons), light the legs of the dancers when they are at the sides of the stage. Because the dancers work closer to these lights than to those mounted higher on the

boom, the shinkickers should be circuited separately so that they can be run at lower intensities. The instruments higher up the boom are focused farther out on the stage so that they shine over the dancers' heads when they are close to the wings.

Sectional drawing of a typical dance boom.

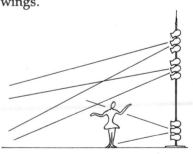

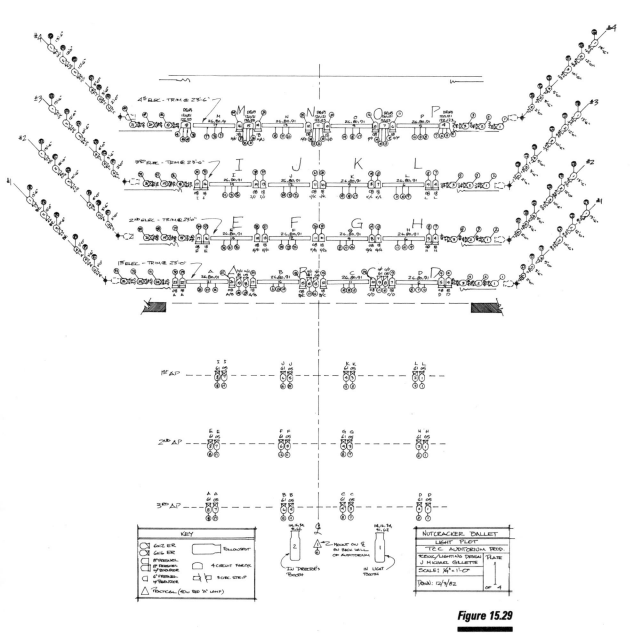

Figure 15.29

Light plot for *The Nutcracker.*

20, Golden Amber; 26, Light Red; 58A, Deep Lavender; and 68, Sky Blue) are used in striplights from the top and in ERSs in the side-front coves to provide the primary color-change mechanisms. The front ERSs (Roscolux 63, Pale Blue) provide a cool visibility light. The side boom ERSs contain Lee 103, Straw; Roscolux 18, Flame; and 62, Booster Blue.

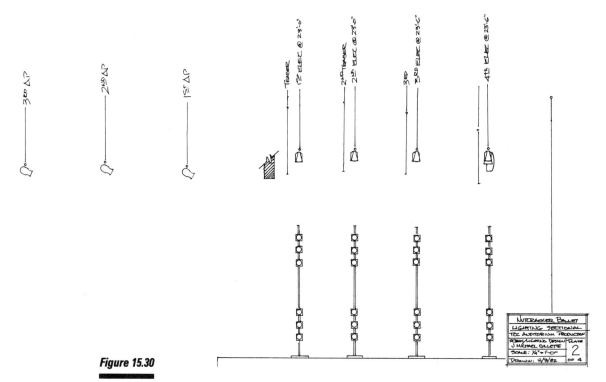

Figure 15.30

Lighting section for *The Nutcracker.*

SAFETY TIP

Dancers are often temporarily blinded by stage lights. As they are exiting the stage there is a real danger that they may run into a boom. Since the area of the side booms at their eye height rarely holds an instrument, it is a good idea to wrap that part of the boom with white and red tape in a barber-pole pattern so that they can see it.

To avoid becoming dizzy and losing their balance, dancers need a visual reference point when executing pirouettes. If you hang a low-wattage red lamp (light bulb) slightly above eye height on the center line and at the back of the auditorium, you will provide them with that point of focus. If your theatre has a balcony, hang the lamp from the balcony rail. If there isn't a balcony, simply hang the lamp on the back wall of the auditorium. If possible, put the light on a dimmer so that you will be able to control its intensity and fade it in and out when necessary.

INSTRUMENT SCHEDULE

PRODUCTION: NUTCRACKER BALLET PAGE 1 OF __

INST #	TYPE	LOCATION	AREA	COLOR	CIR	DIM	LAMP	REMARKS
1AP1	6x16	1ST AP	L	05	1		1K	ALL CIRCUIT
1AP2	6x16	"	L	61	2		1K	ARE PRECEDED W/
1AP3	6x16	"	K	05	8		1K	"1AP..."
1AP4	6x16	"	K	61	9		1K	
1AP5	6x16	"	J	05	15		1K	
1AP6	6x16	"	J	61	16		1K	
1AP7	6x16	"	I	05	17		1K	
1AP8	6x16	"	I	61	18		1K	
2AP1	6x16	2ND AP	H	05	1		1K	ALL CIRCUIT NUMBERS
2AP2	6x16	"	H	61	2		1K	A PREFIX OF
2AP3	6x16	"	G	05	7		1K	"2AP..."
2AP4	6x16	"	G	61	8		1K	
2AP5	6x16	"	F	05	11		1K	
2AP6	6x16	"	F	61	12		1K	
2AP7	6x16	"	E	05	17		1K	
2AP8	6x16	"	E	61	18		1K	
3AP1	6x16	3RD AP	D	05	1		1K	ALL CIRCUIT NUMBERS
3AP2	6x16	"	D	61	2		1K	HAVE A PREFIX OF
3AP3	6x16	"	C	05	7		1K	"3AP..."
3AP4	6x16	"	C	61	8		1K	
3AP5	6x16	"	B	05	11		1K	
3AP6	6x16	"	B	61	12		1K	
3AP7	6x16	"	A	05	17		1K	
3AP8	6x16	"	A	61	18		1K	
1E1	6x16	1ST ELEC	A/B	73	1		1K	ALL CIRCUIT #s HAVE A
1E2	6x16	"	A/B	46	2		1K	PREFIX OF "1E..."
1E3	6x16	"	A/B	22	3		1K	
1E4	8"F	"	D	18	4		1K	w/ BARNDOORS
1E5	8"F	"	D	08	5		1K	w/ BARNDOORS
1E6	STRIP	"	D	26,80,91	6,7,8		300	
1E7	8"F	"	C/D	18	9		1K	w/ BARNDOOR

INSTRUMENT SCHEDULE

PRODUCTION: NUTCRACKER BALLET PAGE 2 OF __

INST #	TYPE	LOCATION	AREA	COLOR	CIR	DIM	LAMP	REMARKS
1E8	6x12	1ST ELEC	O/P	05	10		750	ALL CIRCUIT #s HAVE A
1E9	6x12	"	O/P	61	11		750	PREFIX OF "1E..."
1E10	8"F	"	C/D	08	34		1K	w/ BARNDOOR
1E11	STRIP	"	C	26,80,91	12		300	
1E12	8"F	"	B/C	18	13		1K	w/ BARNDOOR
1E13	6x12	"	N/O	05	14		750	
1E14	6x12	"	N/O	61	15		750	
1E15	8"F	"	B/C	08	16		1K	w/ BARNDOOR
1E16	STRIP	"	B	26,80,91	19,20,21		300	
1E17	8"F	"	A/B	18	22		1K	w/ BARNDOOR
1E18	6x12	"	M/N	05	23		750	
1E19	6x12	"	M/N	61	24		750	
1E20	8"F	"	A/B	08	25		1K	w/ BARNDOOR
1E21	STRIP	"	A	26,80,91	26,27,28		300	
1E22	8"F	"	A	18	29		1K	w/ BARNDOOR
1E23	8"F	"	A	08	30		1K	w/ BARNDOOR
1E24	6x16	"	C/D	73	31		1K	
1E25	6x16	"	C/D	46	32		1K	
1E26	6x16	"	C/D	22	33		1K	
2E1	6x16	2ND ELEC	E/F	22	2		1K	ALL CIRCUIT #s HAVE A
2E2	6x16	"	E/F	46	3		1K	PREFIX OF "2E..."
2E3	6x16	"	EF	73	4		1K	
2E4	8"F	"	H	18	7		1K	w/ BARNDOOR
2E5	8"F	"	H	08	8		1K	w/ BARNDOOR
2E6	STRIP	"	H	26,80,91	9,10,11		300	
2E7	8"F	"	G/H	18	13		1K	
2E8	8"F	"	G/H	08	14		1K	
2E9	STRIP	"	G	26,80,91	16,17,18		300	
2E10	8"F	"	F/G	18	19		1K	
2E11	8"F	"	F/G	08	20		1K	
2E12	STRIP	"	F	26,80,91	22,23,24		300	
2E13	8"F	"	E/F	18	27		1K	
2E14	8"F	"	E/F	08	28		1K	

INSTRUMENT SCHEDULE

PRODUCTION: NUTCRACKER BALLET PAGE 3 OF 6

INST #	TYPE	LOCATION	AREA	COLOR	CIR	DIM	LAMP	REMARKS
2E15	STRIP	2ND ELEC	E	26,80,91	30,31,32		300	
2E16	8"F	"	E	18	33		1K	w/ BARNDOOR
2E17	8"F	"	E	08	34		1K	w/ BARNDOOR
2E18	6x16	"	G/H	73	37		1K	
2E19	6x16	"	G/H	46	38		1K	ALL CIRCUIT #s HAVE
2E20	6x16	"	G/H	22	39		1K	A PREFIX OF "2E..."
3E1	6x16	3RD ELEC	I/J	22	2		1K	ALL CIRCUIT #s HAVE A
3E2	6x16	"	I/J	46	3		1K	PREFIX OF "3E..."
3E3	6x16	"	I/J	73	5		1K	
3E4	8"F	"	L	18	7		1K	w/ BARNDOOR
3E5	8"F	"	L	08	8		1K	w/ BARNDOOR
3E6	STRIP	"	L	26,80,91	9,10,11		300	3 CIRC.
3E7	8"F	"	K/L	18	13		1K	
3E8	8"F	"	K/L	08	14		1K	
3E9	STRIP	"	K	26,80,91	17,18,19		300	3 CIRC.
3E10	8"F	"	J/K	18	20		1K	
3E11	8"F	"	J/K	08	21		1K	
3E12	STRIP	"	U	26,80,91	22,23,24		300	3 CIRC.
3E13	8"F	"	I/J	18	27		1K	
3E14	8"F	"	I/J	08	28		1K	
3E15	STRIP	"	I	26,80,91	30,31,32		300	3 CIRC.
3E16	8"F	"	I	18	33		1K	w/ BARNDOOR
3E17	8"F	"	I	08	34		1K	w/ BARNDOOR
3E18	6x16	"	K/L	73	18		1K	
3E19	6x16	"	K/L	46	19		1K	
3E20	6x16	"	K/L	22	20		1K	
4E1	6x16	4TH ELEC	M	22	1		1K	ALL CIRCUIT #s HAVE A
4E2	6x16	"	M	46	2		1K	PREFIX OF "4E..."
4E3	6x16	"	M	73	3		1K	
4E4	FAR CYC	"	CYC	120,121,122,123	4,5,6,7		4-1K	4 CIRCUIT
4E5	STRIP	"	P	26,80,91	10,9,8		300	3 CIRCUIT
4E6	8"F	"	O/P	18	11		1K	w/ BARNDOOR

INSTRUMENT SCHEDULE

PRODUCTION: NUTCRACKER BALLET PAGE 4 OF 6

INST #	TYPE	LOCATION	AREA	COLOR	CIR	DIM	LAMP	REMARKS
4E7	FAR CYC	4TH ELEC	CYC	120,121,122,123	12,13,14,15		4-1K	4-CIRC
4E8	8"F	"	O/P		16		1K	w/ BARNDOOR
4E9	STRIP	"	O	26,80,91	17,18,19		300	3-CIRC
4E10	8"F	"	N/O		20		1K	w/ BARNDOOR
4E11	FAR CYC	"	CYC	120,121,122,123	21,22,23,24		4-1K	4-CIRC
4E12	8"F	"	N/O		25		1K	w/ BARNDOOR
4E13	STRIP	"	N	26,80,91	26,27,28		300	3-CIRC
4E14	8"F	"	M/N		29		1K	w/ BARNDOOR
4E15	FAR CYC	"	CYC	120,121,122,123	30,31,32,33		4-1K	4-CIRC
4E16	8"F	"	M/N		34		1K	w/ BARNDOOR
4E17	STRIP	"	M	26,80,91	35,36,37		300	3-CIRC
4E18	FAR CYC	"	CYC	120,121,122,123	38,39,40,41		4-1K	4-CIRC
4E19	6x16	"	O/P	7	42		1K	
4E20	6x16	"	O/P	46	43		1K	ALL CIRCUIT #s HAVE
4E21	6x16	"	O/P	22	44		1K	A PREFIX OF "4E..."
— STAGE LEFT BOOM #1 —								
1	6x12	SL SLOT 1	B/C	73	L6		750	
2	6x12	"	B/C	46	L5		750	
3	6x12	"	B/C	22	L4		750	
4	6"F	"	D	73	L3		500	
5	6"F	"	D	46	L2		500	
6	6"F	"	D	22	L1		500	
— STAGE LEFT BOOM #2 —								
1	6x12	SL SLOT 2	F/G	73	L12		750	
2	6x12	"	F/G	46	L11		750	
3	6x12	"	F/G	22	L10		750	
4	6"F	"	H	73	L9		500	
5	6"F	"	H	46	L8		500	
6	6"F	"	H	22	L7		500	

INSTRUMENT SCHEDULE

PRODUCTION: NUTCRACKER BALLET PAGE 5 OF 6

INST #	TYPE	LOCATION	AREA	COLOR	CIR	DIM	LAMP	REMARKS
— STAGE LEFT BOOM #3 —								
1	6x12	SL SLOT	J/K	73	L18		750	
2	6x12	"	J/K	46	L17		750	
3	6x12	"	J/K	22	L16		750	
4	6"F	"	L	73	L15		500	
5	6"F	"	L	46	L14		500	
6	6"F	"	L	22	L13		500	
— STAGE LEFT BOOM #4 —								
1	6x12	SL SLOT 4	O/N	73	L24		750	
2	6x12	"	O/N	46	L23		750	
3	6x12	"	O/N	22	L22		750	
4	6"F	"	P	73	L21		500	
5	6"F	"	P	46	L20		500	
6	6"F	"	P	22	L19		500	
— STAGE RIGHT BOOM #1 —								
1	6x12	SR SLOT 1	B/C	73	R6		750	
2	6x12	"	B/C	46	R5		750	
3	6x12	"	B/C	22	R4		750	
4	6"F	"	A	73	R3		500	
5	6"F	"	A	46	R2		500	
6	6"F	"	A	22	R1		500	
— STAGE RIGHT BOOM #2 —								
1	6x12	SR SLOT 2	F/G	73	R12		750	
2	6x12	"	F/G	46	R11		750	
3	6x12	"	F/G	22	R10		750	
4	6"F	"	E	73	R9		500	
5	6"F	"	E	46	R8		500	
6	6"F	"	E	22	R7		500	

INSTRUMENT SCHEDULE

PRODUCTION: NUTCRACKER BALLET PAGE 6 OF 6

INST #	TYPE	LOCATION	AREA	COLOR	CIR	DIM	LAMP	REMARKS
— STAGE RIGHT BOOM #3 —								
1	6x12	SR SLOT 3	J/K	73	R18		750	
2	6x12	"	J/K	46	R17		750	
3	6x12	"	J/K	22	R16		750	
4	6"F	"	I	73	R15		500	
5	6"F	"	I	46	R14		500	
6	6"F	"	I	22	R13		500	
— STAGE RIGHT BOOM #4 —								
1	6x12	SR SLOT 4	N/O	73	R24		750	
2	6x12	"	N/O	46	R23		750	
3	6x12	"	N/O	22	R22		750	
4	6"F	"	M	73	R21		500	
5	6"F	"	M	46	R20		500	
6	6"F	"	M	22	R19		500	
— FOLLOWSPOTS —								
1	—	DIRECTOR'S BOOTH	—	14,16,34,51,62	—	—	—	XENON SUPER TROUPER
2	—	LIGHT BOOTH	—	14,16,34,51,62	—	—	—	XENON SUPER TROUPER
— PRACTICAL —								
1	—	AUD. WALL	—	RED	BH1		40w	-40w "A" RED IN SOCKET

Figure 15.31

Instrument schedule for *The Nutcracker.*

The Lee 103 and Roscolux 18 on the booms, when used in conjunction with the Roscolux 63 from the front, additively mix to yield a white light on the sides of the dancers. The Roscolux 08, Pale Gold, in the top-back ERSs similarly combines with Roscolux 60, No-Color Blue, in the high side ERSs to produce a white result on the head and shoulders of the dancers. Appropriate specials are used to highlight specific set pieces and locations such as the growing Christmas tree and the throne. Two followspots are located in a booth at the rear of the auditorium.

REHEARSAL AND PERFORMANCE PROCEDURES

t has been said that any lighting design is only as good as its paperwork. The light plot, lighting section, and instrument schedule are only about half of that paperwork. The rest of it is associated with the recording of the dimmer intensity levels and other data that are used when running the lights for a production.

This chapter will present a series of rehearsal and performance procedures, forms, and practices that can be used to assist in the running of the lighting for any production. Every action involving the adjustment of one or more lighting instruments needs to be recorded to ensure that the intensity settings for those dimmers and the timing of each lighting cue remain the same from rehearsal to rehearsal and performance to performance.

ORGANIZATIONAL TOOLS

The forms and practices suggested in this section are not sacrosanct; many different methods can be used to record the information needed to run the lighting for a production. Any well-organized system that works for the lighting designer and electrician can be used. The important point is the necessity of having a clearly written, systematic method of recording the necessary information.

Electrician's Cue Sheet

The electrician's cue sheet is the **board operator's** bible. It contains the primary operating instructions (cue number, what specific action the board operator takes, the timing of the cue, and so forth) for every lighting cue, as shown in Figure 16.1. It is also important to note what information the electrician's cue sheet does not contain. It doesn't give the specific dimmer intensity-level settings (commonly referred to as dimmer settings) for major shifts in the lighting. That information is written on the **preset sheet,** which will be discussed a little later. But the electrician's cue sheet is often used to record the dimmer levels for minor shifts of intensity that involve only one or two dimmers.

If you carefully study the information written on the electrician's cue sheet shown in Figure 16.1, you will be able to follow the progress of the lighting from the lowering of the house lights through the end of the first scene of the play.

Recording Dimmer Intensity Levels

There are actually two methods of recording lighting cues: electronically and in writing.

Electronic Cue Storage   Electronic cue storage is probably the primary advantage of the computer-assisted light board. Although the capabilities of computer-assisted lighting consoles vary from manufacturer to manufacturer, they all provide a basic level of computer memory that

Board operator: An electrician who runs the lighting control console during rehearsals and performances.

Preset sheet: A form used by the electrician to record the intensity levels for each dimmer during major shifts in the lighting.

ELECTRICIAN'S CUE SHEET

Show_____ Script Page_ *1-25*

Cue	Preset	Count	Notations
1	*1*	*—*	House Preset @ 7:30
2	*—*	*8*	House to Half
3	*—*	*4*	House Out
4	*2*	*6*	Apartment ↑ (morning)
5	*3*	*1*	Kitchen when Hal hits switch
6	*4*	*5*	Fade to Black

Figure 16.1
─────────
An electrician's cue sheet.

PRESET SHEET

Production:_____

Preset Bank:_____ Cue:_____

1		16	
2		17	
3		18	
4		19	
5		20	
6		21	
7		22	
8		23	
9		24	
10		25	
11		26	
12		27	
13		28	
14		29	
15		30	

Figure 16.2

A preset sheet.

allows them to electronically store the intensity levels of each dimmer that is used in each cue. Most of them can also store the time associated with each cue. If a production company doesn't have a computer board, that information will have to be recorded manually.

Preset Sheet   The preset sheet (Figure 16.2) is also used to record the intensity levels for each dimmer during major shifts in lighting. The layout and content of the preset sheet is dependent on the type of control system used for the production. But regardless of the exact form of the sheet, it will have an open space adjacent to each dimmer number

PRODUCTION: MEMORY LANE											
CUE #: 38			MEMORY #: 42A			SCRIPT PAGE: 27					
DIM	USE	LVL	DIM	USE	LVL	DIM	USE	LVL	DIM	USE	LVL
1	A↗62	50	11	C↗62	60	21	E↗62	50	31	G↗62	40
2	A↖08	50	12	C↖08	60	22	E↖08	50	32	G↖08	40
3	A→51	70	13	C→51	75	23	E→51	70	33	G→51	45
4	A←51	70	14	C←51	75	24	E←51	70	34	G←51	45
5	A↕CL	60	15	C↕CL	80	25	E↕CL	60	35	G↕CL	30
6	B↗62	60	16	D↗62	60	26	F↗62	60	36	UL DOOR 06	25
7	B↖08	60	17	D↖08	60	27	F↖08	60	37	TABLE 08	10
8	B→51	75	18	D→51	75	28	F→51	70	38	WINDOW 25	—
9	B←51	75	19	D←51	75	29	F←51	70	39	FLASH POT #1	—
10	B↕CL	80	20	D↕CL	80	30	F↕CL	75	40	FLASH POT #2	—

Figure 16.3

Designer's cue sheet (also known as a cheat sheet).

for recording the intensity level of that particular dimmer for that particular cue.

Each time a major shift in the lighting involves more than two or three dimmers, a preset sheet is completed for that cue. The sheet provides the board operators with the information necessary to accurately adjust the dimmers.

Preset sheets are used in conjunction with electrician's cue sheets. The electrician's cue sheets tell the board operator what action is necessary for any particular cue, and the preset sheets are inserted between the cue sheets where they are needed. To keep everything tidy, the cue sheets and preset sheets are usually kept in a three-ring binder.

Designer's Cue Sheet

After the designer has a general idea of the intensity levels for each cue, the levels are recorded on a designer's cue sheet similar to the one illustrated in Figure 16.3. The designer's cue sheet, also known as a cheat sheet, is a form that identifies the function (color, direction) of the light(s) associated with each dimmer and provides a space for recording its intensity level. The cheat sheet allows the designer to record the rough intensity levels and timing of each cue in a systematic manner. Using one page per cue, the designer records the intensity level for each dimmer used in a cue so that he or she will have a clear idea of what

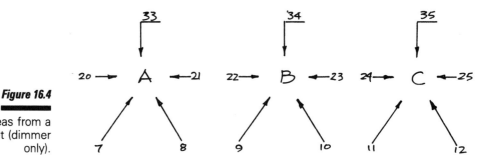

Figure 16.4

Sample areas from a magic sheet (dimmer only).

changes are being made to each dimmer for every cue. Notations can be made on the sheets to indicate the purpose, function, or effect of that particular cue. Designer's cue sheets should be kept in a loose-leaf binder so that cues can be easily added or deleted by inserting or removing sheets from the binder.

Magic Sheet

The magic sheet, another organizational tool of the lighting designer, is a method of visually codifying information that will benefit the lighting designer when he or she is adjusting the dimmer settings during the lighting, technical, and dress rehearsals. In its most basic form, shown in Figure 16.4, the magic sheet provides a clear picture of which dimmers are controlling the various lights for each area. Typically a magic sheet will be drawn on one sheet of paper with all of the lighting areas laid out in their appropriate locations relative to the set, the arrows indicating the direction of the lights and the numbers at the base of the arrows indicating the dimmers.

With designs that make extensive use of color shifts as a primary design motif, it is frequently advantageous to have color indicated on the magic sheet. This can be done in one of several ways. The directional arrows can be overlaid with colors (use wide-tip marking pens) that approximate the hue of each instrument. Alternatively, the numbers of the color media can be placed in front of the directional arrows, as shown in Figure 16.5.

It is essential that the lighting designer and master electrician devise some type of organized system that will ensure that the lighting designer's concepts are accurately recorded and reproduced during each rehearsal and performance of the production. It is of the utmost importance that the various cue and preset sheets be clear and current; any changes in the timing, intensity, or location of any cue must be

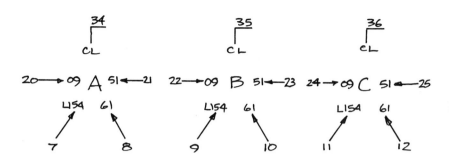

Figure 16.5

Sample areas from a magic sheet (dimmer and color).

recorded so that they can be duplicated during the next rehearsal or performance.

REHEARSALS

The lighting, technical, and dress rehearsals provide the designer with the opportunity to see and adjust the lighting design.

Lighting Rehearsal

The lighting rehearsal is a period devoted to adjusting the intensity levels and timing for each lighting cue. The lighting designer, electrician (board operator), stage manager, a small crew to shift the scenery (if necessary), and the director are the only members of the production team that need be present for this rehearsal.

Before the lighting rehearsal, the lighting designer will have noted the position of any motivated or unmotivated lighting cues that he or she may want to use in the production. The designer will have discussed these cues with the director during one of the production conferences. The extent of this discussion varies greatly. Some directors want to know the exact location, purpose, and function of every cue, whereas other directors will leave the matter entirely up to the lighting designer. The lighting designer and board operator will have "roughed in" the intensity settings for each cue before the lighting rehearsal.

There are two primary reasons for holding a lighting rehearsal: (1) it provides the director and lighting designer with a specific time to discuss the effect, purpose, and content of each cue when they are relatively unencumbered by other elements of the production. Additionally, it gives them an opportunity to discuss any additions, deletions, or other changes that they feel should be made in the location or

Call: To tell specific crew members when to perform their cues.

duration of the cues or anything else affecting the lighting design. (2) It provides the designer, director, stage manager, and board operator with an opportunity to make sure that the paperwork affecting the lighting design is correct. Since the stage manager will be **calling** all of the cues, he or she can use the lighting rehearsal to make sure that the lighting cues have been noted in their appropriate positions in the prompt script. It also gives the board operator a chance to check the accuracy of the electrician's cue sheets and preset sheets.

Technical and Dress Rehearsals

Changes and adjustments to the timing, content, and positioning of lighting cues are normal during the technical and dress rehearsals. Although this can be a very frustrating time, it is essential that the lighting crew understand that the majority of the lighting cues will probably have to be adjusted; intensities and timing will be changed, entire cues will probably need to be added or deleted, instrument focus may need to be shifted, and the color in various instruments may also have to be changed. These adjustments should be considered as normal, rather than extraordinary, because it is part of the lighting designer's responsibility to develop the lighting design to work with the production concept that has evolved during the rehearsal period.

Instrument and Dimmer Check

Several routine equipment checks should be conducted before each technical or dress rehearsal and each performance. All dimmers and

---

HANGING CARDBOARDS

Hanging cardboards are a great time-saver for the electricians hanging the show. Typically, they are pieces of stiff cardboard with specific portions of the light plot (first electric, first ante-proscenium cut, and so forth) taped or glued to them. The master electrician can assign one or two electricians to each position, give them the appropriate hanging cardboard, and send them on their way. With the hanging cardboards (which are mounted on cardboard so the electricians can put them in their pockets without crumpling them), the crew members will have all the information they need and won't have to constantly refer back to the master plot.

DIMMER/INSTRUMENT CHECK SHEET			
Dimmer	Number of Instruments	Instrument Location(s)/Color(s)	Area of Focus

Figure 16.6

A dimmer instrument check sheet.

instruments need to be checked to determine that they are functioning properly. With the aid of a check sheet (Figure 16.6) two crew members can test all the instruments and dimmers in a short time. As the board operator turns on each dimmer, the other electrician checks to see that all of the instruments assigned to that dimmer are functioning properly. At the same time the person checking the instruments can see if any of the color media are bleached out, torn, or otherwise in need of replacement. Each instrument should also be tested to determine if it is focused into its respective area.

The dimmer and instrument check is normally made about an hour and a half before curtain time to allow any necessary repairs, replacements, or adjustments to be made.

GLOSSARY

Acting areas: Those areas of the stage on which specific scenes, or parts of scenes, are played.

Additive color mixing: The transmission of light of varying hues to the eye and the brain's interpretation of the ratio of the light mixture as a specific hue.

Aerial perspective: An optical phenomenon in which objects that are farther away appear less sharply in focus and less fully saturated in color.

Ampere: The unit of measurement of electrical current.

Arc: An electric current that leaps the gap between two closely placed electrodes.

Arena stage: A stage completely surrounded by the audience.

Atom: The smallest particle of a chemical element that retains the structural properties of that element.

Atomic theory: A generally accepted theory concerning the structure and composition of substances.

Autotransformer: A type of dimmer that increases or decreases lamp intensity by varying the voltage within the circuit.

Barn door: An accessory for a Fresnel spotlight whose movable flippers are swung into the beam to control it.

Beam angle: That point where the light emitted by an instrument is diminished by 50 percent when compared with the output of the center of the beam.

Beam projector: A lensless instrument with a parabolic primary reflector and a spherical secondary reflector that creates an intense shaft of light with little diffusion.

Board operator: An electrician who runs the lighting control console during rehearsals and performances.

Boom: A vertical pipe with a heavy base, frequently equipped with horizontal crossbars. Used as a hanging position for lighting instruments.

Bulb: The Pyrex glass or synthetic quartz container for a lamp filament and gaseous environment.

Cable: An electrical extension cord used to connect instruments to dimmers or instruments to permanent stage circuits.

Call: To tell specific crew members when to perform their cues.

Cassette tape: Audio recorder tape, used in computer storage.

Center line: A leader line that runs perpendicular to the set line from the midpoint or center of the opening of the proscenium arch.

Circuit: A conductive path through which electricity flows.

Circuit breaker: A device to protect a circuit from an overload; has a magnetic device that trips open, breaking circuit continuity.

Circuiting: The process of connecting a lighting instrument to its specified stage circuit.

Color: One of the four controllable qualities of light; a perception created in the brain by the stimulation of the retina by light waves of certain lengths; a generic term applied to all light waves contained in the visible spectrum.

Color frame: A lightweight metal holder for color media that fits in a holder at the front of a lighting instrument.

Color media: The plastic, gelatin, or glass material used to color the light emitted by lighting instruments.

Combination circuit: Typically, a circuit where the elements are in a parellel configuration, and the controls are placed in series with the load.

Complementary colors: Two hues that, when combined, yield white in light or black in pigment; colors that are opposite to each other on a color wheel.

Computer board: A lighting control console that uses a computer to store and recall dimmer intensity levels and fade times for each cue; it also stores and recalls various other functions.

Condensing lens: A device that condenses the direct and reflected light from a source and concentrates it on the slide plane aperture of a projector.

Conductor: Any material with many free electrons, such as copper, silver, gold, and aluminum.

Cones: Nerve cells in the retina that are sensitive to bright light; they respond either to red, blue, or green light.

Connecting strip: An electrical gutter or wireway that carries a number of stage circuits; the circuits terminate on the connecting strip in female receptacles.

Control board: A console containing controls for a number of dimmers. Also called a control console.

Cue: A directive for action: for example, a change in the lighting.

Cut list: A list that details the number of gels of specific size and color that will be used on a production; for example, 12 pieces of Roscolux 09 for 6-inch ERSs, 6 pieces of Lee 154 for 8-inch Fresnels, and so forth.

Cyc light: A lensless instrument with an eccentric reflector used to create a smooth wash of light on a cyclorama or skytab from a relatively close distance.

Cyclorama: A large drop used to surround the stage.

Designer's cue sheet: A form used by the lighting designer to record pertinent information (dimmer levels, timing, and so forth) about every cue in the production.

Diffuse: To soften the appearance of light by using a translucent filtering element to scatter the rays.

Dimmer: An electrical device that controls the intensity of a light source connected to it.

Dimmer circuit: An electrical circuit terminating on one end at a dimmer. The other end terminates at either a patch panel or onstage. Synonymous with stage circuit when it terminates onstage.

Distribution: One of the four controllable qualities of light; the direction, shape and size, quality (clarity or diffusion), and character (texture) of light.

Double hang: To place two instruments adjacent to each other to light an area that normally would be lit by one instrument. Normally done to allow a color shift during a scene or to provide an additive color mix.

Double plano-convex lens train: Two plano-convex lenses placed with their curved surfaces facing each other; creates a system that has a shorter focal length than either of its component lenses.

Douser: A mechanical dimming device used in followspots.

Dremel tool: A hand-held router similar to a dentist's drill, which can be equipped with a number of bits for grinding, cutting, or carving of wood, plastic, and metal.

Dress rehearsal: A run-through with all technical elements, including costumes and makeup.

Drop-and-wing set: A setting primarily composed of two-dimensional scenery, normally one or more drops upstage and a series of portals placed between the drops and the proscenium.

Drop box: A small connecting strip, containing four to eight circuits, that can be clamped to a pipe or boom.

Effect: A specialty device designed to give the appearance of being a light source such as a fire effect, candle, torch, or lightning.

Effects head: A motor-driven unit capable of producing relatively crude moving images with a scenic projector.

Electric: Any pipe that is used to hold lighting instruments.

Electrical current: The flow or movement of electrons through a conductor.

Electricians: Those who work on the stage lighting for a production.

Electrician's cue sheet: A form used by the board operator that contains the primary operating instructions for every lighting cue in the production.

Electricity: A directed flow of electrons used to create kinetic energy.

Electron: A negatively charged fundamental particle that orbits around the nucleus of an atom.

Electronics: The field of science and engineering concerned with the behavior and control of electrons within devices and systems and the utilization of those systems.

Ellipsoidal reflector floodlight: A lensless instrument with a conical ellipse reflector; used for lighting cycloramas and drops; also known as a scoop.

Ellipsoidal reflector spotlight (ERS): A lighting instrument characterized by hard-edged light with little diffusion; designed for relatively long throws, it is manufactured with fixed and variable focal-length lenses; the light beam is shaped with internally mounted shutters.

Fade: To increase (fade-in) or decrease (fade-out) the intensity of the lights.

Fader: A device, usually electronic, that effects a gradual changeover from one circuit to another; in lighting, it gradually changes the intensity of one or more dimmer circuits.

Fiber-optic material: Material made of thin transparent fibers of plastic that conduct light throughout their length by internal reflections.

Field angle: That point where the light output diminishes to 10 percent of the output of the center of the beam.

Filament: The light-producing element of a lamp; usually made of tungsten wire.

Fill light: Light used to fill the shadows created by the key light.

First ante-proscenium (AP) cut: A hanging position for lighting instruments; also known as beamport; the slot or opening in the auditorium ceiling closest to the proscenium arch. The second AP is second closest to the proscenium arch, and so on.

First electric: The onstage pipe for lighting instruments that is closest, from the onstage side, to the proscenium arch.

Flash pot: A device used to detonate flash powder.

Floor pocket: A connecting box, usually containing three to six circuits, the top of which is mounted flush with the stage floor.

Floppy disk: A thin piece of plastic coated with metal oxide, used to record the information stored in a computer's memory.

Focal length: The distance from the lens at which the light rays converge into a point; for lenses used in stage lighting instruments the focal length is most frequently measured in even inches.

Focus: In stage lighting, the location onstage where the light from an instrument is directed.

Followspot: A lighting instrument with a high-intensity, narrow beam of light; mounted on a stand that allows it to tilt and swivel so that the beam can "follow" the actor.

Form: In this context, elements that have similar physical characteristics. For example, arena, thrust, and proscenium theatres have different forms of stage configuration.

Free electron: An electron that has broken away from its "home" atom to float free.

Fresnel lens: A type of step lens with the glass cut away from the convex face of the lens.

Fresnel spotlight: A spotlight that produces a soft, diffused light; the Fresnel lens is treated on the plano side to diffuse the light.

Front-of-house: Describing lights that are hung on the audience side of the proscenium arch.

Front projection screen: An opaque, highly reflective, usually white material used to reflect a projected image; the projector is placed on the audience side of the screen.

Funnel: An accessory for a Fresnel or ERS spotlight that masks the beam to create a circular pattern; also called a snoot or top hat.

Fuse: A device to protect a circuit from an overload; has a soft metal strip that melts, breaking circuit continuity.

Gating principle: A rapid switching on and off of electrical power.

Gel: (verb) To insert color media in a color frame and place on a lighting instrument. (noun) Color media made from gelatin.

Ghost load: To connect an offstage, unseen load to the dimmer. An instrument, usually a 500- or 1,000-watt Fresnel, is two-fered with the small onstage load to provide sufficient wattage for the dimmer to operate properly.

Gobo: A thin metal template inserted into an ellipsoidal reflector spotlight to project a shadow pattern of light.

Grid: A network of steel I beams supporting elements of the counterweight system.

Ground plan: A scale mechanical drawing in the form of a horizontal offset section with the cutting plane passing at whatever level, normally a height of 4 feet above the stage floor, is required to produce the most descriptive view of the set.

Ground row: Generally low, horizontal flats used to mask the base of cycs or drops; frequently painted to resemble rows of buildings, hedges, or similar visual elements.

Hanging: The process of placing lighting instruments in their specified locations.

Hanging crew: Those responsible for the hanging, circuiting, patching, focusing, and coloring of the lighting instruments; they are under the supervision of the master electrician.

Hanging positions: The various locations around the stage and auditorium where lighting instruments are placed.

Head: A housing that holds scenic projector lenses in fixed positions to project images of a specific size.

Heat filter: A glass medium that removes much of the infrared spectrum from light.

Heat welding: The use of a heat gun (a high-temperature air gun, visually similar to a hand-held hair dryer) to fuse two pieces of plastic.

Hookup sheet: Another name for instrument schedule.

Hot spot: An intense circle of light created when a projector lens is seen through a rear screen.

Hue: The qualities that differentiate one color from another.

Image of light: A picture or concept of what the light should look like for a production.

Instruments: Lighting fixtures designed for use in the theatre.

Instrument schedule: A form used to record all of the technical data about each instrument used in the production; also known as a hookup sheet.

Insulator: Any material with few free electrons, such as rubber, paper, glass, and certain types of plastics.

Intensity: One of the four controllable qualities of light; the relative brightness of light.

Iris: A device with movable overlapping metal plates, used with an ellipsoidal reflector spotlight to change the size of the circular pattern of light.

Key light: The brightest light in a scene.

Keystoning: The linear distortion created when a projector is placed on some angle other than perpendicular to the projection surface.

Ladder: A vertical pipe with horizontal crossbars hung from the end of an onstage electric pipe. Used as a hanging position for lighting equipment.

Lamp: The stage term for "light bulbs" used in stage lighting instruments.

Law of Charges: The law: Like charges repel and unlike charges attract.

Lensless projector: A projector that works by projecting a shadow image without a lens, such as the Linnebach and curved-image projectors.

Light board: A generic term used to describe all types of lighting control consoles.

Light cue: Generally, some type of action involving lighting; usually the raising or lowering of the intensity of one or more lighting instruments.

Lighting area: Cylindrical space approximately 8–12 feet in diameter and about 7 feet tall; the actual size is roughly determined by the diameter of the beam of light of the instruments that are being used to light the area.

Lighting designer: A person responsible for the appearance of the lighting during the production.

Lighting production team: The personnel who work on lighting for a production.

Lighting rehearsal: A run-through, without action, attended by the director, stage manager, lighting designer, and appropriate running crews to look at the intensity, timing, and placement of the various lighting cues.

Lighting sectional: A composite side view, drawn to scale, of the set, showing the hanging position of the instruments in relationship to the physical structure of the theatre, set, and stage equipment.

Light plot: A scale ground plan drawing that details the placement of the lighting instruments relative to the physical structure of the theatre and the location of the set.

Load: A device that converts electrical energy into another form of energy; a lamp converts electrical energy to light and heat; an electrical motor converts electricity to mechanical energy.

Lumen: The measurement of a lamp's output.

Mask: To block the audience's view—generally of backstage equipment and space.

Master electrician: Person responsible for ensuring that the lighting equipment is hung, focused, and run according to written and verbal instructions from the lighting designer.

Maximum throw distance: The point at which the output of a stage lighting instrument drops to 50 footcandles.

Microcassette tape: A tape cassette approximately 1¼ by 2 inches, used in computer storage; identical to microcassette audio tape.

Micro-floppy disk: A floppy disk 3½ inches in diameter.

Modeling: One of the four functions of stage lighting; the ability of light to reveal form.

Momentary-on switch: A push-button switch without a locking feature. The circuit remains on only as long as the button switch is depressed.

Mood: One of the four functions of stage lighting; the ability of light to create a mood.

Moon box: A device, basically a wooden box with lights inside, for re-creating the moon.

Motivated light cue: Indicated or caused by some specific action within the script, like the beginnings and endings of scenes and acts or a character's turning a light switch on or off.

Movement (in light): One of the four controllable qualities of light; refers to the timing of lighting cues as well as to the movement of onstage and offstage sources.

Neutralization: The result of mixing complementary hues. In light, the creation of white. In pigment, the creation of dark gray.

Neutron: A fundamental particle in the structure of the nucleus of an atom; possesses a neutral charge.

Objective lens: A device to focus a projected image on a screen or other surface.

Ohm's Law: The law that states: As voltage increases, current increases; as resistance increases, current decreases.

Open arc: Light source in which two electrodes operate in the open air.

Paint chip: A small rectangle of paper or thin cardboard painted in a specific hue.

Pan: To rotate an object, such as an ERS, about its vertical axis.

Parabolic aluminized reflector: A sealed-beam lamp similar to the headlight of an automobile.

Parallel circuit: A circuit in which only a portion of the electricity flows through each of the branches of the circuit.

PAR can: A holder for a parabolic aluminized reflector (PAR) lamp; creates a powerful punch of light with a relatively soft edge; the PAR 64 is commonly used for concert lighting.

Patch: To connect a stage circuit to a dimmer circuit.

Patch panel: An interconnecting device that allows you to connect any stage circuit into any dimmer.

Pigment: Material that imparts color to a substance such as paint or dye.

Pipe: A counterweighted batten or fixed metal pipe that holds lighting instruments or equipment.

Plan angle: The ground plan view of an object.

Plano-convex lens: A lens with one flat and one outward curving face.

Plotter: A computer-controlled machine that draws graphic representations on large-sized paper.

Plug: The male portion of a connecting device.

Pop riveter: A tool used to secure rivets in thin metal.

Potential: The difference in electrical charge between two bodies; measured in volts.

Practical: An onstage working light source such as a table lamp, wall sconce, or oil lamp.

Preset light board: A lighting control console that uses electromechanical, variable resistance switches to control the output of the dimmer.

Preset sheet: A form used by the electrician to record the intensity levels for each dimmer during major shifts in the lighting.

Primary colors: Hues that cannot be derived or blended from any other hues. In light, the primaries are red, blue, and green; in pigment, the primary colors are red, blue, and yellow.

Production concept: The creative interpretation of the script that will unify the artistic vision of the production design team.

Production design team: The producer; director; and scenic, costume, lighting, and sound designers who develop the visual and aural concept for the production.

Production meeting: A conference of appropriate production personnel to share information.

Proscenium stage: A stage configuration in which the spectators watch the action through a rectangular opening (the proscenium arch) that resembles a picture frame.

Proton: A fundamental particle in the structure of the nucleus of an atom; possesses a positive charge.

Rear projection screen: Translucent projection material designed to transmit the image through the projection surface; the projector is placed in back of the screen.

Receptacle: The female portion of a connecting device.

Repatch: To remove one circuit from a dimmer and replace it with another during a performance.

Resistance: The opposition to electron flow within a conductor, measured in ohms; the amount of the resistance is dependent on the chemical makeup of the material through which the electricity is flowing.

Rise time: The time that it takes the filament of a lamp to heat to full incandescence.

Rods: Nerve cells in the retina that are sensitive to faint light.

Roundel: A glass color medium for use with striplights; frequently has diffusing properties.

Running: Controlling or operating some aspect of a production.

Running crew: Those electricians responsible for operating lighting equipment during rehearsals and performances.

Saturation: The relative purity of a particular hue.

Scenic projector: A high-wattage instrument used for projecting large-format slides or moving images.

SCR (silicon controlled rectifier): A heavy-duty power transistor.

SCR dimmer: A dimmer that uses two SCRs in a back-to-back configuration to control the load circuit. A low-voltage control circuit uses the gating principle to switch the SCRs to a conducting state.

Secondary colors: The result of mixing two primary colors.

Sectional: A drawing, usually in scale, of an object that shows what it would look like if cut straight through at a given plane.

Sectional angle: The angle of intersection between the axis of the cone of light emitted by an instrument and the working height—usually the height of an actor's face (about 5 feet 6 inches)—of the lighting area.

Selective focus: One of the four functions of stage lighting: the ability of light to direct the audience's attention to a specific location.

Series circuit: A circuit in which all of the electricity flows through every element of the circuit.

Shade: A color of low value; usually created by mixing one or more hues with black.

Shutter: A lever-actuated device used to control the height of the top and bottom edges of a followspot beam; also called a chopper.

Sidelight: Any light striking the side of an object relative to the view of the observer.

Slide plane aperture: The point in a projection system where a slide or other effect is placed.

Slide projector: A reasonably high-output instrument capable of projecting standard 35-mm slides.

Snoot: Another term for funnel.

Source: The origin of electrical potential, such as a battery or 120-volt wall outlet.

Source light: The apparent source of light that is illuminating a scene or object.

Spectrometer: A device for measuring specific wavelengths of light.

Spidering: Running a cable directly from the dimmer to the instrument; also known as direct cabling.

Stage circuits: An electrical circuit terminating on one end in a female receptacle in the vicinity of the stage. The other end is connected to a dimmer or patch panel. Synonymous with dimmer circuit when it terminates at a dimmer.

Stage picture: The visual appearance of the stage during a specific moment in a play.

Step-down transformer: A transformer whose output voltage is lower than its input voltage.

Step lens: A plano-convex lens with the glass on the plano side cut away in steps that are parallel with the plano face.

Step-up transformer: A transformer whose output is lower than its input voltage.

Stream-of-consciousness questioning: Asking whatever relevant questions pop into your mind in the course of a discussion.

Striplight: A long, narrow troughlike instrument with three or four circuits controlling the individual lamps; each circuit is normally equipped with a separate color; used for blending and creating color washes; also known as an x-ray.

Style: In this context, style refers to the specific compositional characteristics that distinguish the appearance of one type of design from another. Using this definition, the various design styles—realism, expressionism, surrealism, and so forth—are delineated by the differences in their compositional principles.

Subtractive color mixing: The selective absorption of light by a filter or pigment.

Technical rehearsals: Run-throughs, in which the sets, lights, props, and sound are integrated into the action of the play.

Texture: The relative roughness or smoothness or the finish of an object.

Throw distance: How far light from an instrument travels from its hanging position to the center of its area of focus.

Thrust stage: A stage projecting into, and surrounded on three sides by, the audience.

Tilt: To rotate an object about its horizontal axis; to pan vertically.

Tint: A color of high value; usually created by mixing one or more hues with white.

Tone: A color of middle value achieved by mixing one or more hues with black and white.

Top hat: Another term for funnel.

Transformer: A device that changes the voltage in an electrical system; the output voltage of a step-down transformer is less than its source; a step-up transformer increases it.

Trim height: Height above the stage floor at which an instrument will be hung.

Two-fer: An electrical Y that has female receptacles at the top of the Y and a male plug at the bottom leg of the Y; used to connect two instruments to the same circuit.

Unit set: A single set in which all of the play's locations are always visible and the audience's attention is usually shifted by alternately lighting various parts of the set.

Unmotivated light cues: Changes in the lights that are not specifically called for in the script.

Valence shell: The outermost plane of orbiting electrons in the structure of an atom.

Value: The relative lightness or darkness of an object.

Variegated gel: A multicolored gel made in the shop from strips of color media of differing hues.

Visibility: One of the four functions of stage lighting; to make the stage selectively visible.

Volatility: Nonpermanence; in computers, a volatile memory will be lost if the computer loses its power supply.

Volts: The unit of measurement of electrical potential.

Wall pocket: A connecting box similar to a floor pocket but mounted in the wall.

Working sectional: A drawing showing the sectional angle for a lighting instrument; used to determine its trim height or hanging position; not to be confused with the lighting section.

Work light: A lighting fixture, frequently a scoop, PAR, or other wide-field-angle instrument, hung over the stage to facilitate work; generally not used to light a production.

X-ray: Another term for striplight.

Zoom ellipse: An ellipsoidal reflector spotlight with movable lenses that allow the focal length to be changed.

I N D E X